Modern Latin Amer

MW00565149

"Modern Latin America: Everyday Life and Politics 1800 to the Present. Covering the sweep of Latin American history from the perspective of the everyday experiences of the people who made it, Modern Latin America, tells the story of the forces that shaped the region and how people from various walks of life negotiated the changing dynamics of race, class, gender, political conflict and power to create the societies of today. Integrating current scholarship, the book covers the major themes and events of Latin American history while breaking away from a dry history of states and institutions to provide a window on the dynamics of how people shaped, were impacted by, and lived their history."

—Paul Hart, *Professor of History and Director of the Center for International Studies, Texas State University, USA*

"*Modern Latin America: Everyday Life and Politics 1800 to the Present* is an engaging account that effectively weaves the economic, cultural, social, and political histories of the region. Wasserman has a keen eye, recognizing the challenges that Latin America's diverse populations have confronted over the centuries. "Nature's Way," one of the special features in each chapter, is a welcome addition at a time when disease and climate change surround us."

—Sandra Mendiola García, *Associate Professor of History, University of North Texas, USA*

"The strength of *Modern Latin America* resides in Wasserman's ability to present to students in jargon-free language a balanced interpretation of Latin American history, one that seamlessly integrates a discussion of political economy with an astute and sympathetic rendering of "everyday life" from the perspective of *los de abajo*. Narrative portals in each chapter help the student to understand the process of historical inquiry and to grasp a deeper sense of historical context, including a new feature that examines environmental forces. This new edition brings the narrative up to the present and offers the instructor ample opportunity to develop the survey course in any number of possible directions."

—Eric Zolov, *Professor of History and Director of Undergraduate Studies, Stony Brook University of The State University of New York, USA*

Mark Wasserman

Modern Latin America Since 1800

Everyday Life and Politics

palgrave
macmillan

Mark Wasserman
Department of History
Rutgers, The State University of New Jersey
New Brunswick, NJ, USA

This book was previously published by Pearson Education, Inc.

ISBN 978-3-030-96184-8   ISBN 978-3-030-96185-5   (eBook)
https://doi.org/10.1007/978-3-030-96185-5

Cover illustration: FRIDO | eStudiioCalamar

This Palgrave Macmillan imprint is published by the registered company Springer Nature Switzerland AG.
The registered company address is: Gewerbestrasse 11, 6330 Cham, Switzerland

To My Children
Aaron, Marcos, Danielle, Hudson, Andrew

Preface

Modern Latin America: Everyday Life and Politics was originally the second volume of *Latin America and Its People*, a textbook coauthored with Cheryl E. Martin through three editions (2005, 2008, 2012). I added a chapter "Legacies" to summarize the period prior to 1800, completely revised and updated Chaps. 8 and 9, and revised more lightly Chaps. 2, 3, 4, 5, 6, and 7. I also added a fourth Special Feature "Nature's Way" to each chapter to inform readers about recent discoveries in the history of the environment, medicine, and disasters.

The goal of Modern Latin America: Everyday Life and Politics is to provide a fresh interpretative survey of Latin American history since 1800. Millions of "ordinary" Latin Americans are the central characters in the story. I explore the many social and political institutions that Latin Americans built and rebuilt—families, governments from the village level to the nation state, churches, political parties, labor unions, schools, and armies— through the lives of the people who forged these institutions and tried to alter them to meet changing circumstances. The texture of everyday life, the daily struggles of men, women, and children as they faced difficult challenges and adapted to changing times, the people of Latin American history "up close and personal," in their houses and on the streets, on the shop floors and in the fields, and at work and at play is my focus. It is everyday life, which makes the history of Latin America so fascinating and compelling.

Despite their different languages, ethnicities, and geographic origins, Latin Americans have faced certain common challenges. European conquest and subsequent shifts in world economic and political configurations have shaped the region's history over the past five centuries. Latin America's rich natural resources attracted foreign investors who profited handsomely, while the people who worked in the mines and oilfields seldom garnered an equitable share of the bounty. The region's ability to produce a stunning variety of agricultural staples shaped patterns of landholding and labor throughout the region, again to the detriment of the many and the benefit of the few. How to achieve political stability in nations divided by class, ethnic, and regional differences is an enduring conundrum for Latin Americans, even if they tried many different means of resolving that dilemma.

The dilemma in writing a book about Latin. Americans is how to explore their common history without losing sight of their diversity, and to compare how the many different peoples of the region responded to similar situations. I organized the book thematically rather than proceeding country-by-country. I have too much ground to cover, five hundred years and twenty countries, to document the history of every Latin American nation. No doubt, some specialists will feel their area slighted, but textbooks are as much about the choices of what to exclude as they are about what to include. Unlike many other texts on Latin American history, Modern Latin America interweaves the history of Brazil with that of its Spanish-speaking neighbors, rather than segregating it in separate chapters, while also pointing out the special features that distinguish it from other Latin American countries.

I found during the many years of teaching introductory courses about Latin America (or anything else) that it is best not to clutter the narrative with too many dates and names. It is more important for students to remember the major themes, such as the struggle to control local affairs, the impact of war, the transformation of women's roles, and the social changes wrought by economic development. They will remember, perhaps even more clearly, that many Latin Americans lived and continue to live in overwhelming poverty.

The overarching theme is how ordinary people struggled over the course of two centuries to maintain control over their daily lives. This meant that they sought to determine their own community leaders, set their local laws and regulations (especially taxes), establish and keep their own traditions, practice their religion, supervise the education of their children, live by their own values and standards, and earn a living. This endless struggle came to involve more than just the narrow view and experience of their village or urban neighborhood or their friends and neighbors. Rather, it brought ordinary people and their local lives into constant, not always pleasant and beneficial, contact with the wider worlds of regional (states, provinces, and territories), national, and international politics, economy, and culture. Although the local struggle forms the backbone of the narrative, I include summaries and analyses of the contexts in which these struggles occurred, as well. Because all Latin Americans, regardless of country, participated in this struggle, the economic and political narratives proceed thematically and chronologically.

Other themes interwoven with that of the struggle for control over everyday life. Unlike many other texts in the field, Modern Latin America gives full and nuanced coverage to the nineteenth century, incorporating the most exciting new scholarship on that period. In the nineteenth century, I assert, chronic war (external and internal) and the accompanying militarization of government and politics profoundly shaped the region's economy and society. I maintain, as well, that race, class, and gender were the crucial underlying elements in Latin American politics. Moreover, warfare, combined with the massive flow of people to the cities, most particularly transformed the place of women.

In the twentieth century, conflict between the upper, middle, and lower classes was the primary moving force behind politics. No ideology from either Left or Right, nor any type of government from democracy to authoritarianism, has brought other than temporary resolutions. The continued changes in the role of women in society and politics in the face of vast transformations caused by technology and globalization are another major concern.

It is also my belief that the history of Latin Americans is primarily the story of Latin America and not of the great powers outside the region. To be sure, Europeans and North Americans invested considerable sums of money and sometimes intervened militarily in Latin America. Their wars and rivalries greatly affected Latin America's possibilities. We do note the importance of such key developments as Mexico's loss of half its national territory to the United States in 1848, the impact of the Cold War on Latin America, and the training that rightwing Latin American military establishments received at the hands of U.S. military forces in the late twentieth century. I prefer to keep the spotlight on the people of Latin America themselves.

Special Features

I included four Special Features in each chapter. (1) "How Historians Understand," a discussion of the way historians go about their work or the ways in which people used historical knowledge and transformed it according to the concerns of a particular time and place; (2) "Latin American Lives," a biography of an individual, whose life illustrates some of the key points of that chapter; (3) "Slice of Life," a vignette that takes students to the scene of the action and that illustrates in detail some of the social processes under discussion; and (4) "Nature's Way," explorations into the histories of disease, natural disasters, environment, and ecology.

New Brunswick, NJ, USA   Mark Wasserman

Acknowledgments

Textbooks are inherently collective enterprises. In synthesizing the work of other scholars, I have come to an extraordinary appreciation for the remarkable researches and analyses of our colleagues all over the world. I have tried to use the best old and new discoveries to illuminate Latin America's past. The list of those to whom we are beholden is endless. Because space constraints forced me to eschew scholarly apparatus, I have not presented formal recognition of these contributions. Many will recognize their work on my pages. They should regard this as my highest compliment. Special thanks go to Cheryl E. Martin, who worked with me through a decade and a half and three editions, adding her extensive knowledge, fine writing, and good sense to the enterprise.

Contents

1 **Legacies**   1
   Timeline   20
   How Historians Understand   21
   Latin American Lives   22
   Slice of Life   24
   Nature's Way   26

2 **New Nations**   29
   Causes   29
   Four Revolutions   32
   Results   38
   Conclusion   39
   Timeline   41
   How Historians Understand   42
   Latin American Lives   43
   Slice of Life   45
   Nature's Way   47

3 **Politics and Economics, 1821–1880**   49
   The Challenges of Nationhood   50
   Nations at War   59
   Popular Participation   63
   Leadership   65
   Economic Recovery   66
   Conclusion   69
   Timeline   71

	How Historians Understand	72
	Latin American Lives	73
	Slice of Life	75
	Nature's Way	77

4 Everyday Life in an Uncertain Age, 1821–1880 — 79
Land and Work in the Countryside — 81
In the Cities — 92
Daily Life — 96
Conclusion — 103
How Historians Understand — 104
Latin American Lives — 106
Slice of Life — 108
Nature's Way — 109

5 Economic Modernization, Society, and Politics, 1880–1920 — 111
Conclusion — 131
Timeline — 132
How Historians Understand — 133
Latin American Lives — 135
Slice of Life — 137
Nature's Way — 139

6 Between Revolutions: The New Politics of Class and the Economies of Import Substitution — 141
Three Crises — 143
Dictators and Populists — 145
Failures on the Left and Right — 156
Conclusion — 158
Timeline — 160
How Historians Understand — 161
Latin American Lives — 163
Slice of Life — 165
Nature's Way — 167

7 People and Progress, 1910–1959 — 169
Proletarianization and Patriarchy — 171
Urbanization and Social Change — 178
The Arts — 183
Conclusion — 186

How Historians Understand   187
Latin American Lives   189
Slice of Life   190
Natures's Way   192

8 The Search for a Better Way, 1959 to the Present   195
The Revolutions: Cuba, Central America, Peru, and Colombia   197
    Cuba   197
    Central America   199
    Peru   202
    Colombia   204
The Tyrannies: Brazil, Argentina, and Chile   205
    Brazil   206
    Argentina   207
    Chile   209
Mexico: The End of the One-Party State   210
The Flow and Ebb of the Pink Tide   212
The Global Economy   216
Conclusion   220
Timeline   222
How Historians Understand   223
Latin American Lives   225
Slice Of Life   227
Nature's Way   229

9 Globalization and Everyday Life, 1959 to the Present   231
Population   232
Poverty   235
Indigenous   238
Inequities   240
Violence   241
Employment   243
Informal Economy   244
Migrations   247
Super-Urbanization   249
Environment   253
Human Capital   254
The New World of Communications   256
Art   257
Sports   258

Music   259
Conclusion   259
How Historians Understand   260
Latin American Lives   261
Slice of Life   262
Nature's Way   263

Epilogue   265

Suggested Reading   267

Index   269

About the Author

Mark Wasserman is a Professor Emeritus of history at Rutgers, The State University of New Jersey, where he taught from 1978 to 2018. Brought up in Marblehead, Massachusetts, he earned his B.A. at Duke University and his M.A. and Ph.D. at the University of Chicago. He is the author of four books on Mexico: *Capitalists, Caciques, and Revolution: The Native Elite and Foreign Enterprise in Chihuahua, Mexico, 1854–1911* (1984); *Persistent Oligarchs: Elites and Politics in Chihuahua, Mexico, 1910–1940* (1993); *Everyday Life and Politics in Nineteenth Century Mexico: Men, Women, and War* (2000); and *Pesos and Politics: Business, Elites, Foreigners, and Government in Mexico, 1854–1940* (2015). He also coauthored the early editions of the bestselling *History of Latin America (1980–1988)* with Benjamin Keen and co-authored three editions of *Latin America and Its People* with Cheryl E. Martin. Professor Wasserman three times won the Arthur P. Whitaker Prize for his books. He received research fellowships from the Tinker Foundation, the American Council of Learned Societies/Social Science Research Council, the American Philosophical Society, and the National Endowment of the Humanities. He was Chair of the Rutgers Department of History. Professor Wasserman was an elected member of the Highland Park, New Jersey, Board of Education for nearly a decade and served as its president for 2 years. He enjoys reading mystery novels, hiking, and travel.

List of Maps

Map 3.1   Latin America in 1830   51
Map 3.2   Brazil, states and their capitals   52
Map 3.3   Mexico and state capitals   53
Map 3.4   Central America   54
Map 3.5   The Wars for Northern Mexico   55
Map 3.6   The Caribbean   60

List of Tables

Table 4.1   The Population of Latin America in the Nineteenth Century   81
Table 5.1   Railways in Latin America, 1880–1920 (number of miles)   117
Table 5.2   Destination of European Emigrants to Latin America,
             c. 1820–1932   121
Table 6.1   Women's enfranchisement   158
Table 7.1   A Typical Middle Class Budget in Mid-Twentieth Century
             Peruvian Soles   180
Table 9.1   Population growth in Latin America, 1950–2000 (Millions)   233
Table 9.2   Population of Latin America, 2020 (In Millions)   234
Table 9.3   Latin Americans living in poverty and extreme
             poverty, 1980–2002   236
Table 9.4   Latin American inflation: regional average 1980–2019   237
Table 9.5   Inflation (Average annual rate) selected Latin American nations   237
Table 9.6   Gini coefficient for Latin America 2018   241
Table 9.7   Homicide rates for Latin America 2020   242
Table 9.8   Global peace index   242
Table 9.9   Informal economy as percentage of total employment in Latin
             America: Selected Countries 2019   245
Table 9.10   Latin America, largest cities   250

1

Legacies

Thousands of years of humankind before 1492 and three hundred years of European colonial rule left indelible legacies for the Western Hemisphere. The nations that came into being during the nineteenth century were heirs to the best and the worst of three continents.

During more than three hundred years after 1492, many ethnicities among three races came together in what white Europeans named the Americas. For the indigenous peoples, of whom there were an estimated eight to forty million, speaking hundreds of languages and having even more varied cultures, the encounter was a nightmarish disaster. For millions of Africans, torn from their homes, imprisoned, and shipped by brutal sea voyages to the Americas, it was nothing less than a catastrophe. In both these cases the result of their encounter with the third race, white Europeans, amounted to genocide unequalled by humankind until the murderous twentieth century. The victorious Europeans wreaked havoc on native and African folk alike, for their diseases, steel and guns, and greed killed millions and ran roughshod over their victims' cultures and economies.

In retrospect, it seems unsurprising that the peoples of the Iberian Peninsula, the Portuguese and Spanish, situated on the great western ocean and its confluence with the Mediterranean Sea were the adventurers who set off to explore the seas. The Portuguese in particular were inveterate marine travelers. The Iberians possessed a troubled and varied history with successive settlements and invasions by the Phoenicians, Greeks, Carthaginians, Romans, Vandals, Visigoths, and Muslims over two thousand years. Christianity arrived during the mid-200s C.E. In response to the Muslim conquest of the peninsula (711–788), in the middle of the eighth century Christians, concentrated in

M. Wasserman, *Modern Latin America Since 1800*,
https://doi.org/10.1007/978-3-030-96185-5_1

the northern regions of the peninsula, embarked on what we now know as the *Reconquista* (Reconquest), which went on in fits and starts for seven hundred years, in order to take control of the peninsula from the Muslim state entities. Alternating periods of peace and war, including shifting alliances between Christians and Muslims, created a highly militarized society. Its great fighters, called knights, occupied the highest echelons. Portugal was first to emerge as an independent kingdom in the late fourteenth century. A century later, under the leadership of King Ferdinand and Queen Isabella, Spain united. They used aggressive Catholicism as the glue that held together the long-warring polities. Consequently, the monarchs purged non-Christians (Muslims and Jews), who, to a considerable extent, formed the financial and cultural backbone of their new nation. Less militarized and more stable, Portugal led the way in exploration, its sailors working their way down the African coast, eventually finding a route to India. The Catholic monarchs, perhaps encouraged by the heady triumphs of the unification of Spain in 1492, that same year backed a visionary Genoese, Christopher Columbus, in a risky venture to discover an alternate route to the Indies (India, China).

The two Iberian nations soon came to rule the vast lands of what we came to know as the Americas. The character of their subsequent rule evolved in great part from their formation. Portugal, unified earlier with less bloodshed and, thus less militarized, and perhaps less imbued with aggressive Christianity, because it did not experience the last bitter century of Reconquista, was more secure and less rigid in its administrative practices than Spain. Unemployed military with few skills other than the ability for violence and mayhem were a plague for Spain. They were men filled with self-importance and lust for glory. The Crown expelled the people with commercial and financial skills, so those it could send to the newly found lands were adventurers not settlers. They sought glory and quickly acquired wealth. Centuries of reunification wars cloaked as Christian crusades inculcated a thorough intolerance in them. Newly unified Spain's history of regional loyalties and distrust of central authority was ingrained. All of these factors helped shape both the conquest and administration of their new empire.

Columbus, of course, discovered lands hitherto unknown to Europeans, many of whom thought the world was flat. He mistakenly thought he found the Indies. In his attempt to obtain power and riches, he overreached, ending up imprisoned and impoverished. Spanish settlement of the Caribbean during the period from 1492 to 1519 resulted in widespread destruction of indigenous societies. It also served as the staging area for further discoveries. Even immense an island as Cuba, devoid of easy riches, though fertile beyond imagination, did not satisfy the ambitious near-do-well warriors. Led by

Hernán Cortés, a small group sailed west from Cuba in 1519, impelled by rumors of cities of gold.

When Europeans first set foot in these lands, until then unknown to them, many extraordinary civilizations existed which were in many ways far superior to theirs. Three of these civilizations, the Aztecs, Incas and Mayas, the new arrivals quickly discovered. The Aztecs and Incas created enormous empires dominating Mesoamerica and the west coast of South America, respectively. Their achievements in architecture, engineering, hydraulics, and organization were extraordinary. The Maya, whose heyday had gone by, possessed unrivaled skills in art, architecture, irrigation, mathematics and astronomy.

The two great empires, which the Europeans brutally defeated, were in some ways only the consolidators and imitators of their predecessors, who flourished before them. The extraordinary accomplishments of the Olmec, Monte Albán, Teotihuacán, Mixtec, and Toltec in Mesoamerica and the Chavín de Huantar, Tiwanaku, Moche, Nazca, Wari and Chimu in Peru laid the foundation for the great empires, which succeeded them. These civilizations built some of the world's greatest cities and amazing communications and agricultural systems, and created spectacular art works.

The first great civilization in Mesoamerica arose in the tropical coast of the Gulf of Mexico in what are now the states of Veracruz and Tabasco between 1200 and 400 BCE. The Olmecs created impressive religious ceremonial centers at San Lorenzo and La Venta with remarkable giant basalt heads, weighing twenty tons and standing eight feet high. These required engineering feats to transport them. They also produced large mosaics in the form of jaguar masks and smaller objects such as jewelry, figurines, and tools. Archaeologists often call the Olmecs the "mother culture" of Mesoamerica, because they introduced several practices that appeared in later civilizations, such as the Mesoamerican ball game (played with a rubber ball), glyphs (writing) with dots and dashes, and tortillas, which became the staple food of the region.

Simultaneously the Chavín de Huantar emerged in the Andes, reaching its peak between 400 and 200 BCE. The Chavín brilliantly engineered drainage, ventilation and acoustics in their temple and produced innovative textile designs from llama, alpaca, and cotton and metal working techniques. They were the first to craft three-dimensional objects from metal.

The first cities arose in Mesoamerica as the Olmecs declined. Zapotec people began Monte Albán in the Oaxaca Valley in southern Mexico around 500 BCE and it lasted for a millennium, becoming a trading and religious center with as many as 25,000 inhabitants. Somewhat later Teotihuacán in the Valley of Mexico (not far from current day's Mexico City) became one of the largest cities in the world with more than 100,000 residents in 500 CE. It has more than 600 pyramids including the spectacular, enormous pyramids of the Sun and Moon. Teotihuacán was a military, commercial and religious center. Its people's engineering and artistic accomplishments are notable in its pyramids. It declined through the 700s CE.

In the third century BCE, an extraordinary civilization appeared in the lowland rainforests in southern Mexico, Guatemala, Honduras, and Belize. The Maya invented a writing system that stumped scholars for decades before they were able to interpret it, thereby altering almost everything they thought they had known about the Maya until that time. The Maya did not build huge cities such as Teotihuacán, but they constructed more than fifty closely connected though separate city-states. The most important were Tikal in Guatemala and Copán in Honduras which each had approximately 50,000 residents. The Maya invented a complex agriculture based on canals and raised fields that took advantage of tropical resources that required scrupulous maintenance. They also came up with a system of mathematics based on units of twenty and were the first people to develop the concept of zero. (Europeans adopted this from the Arabs eight hundred years later.) The Maya also had a 365-day calendar. Their artwork was exquisite. The once flourishing civilization collapsed beginning around 800 CE.

After the Chavín culture dissipated in the second century CE, new city states arose. In northern coastal Peru, the Moche people built a 300-mile sphere of influence that coincided with Teotihuacán in Mesoamerica. They, too, were great builders, engineering pyramid mounds, fortresses, roads, and irrigation works. The most impressive structure was found at Cerro Blanco, the Huaca del Sol, which was 500 by 1000 feet at its base and 130 feet high. The immense palace and mausoleum required 143 million adobe bricks. The Moche were notable artists as well producing brilliant carvings, ceramics, metal works, and textiles. At the same period in the river valleys along the southern coast of Peru another civilization, known as the Nazca, flourished. They were ingenious hydraulic engineers. They were also responsible for the large designs—some five miles in length—traced on the flat desert north of the Nazca River that are visible from the sky. Along the shores of Lake Titicaca in present-day Bolivia Tiwanaku arose between 100 and 1200 CE to extend its influence over a wide area including southern Peru, northern Chile and eastern Bolivia. These people built their most imposing ceremonial site in the lake. They seem to preview some of the innovations in empire administration the Incas practiced later, such as labor extraction and establishment of agricultural colonies. The Wari Empire rose in the sixth century CE with its capital near what is now Ayacucho. It extended four hundred miles. The rulers also employed administrative strategies the Incas employed later, including the use

of quipus, centralized control over agricultural production, population reloca-
tion, maintaining storehouses, building terracing, and road construction. The
inhabitants of both Tiwanaku and Wari abruptly abandoned their capitals in
1200 CE and 850 CE, respectively.

The end of the Olmecs, Monte Alban, and Teotihuacán in Mesoamerica
and Tiwanaku and Wari in Peru led to five hundred years of relative turmoil.
The fall of Teotihuacán allowed the migration of northern peoples into central
Mexico. The warlike hunter-gatherers settled down. One of those peoples, the
Toltecs, built the city of Tula, northwest of current day Mexico City, where
they left ample evidence of warfare and human sacrifice. They introduced the
serpent god Quetzalcoatl. Although Tula collapsed in the twelfth century,
Toltec influence was widespread and the Toltecs were role models for the
Aztecs. Meanwhile, the Mixtecs dominated in Oaxaca. They produced exqui-
site gold jewelry, woodcarvings, mosaics, and especially pictorial books composed on deerskins, the latter of which recorded centuries of history. The
Mixtec dominion included seventy-five cities and lasted into the 1300s. The
Maya continued to flourish in Guatemala, Chiapas, and Yucatán, heavily
influenced by the Toltecs.

Another of the peoples who came from the northern wilds to settle in the
Valley of Mexico were the Mexica (Me-SHEE-Ka). By the early 1300s, they
settled on a small island in the middle of Lake Texcoco that was located where
Mexico City is today. Generally unwelcomed by their neighbors, they survived as mercenaries for the strongest of the quarreling city-states in the valley.
By virtue of a series of exceptionally talented rulers, the Mexica, in a triple
alliance with two other city-states, Texcoco and Tlacopan, constructed the
vast domain that eventually incorporated territories from the central plateau
in the north to the Petén forests in the south, an area roughly the size of
today's Italy. Using the tribute paid in cacao, gold, gems, cotton, textile, maize,
feathers, and honey the Mexica compiled great wealth and built a magnificent
city on the lake, Tenochtitlan.

The basis of the Mexica/Aztec state was war. The flow of tribute financed
the growing city, its spectacular arts and crafts, and its expanding noble class.
Individual status resulted from accomplishments as a warrior (reserved only
for males). Two limitations arose from its military foundation. First, the
Tlaxcalans to the east and the Mixteca to the west defeated the Mexica, so
they could not expand in these regions. To maintain an uneasy peace the
Tlaxcalans agreed to an annual rite, the Flowery Wars, which provided all of
the trappings of war without major battles, thus enabling the Mexica to save
face and train. The peoples of Mesoamerica feared the Mexica. To oppose
them and lose meant certain annihilation. To surrender led to heavy tribute

payments. The Mexica brutally quelled rebellions. The victors were not particularly interested in ruling their conquests, however, rather in squeezing out the payments demanded. The Mexica were also adept at forging alliances with the ruling families of the other city-states through marriage.

Although the Mexica were powerful and feared, their empire rested on uncertain grounds. Bitterness underlay the relations between the Mexica and the other city-states. The states they subdued bristled under Mexica rule, for everyone resented the tribute and their haughty attitudes. Decline in the pace of conquest, the flow of tribute payments or defeat in battle undermined their credibility. Any show of weakness might lead to rebellion. The Valley Mexico had a long history of rancorous relations among the different entities. The Mexica were another in a long line of strong states that eventually lost out to yet another.

However mighty the Mexica ruler (known as *tlatoani*) appeared, Mesoamerican politics were locally- based. Each entity or *altepetl* ruled itself "as their own people felt best, rotating tasks and responsibilities among the various segments that composed it...." Sometimes several altepetls joined to conduct external relations. Local traditions and local people governed everyday life. When the Mexica and their allies took over, they left local rule intact and required only that subordinate altepetls fight in their armies, participate in their public works, when called upon, and pay tribute. The Mexica had no interest in imposing their culture or language on their subalterns.[1]

The Incas built an even greater empire than the Aztecs. It extended from what is today the northern border of Ecuador into Bolivia, Argentina and Chile, 2500 miles. Somewhere between three and twelve million people resided in its territories. Cuzco, its largest city, had a population between 60,000 and 150,000. The Inca expansion proceeded in a unique fashion. First, they offered regional leaders a peaceful alternative, including gifts and the promise that they would maintain their positions. A rejection of these terms resulted in the execution of these leaders. The Inca armies consisted of warriors taken from recently conquered areas. Like Mesoamerica, in the Andes, the many political entities maintained long, bitter rivalries. Unlike the Aztecs, the Incas administered their empire, forcing their subjects to build roads, palaces, and temples, in addition to toiling on farms, tending to herds of llamas and alpacas, and working in the mines controlled by the state. Conquered people paid tribute as well. The Incas also relocated large numbers of people in order to consolidate their rule; they moved recalcitrant subjects

[1] Camilla Townsend, *Fifth Sun: A New History of the Aztecs* (NY: Oxford University Press, 2019), pp. 46-47.

to regions far from their homes into completely different ecologies. They also transferred skilled crafts people to the bigger cities. To insure loyalty, the Inca sent colonists from the heart of the empire to outlying places. Like the Aztecs, however, the Incas did not succeed in homogenizing the cultures of the empire. Quechua did become the common language.

If Tenochtitlán was the great achievement of the Mexica/Aztecs, then the road system was the Incas'. They built 20,000 miles of highway, much of it through mountainous terrain, with inns along the way. These provided a remarkable communications system that enabled the Inca to compile data invaluable for maintaining a centralized state. Another unique aspect of Inca rule was the role of mutual obligations between the Incas and their subjects. In return for tribute in kind and services, the Inca rulers were to take care of the people when in need. To accomplish this they maintained strategically placed warehouses along the highways stocked with large quantities of food and cloth. Thus, the Incas were able to care for their subjects, provision their military, and govern staple markets.

Both Mexica and Inca based their everyday lives on family units, on farming in ingenious ways and on increasing militarization. Family was at the center of daily life, obligations, and politics. In Mesoamerica the calpulli, comprised of a dozen or so households, oversaw the allocation of lands and local governance. In the Andes, the ayllu, a group of people who claimed common ancestry, worked the land together. Both were brilliant agriculturalists. The Mexica cultivated the lake with *chinampas* that were enormously productive floating gardens. The Inca employed carefully constructed terracing on the steep mountain slopes.

Militarization deeply affected gender relations. In both Mexica and Inca societies women did not participate in warfare. Consequently, whatever equalities they enjoyed during the early years of empire eroded substantially over time as warfare gained ever more importance.

As the sixteenth century began, in Mesoamerica and the Andes, two empires at the peak of their power and glory ruled. Their achievements in architecture, art, science, mathematics, astronomy, construction, and agriculture at the very least equaled and in many cases surpassed those of the civilizations of Europe and Asia. By the mid-1500s, both empires were in ruins, destroyed by Europeans far less advanced, except in the technology of destruction.

The conquest of the Americas by the Europeans elicits considerable debate. The first question usually posed is how could so few defeat so many in so little time? The very fact of the native defeat was for centuries used as evidence of the superiority of Caucasians. There were actually at least two stages to the conquest by the Europeans. The first was the relatively rapid military defeats of the two mighty, indigenous empires ruled by the Aztecs and the Incas, respectively. These bloody, brutal, epic struggles lasted for only a year or so with the capture or murder of their leadership and in the case of the Aztecs the total destruction of their remarkable capital city, Tenochtitlan. The second stage of the conquest took more than a century and was multi-dimensional. It involved military, economic, biological, religious, and administrative aspects. It also encompassed several levels of struggles. The analysis of these stages revolves around two basic questions. The first, asked earlier above, seeks explanations for the why the Spaniards were able to overcome the Aztecs with less than 1500 soldiers and then overcome the Incas with even fewer. The second looks to understand how the Iberians with the bare bones of bureaucracy and no standing occupying military force ruled these vast territories for three hundred years.

Criminals founded the greatest empire in the world. Cortés and his band were outlaws from the outset. They left Cuba illegally. They lied repeatedly to their superiors in order to justify their military operations. Cortés's letters to Charles V, reporting his activities, were at worst prevarications and at best deceptions. They deceived and lied to the native people they encountered; Moctezuma, the leader of the Aztecs, was only their most prominent victim. The Pizarro brothers in Peru also were murderers and thieves. All of this is worthy of mention for two reasons. First, because the Spaniards were the winners, they wrote the history, whitewashing their crimes. This was not always successful, as we shall see, for there arose a "Black Legend," that exposed them. Second, the fact that they founded their empire on criminality, cloaked in ardent Christianity and loyalty to the monarchy, inculcated lawlessness into the subsequent colonial enterprise.

As told by the conquerors, the encounter between the Aztecs and Spaniards was a heroic tale. The small army of Europeans vastly outnumbered through their persistence and valor defeated the cruel, savage Aztec empire. The Spaniards hated their foes for their religious practices, especially their worship of non-Christian gods and their use of human sacrifice to please these deities. The Aztecs, on the other hand, also despised their enemies as cowards who hid behind armor and horses, firing their weapons from afar, avoiding hand-to-hand combat.

The Spaniards were undoubtedly awestruck when they approached the remarkable view of Tenochtitlan in 1519. It spectacularly rose from the lake with its huge temples and palaces, abundant, lush market, and impressive causeways to the shore. Fifty thousand or more people inhabited the city making it perhaps the largest urban entity in the world. They had come in search of riches, to bring honor to themselves and their king, and (perhaps) to spread the word of their Christian god. Their priority was obvious—the native chronicles described them as having bulging eyes and distorted faces with their greed. Lust for gold was not enough to defeat an empire that for decades elicited nothing less than terror from its opponents.

How then did the Spaniards beat the Aztecs? Four factors were crucial. First, the catastrophic transfer of European diseases, such as smallpox, measles, and cholera, to the Americas; second, the assistance of indigenous allies, who hated the Aztecs and saw an opportunity to rid themselves of their oppressors. The virulent diseases had both short and long-term effects. Immediately, they wreaked havoc on the leadership of the Aztecs and severe loss of population badly weakened their ability to withstand Spanish attacks, especially during the siege of Tenochtitlan in 1521. In the years following, disease killed over ninety percent of the indigenous people, allowing the Spaniards to install their rule with far less resistance than if the population had remained at 1520 levels. It was so much easier to take over the land and install Spanish agriculture when there were so few people to resist. No less important were the indigenous allies the Spaniards acquired, most prominently the Tlaxcalans. Tens of thousands of the Mexica's enemies, not hundreds of Spaniards bore the brunt of the war for Mesoamerica. Third, the Europeans possessed weapons that were far superior, specifically their steel swords and guns. Fourth, the Aztec leadership miscalculated the motivations of the Europeans, not from cowardice or from mistakenly believing that the Spanish commander was a deity (allegedly tradition predicted the return of Quetzalcoatl), but because they did not understand their enemies' worldview. The Mexica were accomplished warriors, but their protective gear and arrows were no match for steel blades, guns, and cannon. Cortés himself received numerous wounds from these arrows, but, of course, survived. In the siege of Tenochtitlan, the Spaniards added ships with cannon to their technological advantages. The Aztec ruler Moctezuma II was well aware of the capabilities of the Europeans; his spies reported the crushing defeat of the Tlaxcalans and Cholulans on the road to the central plateau. He had two possible strategies. He could confront the invaders, but he was certain that he could not defeat them. He realized, too, that any massive defeat would jeopardize his empire. Subject people, ruled for decades in terror, would surely rebel against the weakened Mexica. Moctezuma instead chose to offer for his domain to become a tributary to the Spaniards. He envisioned the Mexica assuming a similar position to all those entities he and his predecessors had subjugated in the previous century.

Moctezuma was not afraid, as some concluded, but rather pragmatic. Cortés tried to foist off the story that Moctezuma surrendered to him giving the Spaniard his kingdom, believing that he was a god, whom prophesies long predicted would return. This was nonsense! Cortés made this up so that he could claim his escapades were just under Spanish law. Moctezuma's mistake was to underestimate the greed and ambition of the Europeans. They would not settle for tribute, for they wanted the glory and riches of conquest in European terms.

As it turned out, the Mexica nearly defeated the Spaniards despite the Europeans' advantages. While Cortés in panic left Tenochtitlan to head off an expedition sent by his superiors in Cuba to arrest him for insubordination and traveled to the coast, the Mexica rebelled. The Mexica slaughtered one group Cortés sent back to Tenochtitlan in advance of his force. As soon as Cortés returned, the Mexica attacked again. The *Noche Triste* or Sad Night resulted in heavy Spanish losses and humiliating retreat. The Europeans lost 600 men, two-thirds of their force. Two thousand or more Tlaxcalans perished as well. The Mexica followed them, but could not prevent their enemies from escaping. In May 1521, Cortés returned. By November, Tenochtitlán lay in ruins. The Spaniards were the masters of the Valley of Mexico. The siege illustrated very clearly the Europeans' advantages in technology, their alliance with the Mexica's enemies, and the devastating impact of disease. The Spaniards employed a fleet of ships with cannons on the lake to level the city. They brought with them an enormous indigenous army. During the siege, disease decimated the defenders. The Spaniards almost certainly murdered Moctezuma. His successor fell to disease. Virtually leaderless, starving, and demoralized (at least temporarily) the Mexica surrendered.

In the case of the Incas, the first two of the factors brought the Spaniards victory. Disease killed the leadership, causing internal strife. A civil war between rival heirs to the throne badly weakened the Inca Empire. The Spaniards, led by shady adventurer Francisco Pizarro, arrived in Peru in 1531. Native allies came from the ranks of the defeated faction in the struggle over succession. The Spaniards took advantage of divisions among the Incas, who recently experienced civil war between two contending factions. Military defeat was much more gradual than in the north, however. Duplicating the strategy employed against the Mexica, the Spaniards murdered the Inca leader, Atahualpa, despite his willingness to pay an enormous ransom. Pizarro then made a nearly fatal mistake, installing Atahualpa's half-brother as emperor. Instead of cooperating with the Europeans, Manca Inca led a rebellion in 1536, attacked Lima, besieged the city of Cuzco for eight months, and then retreated to the mountains, where his forces held out until the 1570s. To add to the disorder, a dissident group of Spaniards rebelled against the Pizarro family, resulting in more than a decade of civil strife.

For the first century after the Spaniards defeated the great indigenous empires, two struggles occurred simultaneously. The first was between the Spanish Crown and the conquistadors, such as Columbus, Cortés and his minions, and the Pizarro family. Ferdinand and Isabella and then Charles V, jealously guarded their prerogatives. With their kingdom united for barely a decade, tormented by uncooperative nobility in Spain, vastly ambitious, but with minimal resources, the monarchs were wary of the adventurers who claimed new lands for their realm. Their ability to bring under control this ungrateful rabble was limited, for the treasury was always nearly bankrupt and thousands of miles of sea and land separated them. The enormously greedy, self-gratulatory conquistadors proved an unruly lot, not easily repressed. The monarchs had two useful allies in their conflicts with their new world subordinates, the Catholic Church and the very same nobility, which once formidably opposed them at home. The Church allies comprised two separate groups, often themselves in conflict, the regular clergy, who were missionaries, bringing the Christian god to the indigenous, and the secular clergy, who did not belong to orders and presided over the churches and ceremonies. The regular clergy acted counterweight to the conquistadors, opposing their exploitation of the native population. The secular clergy played a role as an administrative balance. The nobility, particularly at the lower and middle ranges, seemed always in financial straits. The opportunity to purchase (or less frequently obtain by merit) bureaucratic posts in the American empire was an almost surefire way to get rich. At the same time, in order to facilitate the acquisition of wealth and to stay out of prison for their misdeeds, they maintained loyalty to the Crown.

Ferdinand and Isabella quickly tired of Christopher Columbus, whose pretensions and demands were endless. He spent time in chains and died unheralded. Cortés from the outset operated on the margins of legality. The Crown could not argue he did not deserve his rewards, however. Cortés became the Marqués del Valle de Oaxaca and received an encomienda, which bestowed on him the labor of 100,000 indigenous people. The Crown sent a Viceroy to rule in his name in 1535 to prevent Cortés from establishing a kingdom of his own. It took the Crown until 1569 to install a Viceroy in Peru. The colonists killed the first representative the monarch sent to Peru. In both regions, the Spanish kings confronted a serious dilemma. On one hand, they had conquistadors who demanded their just rewards in terms of honors and wealth. The Crown had few resources to finance the rewards owed. The great mineral riches required considerable investment to realize. The near-do-well, uneducated soldiers who comprised the victorious armies had neither the capital nor the skills for such enterprises. The Crown found the answer in the institution

of the encomienda. The King granted the right to collect tribute from a speci-
fied group of native people. The tribute initially could take the form of payment in kind or in labor. It included no land. On the other hand, the Crown
had no interest in creating an American nobility; its experience at home it
wanted to avoid at all costs. The Crown attempted to prevent the creation of
a hereditary nobility in 1542 when it presented the New Laws, which forbade
encomienda recipients from passing them down to their heirs, excluded indigenous labor as payment of tribute, and expressly limited the further enslave-
ment of native peoples. The New Laws resulted from an alliance between the
Crown and the regular clergy.

In keeping with their dual purposes of preventing the rise of an American
nobility and generating revenue, the Spanish Kings established a somewhat
cumbersome administrative structure. It included just enough personnel to
generate funds to support the expenses of the colonial government and to
provide a steady flow of income to the Crown to pay for its profligate court
and European wars. They set up a system of overlapping jurisdictions and
regulations aimed at preventing any group or individual from getting too
powerful. The parsimonious Crown was never willing to invest in either physical infrastructure or human capital. The monarchs were interested primarily
in the extraction of mineral wealth, particularly gold and silver, and collecting
the *Quinto* or fifth in taxes. For the most part, in New Spain they administered the mining districts in the northern plateau, the capital, and the ports of
Veracruz and Acapulco, leaving the rest of the colony to local elites and villages. In South America, they focused their attention on the silver and mer-
cury mines in what is now Bolivia and southern Peru, respectively.

At the top of the administrative hierarchy were two Vice Kings or Viceroys,
one based in Mexico City and the other in Lima, Peru, the Viceroyalties of
New Spain and of Peru. The Viceroys delegated executive, military, and judicial authority in outlying areas to provincial governors, sometimes known as
governor-generals. In the area of today's Mexico, there were twenty-one jurisdictions. Counterbalanced to the viceroys were the *Audiencias*, three person
councils that exercised executive functions and acted as courts of appeal, with
jurisdiction over large metropolitan areas. Town councils or *cabildos*, supervised the markets, administered justice, and sponsored religious festivals.
Counterbalanced locally officials known as *corregidores* or *alcaldes mayors* also
had administrative and judicial responsibilities. In theory, the monarchy
tightly regulated these organizations and individuals. In reality, however, the
nearly 6000 miles between Madrid and Mexico City and Madrid and Lima
limited its reach. When local conditions did not fit new laws emitting from
Spain, the various government entities adopted the motto "*Obedezco pero no*

cumplo" (I obey, but I do not comply). Colonial officials recognized the Crown's authority, but local circumstances dictated alternatives. The audiencias often conflicted with the viceroys, the cabildos with the corregidores, the corregidores with the provincial governors. The Crown trusted no one, consequently the king often sent a *visitador* or inspector to examine the finances and conduct of the viceroys and other officials at the end of their terms.

The monarchs encouraged other layers of conflict as well. The Church had its own bureaucratic hierarchy consisting of bishops and archbishops. These clerics often had differences of policy and procedure with the viceroys and other lay administrators. The Church divided into two competing groups, the regular orders and the secular clergy. In addition, the Inquisition operated almost totally beyond the control of either civil or religious authority. The Church assigned particular duties to each of the groups. The regular orders, the Jesuits most prominent of them, looked after the conversion of the indigenous peoples to Christianity. They learned native languages and customs. It fell to them to protect the indigenous from the conquistadors and settlers who followed them. This duty brought the orders into bitter conflict with the colonists. For the monarchs the orders were crucial to keeping the colonists under control, most importantly in the first hundred years. The secular clergy tended to the non-indigenous folks. They presided over the rites of passage, such as baptisms, marriages, and funerals, saints days, and holy days. Over time, the Church became the empire's largest landowner and banker. Eventually the Church's wealth engendered the enmity of the Spanish kings.

When the population was higher at the beginning of colonial rule, the Spaniards removed themselves from daily supervision. They established two separate republics, one for the native peoples and the other for colonists. In the *república de los indios*, the native peoples administered their lives at the local level. Many of the leaders were members of pre-colonial prominent families. After a century, the death toll from the various diseases rendered this strategy unusable. Villages disappeared. No one remained alive to occupy vast tracts. As the population recovered, in 1650 or so, local governance reappeared.

The colonial administrators cared about four matters: first, that the indigenous population provide labor to feed the settlers; second, that the indigenous supply sufficient labor to operate the mines, in order to assure the Crown's revenue flow; third, that the native people did not revert to their prior religious practices; and fourth, that they enrich themselves.

The colonial system was messy and inefficient. The settlers ignored, sometimes flouted rules, regulations, and laws, nearly always with the complicity of authorities at all levels, going far beyond the "I obey, but do not comply." Smuggling, for example, was commonplace. Little doubt exists that mine owners cheated on their taxes. Local officials siphoned off tribute. Despite these obvious inadequacies, at least through 1700, the Spanish kings seemed satisfied with what they got. Ironically, Spanish governance was not much different from that of the Aztecs. Neither empire was much interested in daily governance; both focused on tax collections in the form of goods and services.

One other aspect of rule that the Spanish colonial regime had in common with the Aztecs was governing by fear. Certainly, the prospect of Mexica vengeance on their opposition instilled cooperation. The specter of human sacrifice was an element of this. The Spanish equivalent was the Inquisition. It tortured and executed those it judged as heretics. The Inquisition crushed any hint of rebellion, making examples by burning at the stake. Was there any real difference between the Mexica tearing out the hearts of their enemies in the name of their gods and the Inquisition torturing, drawing and quartering for their religion?

In Peru, the Spaniards also concentrated on the extraction of minerals. The crucial aspect of their rule was the procurement of sufficient labor to work the mines. Perhaps taking their lesson from the Incas, the Spaniards instituted a forced labor system, which required each village to provide a quota of labor. The Inca, however, unlike the Spaniards supplied protection and provisions in return. The Spaniards gave nothing. Voluntary labor was virtually unheard of, because indigenous folks refused to toil in the dangerous mines unless coerced.

The question of indigenous resistance provides some interesting discussions. The great empires suffered terrible defeats, to be sure. On the surface, it appears they gave in rather abruptly, especially in the case of the Mexica. In fact, rebellions continued against the Spaniards through the colonial era. In some areas, such as the northern regions of New Spain, indigenous peoples fought for three hundred years (Yaquis, Mayos, Tarahumara, Apaches, Comanches, for example) and in the south in the Pampas of the Rio de la Plata, Araucanians never succumbed to colonial governance. Nor did the Mayas. At times, the colonial government reached uneasy truces involving trade agreements, but could not exert control.

Portugal, with a smaller population (one million) than Spain and even fewer resources, faced a daunting task after Pedro Álvaro Cabral sailing under its flag discovered Brazil and claimed it for his sponsors in 1500. No great indigenous empires opposed the Portuguese, but the vast territory and large population, estimates range from two to seven million inhabitants, presented an enormous challenge. For nearly a half century, the Crown assigned exploitation of the colony to private entrepreneurs granted *sesmarías* or proprietary captaincies. Since there were no immediate discoveries of precious metals, the settlers, who numbered a few thousand by the mid-sixteenth century, relied on the export of brazilwood and then sugar. The colonists required considerable labor, which the indigenous peoples loathed to provide. Joao III finally sent a governor-general in the late 1540s, only because France threatened to takeover. By the end of the sixteenth century successor governors-general ousted the French, subdued a native people's rebellion in the northeast, and established a bare-bones bureaucracy. The governors did not attain the power wielded by the Spanish Viceroys. Instead municipal councils, or *senados de Camara*, presided over local affairs, ensuring labor supplies and administering justice.

For the first two centuries of colonial rule, Brazil's economy revolved around sugar production. Like the Spaniards, the Portuguese colonists required considerable labor. The population decline caused by European diseases was as dreadful in Brazil as in Spanish America. The solution for the shortage of workers was to import slaves from Africa. Slave traders from Portugal, the Netherlands, and England brought over millions of people of different ethnic groups from all over Africa. The Atlantic crossing was nightmarish with slaves chained below decks with little food or water. More than two million died over the centuries making these voyages. The enslaved people came from all over Africa, with different languages, religions, customs, and traditions. The traders and settlers ignored all of these. They were concerned solely with forging a docile, productive workforce.

The Iberians employed four strategies to keep their subaltern peoples obedient, or at least accepting of their circumstances. First, and most crucial, was the cooptation of indigenous elites and intermediaries. The local indigenous leaders, known as *caciques* in Mesoamerica and *kurakas* in the Andes, were indispensable for maintaining order and peace. Spanish colonial rule was not possible without them. As time went on and more and more mixed blood people (mestizos, mulattos, etc.) were born, they often provided important links between the indigenous folks and the Spaniards, because they spoke both indigenous languages and Spanish. On the plantations, slaves often served as foremen. Conversion to Christianity was a third important tool of colonialism. Priests acted as secret police (the confessional was not in reality confidential). The Catholic faith favored acceptance of one's plight, while awaiting a better place. Lastly, the Iberians employed coercion. Forced labor ensured the supply of miners and cultivators. Whipping and other corporal punishments maintained discipline on the slave plantations. The Inquisition ensured obedience to Catholicism, but to the Crown as well.

The colonial enterprise rested on the principle of everyone knowing his or her place and remaining in it. There was a strict racial and gender hierarchy. At the top were those of "pure blood," those of one hundred percent

Spanish or Portuguese descent. Other Europeans were white, but often viewed as outsiders. As time went on, a second sector within white arose including Iberians born in the colonies, or creoles (*criollos*). Spanish born whites were peninsulars (*peninsulares*) or the non-complimentary *gachupines*. Next in the pyramid were the castes (*castas*), comprised of the progeny of whites and indigenous, mestizos; whites and Africans, mulattos; and dozens other racial mixtures, all named and meticulously ranked. Then came indigenous people. Last were Africans. Two factors complicated the hierarchy. First, it was often difficult to differentiate between the various castas, indigenous, and Africans. The Spaniards enacted dress codes to identify indigenous, but people ignored them. Second, the concept of *limpieza de sangre*, pureness of blood, was fungible, that is if a person of color attained wealth, he or she could purchase whiteness. This was particularly true in the Spanish colonies that had a considerable African population, like New Granada and Venezuela, and in Brazil. Besides knowing one's place, patriarchy was the other pillar of Iberian colonial society. Males were to rule over family and society; all others, women and children were subordinate. Wives and unmarried daughters were to stay at home, leaving only to go to church and family events chaperoned. Manhood depended on the ability to provide for one's family and to govern his household. Marriage was the basis of family. Like everything else in colonial society, people honored such norms more in their breach than in following them. Women had to leave their homes to work. Most marriages were common law not sanctified in the church. The rite was too costly for most folks.

The colonial economic systems operated primarily for the benefit of the metropole. In both Spanish and Portuguese America the economy centered on the exports of agricultural products and minerals. The monarchies exerted tight control over the flow of precious metals in particular. The Spaniards attempted to limit trade to their advantage. The Crown went to extremes to safeguard the export of gold and silver from the mines of New Spain and Peru, which were the heart of the colonial enterprise. To defend the shipments of precious cargoes, Spanish kings limited them to twice a year treasure fleets. They also limited all trade to the ports of Cadíz in Spain and Veracruz and Acapulco in New Spain and Porto Bello in Panama. The fleets arrived in the American ports loaded with goods from Spain and other European countries. Great merchant houses emerged to manage commerce; these cooperated in organizations known as *consulados* or guilds. The fleet system, which was not always successful at protecting trade from predatory English and Dutch, encouraged contraband and added considerably to the cost of imports. It was an inefficient system that benefited only a very few privileged merchants and the monarchy. It provides yet another instance of the colonial enterprise resulting in corruption, for under the fleet system avoidance of taxes and smuggling were inevitable. The Portuguese were more pragmatic and opened their ports to foreigners. The macro-economic effect of the Spanish trade restrictions was detrimental to the colonies and the metropole. Spain could not come close to satisfying the demand for manufactured products, consequently England and the Netherlands shipped these goods to Spain, which paid for them with American gold and silver. This, of course, increased the cost of all to the colonies. Spain received little benefit, for only a small portion of the precious metals remained in Spain. Another problematic policy of both metropoles was the grant of monopolies of certain products, such as tobacco and cacao. The Crowns bestowed these upon politically connected companies. These, too, added to the cost of the commodities.

The arrival of the white Europeans and black Africans brought vast changes to governance, economics, biology, daily life, and traditions. At the same time, for indigenous people much remained unchanged. Historians once thought that the defeat of the Aztec and Inca empires combined with the terrible impact of disease devastated the indigenous people. It appears, however, that the effects of the conquest were not so extensive, although the drastic population decline was catastrophic. The subjugation to the Spaniards hit the Mexica the hardest, for they lost their position as the mightiest residents of Mesoamerica. But, for most of the peoples of the region, Spain was just another in a long line of repressive masters. They paid their tribute and continued to live their lives. Probably the crucial transformation was the adoption of a new religion. Unlike past conquerors, the Spaniards insisted on conversion to their religion. To this end, the Iberian Crowns sent missionaries, the most prominent of them Jesuits and Franciscans. The orders learned the native languages and customs and (to the chagrin of historians) destroyed many of the records of their history, religious practices, and culture. The defeated people were willing to accept the new god, for it was clearly more powerful than their old gods. Whether or not they were willing to give up all their old gods entirely was altogether a different question. The missionaries, quite cleverly, made the transition easier by building churches on the sites of old temples and by adapting the characteristics of Christian saints to resemble those of some of the old gods. Many indigenous became devout Christians. It is clear, however, a kind of folk culture evolved, particularly in the countryside, that was not quite the Catholicism of the urban cathedrals. In Brazil, the Crown also insisted on the conversion of both the indigenous people and African slaves. The latter evolved their versions of folk Catholicism, mixing their African religious traditions with those of their masters.

The biological and ecological consequences of the European takeover were profound. The Portuguese cleared vast tracts of virgin lands for sugar cane. Eventually these plantations destroyed the environment of the northeastern regions. The Iberians introduced large domestic animals, cattle, horses, sheep, goats, pigs, which altered the landscape. The transformation from cropland to pasture led to widespread erosion, rendering it useless. The Spaniards preferred wheat to corn and bread to tortillas. As a result, over the decades diets changed, mostly in the cities. In the countryside maize, beans, and peppers remained the staple foods.

Aside from mining, the most important economic introductions of the Iberian colonies were the large estates, known as *haciendas* in Spanish America and *fazendas* in Brazil. The haciendas grew from the need to produce large animals and wheat, which required extensive lands to be profitable. They filled the empty spaces left by the precipitous fall in population. The haciendas and their neighboring indigenous and casta villages engaged in a simultaneously symbiotic and conflicting relationship. The haciendas required labor, which villagers, seeking to supplement their subsistence plots, supplied. The widespread uncertainty about titles and boundaries led to many disputes over these and water rights. The sugar cane plantations needed intensive labor, which they obtained from slaves. Sugar growing and processing were dangerous occupations; the enslaved did not last long.

While Spaniards ruled the hemisphere, its enemies propagated a "Black Legend," accusing them of exceptional mistreatment of the native peoples. Many later historians came to similar conclusions. The Portuguese perhaps avoided contemporary disapproval, but their slave hunters, known as *bandeirantes*, earned a reputation among historians for their cruelty. Historians were also clear about the horrendous conditions of the slave trade and slavery in Brazil. Contrarily, a "White Legend" arose among twentieth century historians arguing that the Spaniards acted much more benignly with religious underpinnings for their interactions with the native peoples. At the same time, another view held that Iberian slavery was not nearly as harsh as the English/United States version. There is little doubt that the Spanish colonial system was exploitative and that the harshness of its rule was a contributing factor in the population catastrophe. The Spaniards invested nothing in human beings or in public works. They constructed no body of law to govern commerce industry or finance. The notion that the system was benign in its treatment of native people derives entirely from a body of laws decreed in the sixteenth century by the monarchs and philosophical discussions by learned academicians about the status of indigenous. The colonists angrily disobeyed the former. Almost everyone except a few dissident clerics ignored the latter. The assertion that Brazilian slavery was less destructive than U.S. slavery does not hold up either. The argument centers on the status of slaves under Portuguese and Spanish law as human, rather than as property as regarded in the United States. Similar to the case of the indigenous, the colonists ignored the laws.

Regionalism, disrespect for law, hands-off administration, and corruption were the strongest political legacies of colonial rule in Spanish America. Alongside these inheritances was a strict social hierarchy of class, based almost totally, on race. The economic legacy was the exploitation of non-whites and the protection of wealth privilege. The effects of Iberian colonial rule were no different from the impact of the British or any other European colonial empires, so perhaps we cannot single out the Iberians for particular admonition. Nonetheless, three hundred years of Spanish and Portuguese rule left the nations that emerged in the nineteenth century badly disadvantaged to compete in the industrialized age of capitalism.

Timeline

1300	Mexica arrive in the Valley of Mexico
1429	Triple Alliance takes control of the Valley of Mexico
1492	Spain united under the rule of Ferdinand and Isabella
	Columbus discovers the Caribbean Islands
1500	Cabral lands in Brazil
1518	First recorded smallpox outbreak in the Americas
1519–1521	Cortés defeats the Mexica
1532	Pizarro defeats the Incas
1538	Manco Inca revolt
1537–1548	Civil Wars in Peru
1540s	Silver discovered in Zacatecas, New Spain
1542	New Laws
1556	Philip II becomes King of Spain
1568–1572	Jesuits arrive in New Spain and Peru
1572	Defeat of neo-Inca state
1580	Brazil becomes world's leading sugar producer
1610	Portuguese put down santidade revolt
1690	First gold found in Brazil

How Historians Understand

Documenting the Colonial Enterprise

The documentation for studying the history of the Iberian American colonies is enormous. The Spanish and Portuguese colonial bureaucracies monitored economic activity in their overseas empires with the aim of enforcing mercantile restrictions and maximizing revenues for the Crown. These administrative records, of course, are not flawless. They show taxes collected, but not those evaded; they itemize goods shipped legally but not those smuggled. While exact totals are illusive, it is possible to track trends. It is an irony of Iberian colonial regimes, that their corrupt, inefficient rule produced enormous archives in Seville, Madrid, Mexico City, and elsewhere for historians to sift through.

Various types of documents enable us to reconstruct colonial enterprises. The records of the courts and notaries are especially revealing. Copies of land titles ended up in the archives when landownership was the subject of litigation. Wills typically included information on a person's place of birth, marriages, children, dowries brought into the marriages, inheritances, personal earnings, outstanding debts, and accounts payable. The executor made a careful inventory of the testator's estate, complete with the appraised value of all possessions, down to individual items of clothing and household effects. Litigation among the heirs sometimes also created a quite long paper trail. Owners and overseers often kept meticulous accounts of the daily operations of mines, haciendas, and businesses.

To appear in the written records one probably had to accumulate assets worth a court fight among heirs or creditors. Thus, the official records skew towards those of considerable means. The documents also weigh toward enterprises that remained in the same family or institution for generations. For example, many hacienda studies investigate the properties owned by the Jesuits. Luckily for historians, when the Spanish and Portuguese expelled the order in the late eighteenth century and confiscated their property, they included their well-kept records, which the governments deposited in archives accessible to this day. Much of what we know about Brazilian sugar plantations derives from the records of the Jesuits estates. Historians have to take care not to assume that the operations of these plantations were universal to all.

The further down the social scale, the harder it is to document the activities of specific individuals. Notarial archives provide one track the everyday activities of artisans, petty entrepreneurs, and other ordinary folks. Notaries certified apprentice contracts, bills of sale for all kinds of property, letters granting freedom to slaves, and wills. Those of more humble status also appear in the court records. Historians might find the record of a complaint brought by a small farmer whose cow someone stole, or a worker whose boss mistreated him. These files are often slimmer than the great bundles of papers delineating the disputes of the great landowners, miners or merchants, but they are revealing nonetheless. Smaller towns maintained record in indigenous languages, evidence that the people did have a voice.

Historians must thank the thousands of accountants, notaries, clerks, and scribes, who in their meticulous penmanship created the records that permit them to illuminate the business and lives of colonial Latin Americans.

Latin American Lives

Domingos Fernandes Nobre, Mameluco of Brazil

Both the Spanish and Portuguese colonial enterprises depended on the forced or voluntary cooperation of native peoples. This collaboration in turn relied on individuals who understood enough about indigenous cultures and European demands to broker the two. At times, the intermediaries were indigenous or other times Europeans who lived among the native peoples. Still others were the offspring of European men and indigenous women, like Domingos Fernandes Nobre. Born in Pernambuco in northeast Brazil in 1564, the son of a Portuguese stonemason and an indigenous woman, baptized a Catholic, fluent in Portuguese, and married to a Portuguese woman himself, Nobre lived, in the words of historian Alida Metcalf, "on the margins of respectability" in the Brazilian capital of Salvador. He was deeply familiar with the customs and traditions of native people, for he spent a good part of his life among them in the sertão, the poorest region of the Brazilian interior. During those years, he tattooed his body in the style of the Tupi and adopted the indigenous name "Tomacaúna" ("black ant-bird") and lived as one, "walking naked as they do" and "neither praying nor commending himself to God."

Nobre's ability to speak the Tupi language and to live in two worlds facilitated his work as a leader of "*entradas*," expeditions into the interior that captured indigenous and delivered them as slaves to sugar plantations along the coast. His activities brought him into conflict with Jesuit missionaries, who opposed this treatment, preferring that the entradas brought the indigenous to them for indoctrination. His strategies for gathering slave labor eventually brought him to an even more dangerous encounter with church authorities.

In 1585 sugar planter Fernão Cabral commissioned Nobre to lead a large entrada with a hundred mamelucos like himself and indigenous into the sertão to round up workers for his estate. This venture led him into the purview of the Inquisition. In the last part of the sixteenth century, a series of messianic revolts arose in northeast Brazil that came to be known collectively as *santidade*. Indigenous, who had come into close contact with the Portuguese settlers, either as residents of mission villages or as slaves, and Africans, who escaped their Portuguese masters, established their own communities. The rebels fashioned a hybrid religion with idols to ward off whites and rosaries. They had popes, bishops, and missionaries to spread the word. By 1610, there were, perhaps, 20,000 indigenous and blacks, who fled to the santidade communities. The Portuguese, of course, regarded them as a threat. In his hunt for labor for the plantation, Nobre encountered Antonio, a baptized indigenous who had pronounced himself "pope," claimed to be God, and took over leadership of the rebellion. Nobre joined with him in dancing, singing, and smoking tobacco. Acting on instructions from Cabral, Nobre promised the rebels that if they were to accompany him to Cabral's plantation, the owner would allow them to practice their beliefs without interference. Sixty or so adherents to santidade accepted and received a warm welcome when they arrived at Cabral's estate. They erected a "church" and Cabral permitted the rebels to baptize his own African slaves into their sect.

(*continued*)

(continued)

A few years later, in 1591 the Portuguese Inquisition arrived in Brazil with the goal of ending alleged abuses in the colony. Mamelucos like Nobre, who both enslaved indigenous to the disapproval of the Church, and, then, to make matters worse, practiced santidade themselves, were obvious targets for the Inquisition. At his trial Nobre confessed to several transgressions, including sexual relations with numerous indigenous women, two of whom were his goddaughters. He also admitted to neglecting his Christian obligations while in the sertão and bowing in worship to Antonio. He explained to the inquisitor that he adopted indigenous ways in order to gain acceptance into their community. Probably much to his surprise (and ours) Nobre got off lightly. He paid a fine and participated in penitential rites. At some point, he later received a land grant.

The Portuguese apparently no longer found use for such intermediaries after the end of the sixteenth century. They instead turned to imported African slaves to perform the hard labor of the sugar plantations. Cultural brokers of mixed and indigenous ancestry, however, did not disappear from other regions in Latin America. They were in many ways the pillars of Spanish colonial rule, assuring the flow of village labor, seeing to the payment of tribute, and offering assistance for indigenous in their dealings with the outside world. Like Nobre, they were usually out for their own profit. Nonetheless, they were crucial in the functioning of the colonial system.

Slice of Life

The Indigenous Peoples of Oaxtepec Defend Their Land and Water

Profound change for the residents of Oaxtepec (now in the state of Morelos sixty miles southeast of Mexico City) accompanied the Spanish invasion of Mesoamerica. The introduction of new plants and animals extensively altered their material environment. The Europeans reshaped the landscape to accommodate newly created haciendas, plantations, and mines. The structure of community life transformed as well, for the people answered to new rulers and prayed to new gods. Some of the changes were good. They enjoyed new foods, such as melons, figs, oranges, limes, and quinces. They became enthusiastic participants in the market economy, selling produce to the cities and mines. But certainly in the late days of the sixteenth century the people of the village could not help but look back fondly on the days before the Spaniards came, when people worked hard, bathed three times a day, and "did not know what sickness was."

Much also remained the same over the decades. The familiar crops, such as maize and beans still formed the basis of their subsistence. Most spoke the language of the forebearers. The people of the village continued to govern themselves. The Spaniards did not have sufficient coercive force or administrators to rule closely at the local level.

The challenges for Oaxtepec were legion. Terrible epidemics killed ninety percent of the population. Haciendas developed as neighbors constantly challenging their rights to property and water and demanding the labor of its residents. Plantations endlessly pressed to take its lands for the production of sugar cane, taking away precious land for staple crops crucial for the subsistence of its people. As the population recovered generally, the village's fertile soil and agreeable climate attracted a growing numbers of non-indigenous who bought or rented lands from indigenous leaders and took up permanent residence in violation of royal prohibitions.

The most troublesome adversary was the Hacienda Pantitlán, which contested the rights to the water from a spring located near the church. For many years, the estate was in ruins and the hacienda owners did not challenge the village's use of the spring. However, in 1750 a new owner refurbished the sugar mill on the property and expanded production. Initially, the village and the hacienda compromised to allow each access to the water, but in1776 the owner sued the villagers, claiming they had taken most of the water at the height of his harvest, thereby halting his mill. Two decades of litigation ensued with no settlement. Rumors flew that the villagers planned a general uprising with support from neighboring indigenous communities. This threat seemed to convince the owner of Panititlán to look instead for his water in a local river from which he built an aqueduct. The bickering over the water continued, but the village won a victory, conceding only the right of way across their property for the construction of the aqueduct.

(continued)

(continued)

This was not the only conflict over water. Another hacienda owner accused them of diverting water from his aqueduct in order to supply thousands of banana plants cultivated by the local priest, a doctor and a number of other non-indigenous, who rented village lands. The feud grew particularly acrimonious in 1786, when demand for Oaxtepec's crops was unusually high. The village won one round in that year but the courts reversed their ruling two years later. In an effort to recoup the needed water supply, the village then renewed its dispute with Panititlán. Litigation continued for another century.

Oaxtepec's story illustrates the willingness and ability of indigenous communities to govern themselves and, perhaps as important, to defend against aggressive European landowners. The persistence of these villages was at times truly remarkable. It also shows the complexity of the relations between indigenous villagers, haciendas, and mestizo emigrants. These collaborations and conflicts continued throughout the nineteenth and well into the twentieth century.

Nature's Way

Columbian Exchanges

Europeans not only brought with them to the newly discovered lands great horror and suffering in the form of diseases hitherto non-existent in the western hemisphere, but also brought new plants and animals that profoundly altered the ecology, demography, and geography. The newly found lands reciprocated, sending in return new crops that bettered the lives of Europeans.

The Europeans came with many animals unknown in the western hemisphere, such as horses, cattle, oxen, sheep, donkeys, goats, pigs, and chickens. These introductions immediately badly altered the ecosystem. Animals spread disease, polluted water resources, and trampled crops. Grazing denuded the land, which caused soil erosion. The Europeans made erosion worse by cutting down the forests for lumber and firewood. Once productive land in a few years became barren. The transition in some areas to plantation crops like sugar and coffee (to feed European demand) transformed the ecology as well. Large-scale agriculture replaced the collectives and family plots reducing the production of traditional staples, such as maize, beans, and chili peppers.

Historians focused much of their discussions of the Columbian exchange on the transmission of Euro-African diseases, which devastated the indigenous population. The biological transformation went far beyond. The introduction of new foods changed diets and health; animal protein and wheat were probably the most important. They did not entirely replace the staple diet of corn (tortillas), frijol (beans), and chili, but the addition of more protein certainly altered metabolisms.

The most controversial aspect of the agricultural Columbian exchange is the introduction of livestock, especially cattle. Some historians argue that the introduction of hoofed animals was an ecological disaster, because it detrimentally affected the existing ecosystems. Cattle ranching caused the destruction of native species, their replacement by foreign varieties, and the alteration of soils. The prolific reproduction rate of cattle, their numbers doubled every fifteen years, compounded their impact. The herds changed the landscape, particularly in arid and semi-arid highlands. These transformations sped up erosion, which in turn led to flooding, and crop loss. In some areas, what once was green and productive became moonscape. In a few areas, ranchers mitigated the destructive effects of livestock by cyclically alternating land usage between pasturage and crop growing. Employing a system of "nomadic herding," which limited overgrazing, also lessened the impact of the cattle.

Cattle probably arrived in New Spain in the 1520s. They found among their first homes the region of Veracruz extending from the wetlands near the port to the piedmont. Interestingly, indigenous people intensely farmed the region in an earlier time. Archaeologists found that the native people dug a system of ditches, dumping the excavated soil into mounds between them. This method assured a year-round water supply. In addition, dredging the ditches supplied fertilized soil. The system yielded two crops annually. By the late 1500s, the ditches filled in, likely from neglect by a rapidly shrinking population. Cattle

(continued)

(continued)

moved into the empty spaces. Ranchers alternated their herds between the wetlands and the hills. Veracruz continued to the present day as one of the largest cattle producing areas in Mexico.

The introduction of livestock had another important detrimental effect, because it created constant tensions between ranchers and indigenous villages. The cattle trampled staple crop fields. The Spanish Crown early on in the sixteenth century attempted to protect the native people from the cattle herds. The Crown forbade raising cattle on encomiendas (the grants of territories from which recipients collected tax revenue), for example. Like every other such effort, it fell victim to market forces (greed). The pueblos and haciendas engaged in conflict everywhere in Mexico over land and water for the next five centuries.

Like everything we study in history, we can view the Columbian exchanges from different perspectives. On one hand, they brought on the deaths of over ninety percent of the pre-European invasion population from a wide variety of diseases. They changed the very nature of the land, not always positively. The disruption of land holding patterns and rural agricultural relationships, because of the changes in crops, introduction of livestock, and precipitous population decline was traumatic and, arguably, destructive. On the other hand, the insertion of new crops probably enhanced nutrition. The presence of large work animals, such as horses, oxen, and donkeys revolutionized farming and transportation.

2

New Nations

After three hundred years, the Spanish and Portuguese empires disintegrated between 1808 and 1824. Most of Spanish America and Brazil won their independence with only Cuba and Puerto Rico remaining colonies. The new nations of Spanish America emerged from long, costly wars. Brazil gained its separation from Portugal more peacefully, when the heir to the Crown proclaimed himself emperor of the former colony.

Causes

Independence movements resulted from the convergence of two sets of factors. The first was external. The age of revolution, which produced upheavals in North America, the Caribbean, and Europe, profoundly affected Latin America. The French Revolution (1789) and the ensuing conquest of Europe by Napoleon I, the slave rebellion in Sainte Domingue which led to the birth of Haiti, and the uprising of British colonists that created the United States changed how Latin Americans regarded Spanish and Portuguese colonial rule. Events in Spain and Portugal influenced both the timing and the path of the upheavals. Second and most important was internal, the insistence by people all over the region that they obtain more control over their daily lives, particularly local governance, the practice of their traditions, and the conduct of business. The geographical and historical diversity of the region dictated the character of the struggles and the nations that emerged from them.

© The Author(s), under exclusive license to Springer Nature Switzerland AG 2022
M. Wasserman, *Modern Latin America Since 1800*,
https://doi.org/10.1007/978-3-030-96185-5_2

The trigger for rebellion occurred in Spain, where the French Revolution and subsequent ascendance of Napoleon Bonaparte disrupted foreign relations and domestic politics. At the end of the radical phase of the French Revolution in the mid-1790s, the inept Spanish King Charles IV allied with France against England. This brought about a highly costly war, which elevated taxes in the colonies and brought on an English naval blockade that badly disrupted Atlantic commerce. The worst was to come for Spain. France's new Emperor Napoleon I invaded Iberia in 1808, forcing the recently installed King Ferdinand VII from the throne and replacing him with Joseph Bonaparte. Spaniards rebelled against the imposition of a French monarch, establishing juntas all across the country to govern in opposition. In 1810, the rebels established a legislative body, known as the Cortés, and wrote a new constitution in 1812. In response, Creoles organized juntas all over the colonies, in response to the events in Spain. Some colonists went a step further, claiming they were not colonies but separate kingdoms, equal to Castile and the other territories united by Ferdinand and Isabella in 1492. They argued the term colony came into use only in the mid-eighteenth century. By this reasoning, the imposition of Joseph severed their relationship with the monarchy. Initially, the creoles disagreed among themselves about whether to advocate self-rule and cooperation with the Cortés or complete separation from Spain. On the local level, the colonists elected hundreds of new cabildos, almost a thousand in New Spain alone.

The chaos in Spain instigated two simultaneous debates that would set the course of Latin American politics for a century. The first was between Spaniards and Creoles over how much self-governance to allow the colonies. The second was among the creoles over whether they were willing to advocate separation from Spain at the risk of setting off an uncontrollable revolution-from-below. The two questions came to a head during the creation of Spain's Constitution of 1812. Originally, the writers of the Liberal constitution thought to allocate representation according to population. The problem to the Spaniards was twofold: the inhabitants of the colonies far outnumbered those in Spain and most of the population of the colonies were indigenous, African, and mixed blood. Eventually the authors compromised allowing indigenous and mestizos the franchise, but no one of African descent. The creoles' dilemma was how to achieve their political goals—to get fair hearing—while protecting themselves from the feared masses. The Spaniards rigged the representation in the Cortés in order to maintain their majority in the body, despite their minority status in the empire as a whole. The Cortés consistently ignored the demands of the creoles.

As they developed, the rebellions bitterly divided along class and racial lines. The upper class creoles who led the movements despised the masses of poor indigenous, Africans, and castas upon whom they relied for support in the wars for independence and the political battles that ensued to form their new nations. It is likely that these wealthy whites endured the disadvantages of colonial rule as long as they did only because they feared they might unleash unmanageable popular unrest. They had good reason for their assessment. As the population recovered from the devastating epidemic diseases and increased substantially during the eighteenth century, access to land and employment decreased, leading to widespread discontent. A dangerous revolt broke out in Peru in 1780, led by a descendant of the Incas, Tupac Amaru. More than 150 village riots erupted in New Spain from 1700 through 1820. The Haitian revolution of the 1790s frightened slaveholders throughout the Western Hemisphere. The classes had differing goals. The masses sought to unbind themselves from the instruments of colonial oppression, such as slavery and the capitación or tax on indigenous people, and to assert local autonomy for their villages. The upper classes looked to gain access to government offices and thought in terms of nationhood. Further divisions arose from geographic loyalties; the interior provinces of the Rio de la Plata opposed Buenos Aires; Colombians distrusted Venezuelans. The prolonged wars of independence revealed and exacerbated these problems, which subsequently shaped Latin American politics during the nineteenth century and beyond.

The century of discontent that preceded independence originated in the demographic recovery that occurred after 1650 and accelerated after 1700, and in the alterations in colonial governance instigated by the kings of the House of Bourbon after 1714. Epidemic diseases continued devastate the region through the eighteenth century. As a result, rebuilding the population went slowly. Nonetheless, the increases put enormous pressure on land and water resources. This alone was not likely sufficient cause for the upheaval. At the same time, however, the new Bourbon regime instituted new policies meant to tighten royal control, making government more efficient, in order to squeeze more revenue from the colonies. The reforms adversely affected Americans of all classes. At the top, a horde of Spanish bureaucrats stomped into the colonies, pushing aside ambitious creoles, who thought themselves deserving of these positions. The new monarchs distrusted the creoles, believing them too attached by family and custom to carry out the new policies. The Spaniards disdained the Americans as lazy and inefficient. The Bourbons expanded the royal army; the conscription required to fill its ranks caused widespread discontent. The higher taxes they demanded exacerbated the situation. After nearly two centuries of inefficient, often inattentive rule, the Spanish monarchy attempted assert its control. Instead, it engendered bitter opposition.

Four Revolutions

Four separate independence movements emerged from the domestic discontent and international chaos of the first decade of the nineteenth century. The first began in Buenos Aires in 1808, then New Spain exploded in 1810, Venezuela in 1810, and, finally, Brazil in 1822. In only one region, separation occurred without difficulties. In each case, except Brazil, the wars that resulted lasted for more than a decade and cost the colonies dearly in blood and treasure. The military aspect of the wars of independence in Spanish America proceeded in two stages. The first, from 1810 to 1816, brought defeat and despair. The second, from 1816 to 1824, brought victory.

The Bourbon reforms established two additional Viceroyalties, New Granada (currently Venezuela and Colombia) in 1717 and Rio de la Plata (today Argentina) in 1776. Not coincidentally, these were the areas of origin of the two major independence movements in South America. The new commercial openings and local administration must have opened the eyes of the rich creole merchants and landowners to the possibilities separation from Spain offered. In New Granada, they took advantage of the disruptions in Spain in 1808 to attempt to start a self-governing junta, succeeding in 1810 by ousting the governor and the audiencia. The rebels set up a three-person executive and drafted a constitution. In keeping with the creoles' fear of the lower classes, it excluded them from political participation. The royalists regained the upper hand in 1812 after a severe earthquake struck Caracas. Somehow, they convinced enough of the population that the disaster was punishment for their defying divine intent by their rejecting the Crown. In 1813, a charismatic young wealthy creole, Simón Bolívar, emerged as the leader of a renewed movement for independence. Perhaps, more than any other leader of these times, he represented the creoles' dilemma. He despised the lower classes, but as he was to discover to his misfortune he could not defeat the Spanish without them. He suffered a humiliating defeat in 1814 to a royalist army comprised mostly of black and mulatto *llaneros* (cowboys), led by a black general, José Tomás Boves. Race and class war raged as the lower classes sought retribution for mistreatment by the creole advocates of independence. Boves died in battle, but his army forced Bolívar into exile.

Río de la Plata boomed after it became a Viceroyalty. For two hundred years, it had fallen under the authority of the Viceroy in Lima. At the same time, the Spanish Crown, which had once forbidden direct trade through Buenos Aires, opened the port to foreign commerce and it quickly emerged as the primary outlet for silver from Bolivia and for shipment of hides and tallow produced from the cattle that roamed the vast nearby plains. Buenos Aires' population reached 40,000 by 1800. The city had an independent streak from the outset. It was far from authority—2500 miles through mountains from Lima—and smuggling flourished during the decades before 1776. The sense of independence strengthened in 1806 and 1807 when a coalition of creoles, blacks, and mulattos joined to repel two attempts by the British navy to occupy successively Buenos Aires and Montevideo. In May 1810 amidst the crisis in Spain, a meeting of the upper class organized a junta that assumed governance. They proclaimed allegiance to the King, but in reality Spanish rule ended.

In New Spain, too, the popular classes played a major role, but in this instance, a wealthy creole with empathy led. The Bajío, a region one hundred or so miles northwest of Mexico City, illustrated the impact of the widespread changes brought on by the Bourbon reforms. Because of the growing market for staples crops caused by the increase in population, the owners of large estates sought to expand their holdings. The region was then the "bread basket" of New Spain with its fertile soil and proximity to the colony's largest city and the great mining camps. The Bajío was also an area with many cloth factories and artisans who produced textiles at home. The Bourbon reforms included opening up colonial trade to foreign merchants, who could supply manufactured textiles more cheaply, thus forcing the factories and artisans out of business. At the turn of the century, silver production in the Bajío plummeted, leaving additional thousands without employment. A series of droughts and crop failures compounded the misery. In the worst of these agricultural crises fifteen percent of the Bajío's inhabitants perished of hunger. More crop failures occurred in 1809. Between the changes brought on the Bourbon kings and the natural disasters, thousands of people were in dire difficulties. The heartland of New Spain was a simmering pot ready to boil over.

Father Miguel Hidalgo y Costilla was a priest in Dolores, a town twenty miles from the mining center of Guanajuato in the Bajío. Fifty-seven in 1810, Father Hidalgo, a middle class creole, had more than one grudge against the Spaniards. Jesuit-trained, he deeply resented the expulsion of the Order. His training led him to the philosophers of the Enlightenment and his subsequent advocacy of unorthodox ideas resulted in his dismissal from the prestigious position as rector of the college at Valladolid (Morelia today). He narrowly avoided prosecution by the Inquisition. Father Hidalgo, who lived well, sought to become wealthy beyond his meager income as a parish priest. Toward this end, he owned a small hacienda. Royal officials, however, confiscated his property in 1804, because he failed to pay the special tax levied by the colonial government to finance Spain's European wars. In Dolores, he often met with others of similar, disruptive intellectual interests and tried, too, to start up a number of business ventures.

As the Bajío in general and Father Hidalgo individually built their resentments against Spanish authority, conservatives in the capital overthrew the Viceroy in order to prevent independence. The disgruntled priest joined one of many conspiracies. Somehow, the colonial authorities discovered his plot. Consequently, he issued his famous "Grito de Dolores" (Cry of Dolores) on September 16, 1810, ahead of schedule. The region exploded as thousands joined his insurgency. At its peak, his army comprised 60,000, mostly mestizos and indigenous. The ranks filled with hungry, unemployed men, motivated in part by the prospect of daily wages, the prospect of booty from looting, the possibility of escape from dismal conditions, or other grievances against the status quo. The indigenous folk sought to retain control over their own communities. It is not likely independence was a concern.

The Hidalgo revolt was, of course, the creoles' worst nightmare. The priest's followers sacked several towns. The event that remained in the memories of the upper classes for a century was the attack on the grain warehouse (*alhondiga*) in Guanajuato in November 1810, when the rebels killed hundreds of Spaniards and creoles. As a result, frightened creoles fled the independence cause and joined the royalists. Within a few months, the reinvigorated Spanish army defeated Hidalgo's disorganized forces and executed him and its other leaders.

The rebellion did not end with the death of Hidalgo, however. Another priest, José María Morelos, took up arms, coming to control virtually all of southern Mexico from 1811 to 1815, until he, too, met defeat. The casta Vicente Guerrero took the mantle of Morelos and conducted guerrilla warfare into the early 1820s.

The road to independence was not a smooth one. Although in the Río de la Plata, Spanish rule was finished, everywhere else the prospects for separation from Spain appeared doomed. In New Spain, Hidalgo and Morelos were dead. Thousands of other rebels accepted amnesty. Bolívar was in exile in Jamaica. King Ferdinand, restored to his throne in 1814, sent a new army to northern South America to impose order. The Crown, at the same time, rejected all of the reforms of the Cortés and the Constitution, leaving the colonies once again under the thumb of the metropole.

Spanish liberals and army officers, who had opposed the French at great cost, when their kings abdicated and fled to luxurious exile, governed without the monarchy for six years, and for their sacrifices received nothing but contempt from the returning Ferdinand, in 1820 rebelled. They forced the king to reconvene the Cortés and reinstitute the 1812 constitution. The new leadership, however, committed a serious mistake when they refused to accept the colonies as equals or to maintain the earlier commercial reforms. This foolish stubbornness led the way to American independence.

Creoles, at least temporarily learning their lesson, in their renewed efforts incorporated the popular classes. Their mistrust continued, but they realized their goal of independence was unattainable without popular support. In Venezuela, Simón Bolívar returned from his exile and led a new army, soldiered by black troops, to a series of victories. Tropical diseases ravaged the Spanish army, which immeasurably helped the rebels to a long series of victories. By 1822, Bolívar won the long, hard-fought war and assured the independence of Gran Colombia, comprised of current day Venezuela, Colombia, and Ecuador.

José de San Martín, a Río de la Plata-born, veteran Spanish army officer, returned home in 1812 with the aim of liberating the rest of South America. After years of preparations, in 1817 he crossed the Andes, through the difficult mountain passes, to defeat the Spanish in Chile and proclaim its independence in 1818.

An indication of what was to follow during the nineteenth century appeared after San Martín sought to complete the second part of his plan, which was to liberate Peru. This required considerably more preparations (it took him five years to prepare the Chilean expedition), including construction of a Chilean navy. Additional difficulties arose because Peru was a royalist stronghold. Yet another obstacle rose, when San Martín and Bolívar seemingly could not agree on who was to free Peru. The two met in Guayaquil, Ecuador in 1822. San Martín withdrew and retired, leaving it to Bolívar to occupy Lima the following year. His lieutenant Antonio José de Sucre secured the victory in 1824 at the Battle of Ayacucho. The royalist army surrendered in Bolivia in 1825, ending the wars of Independence in South America.

In New Spain, soon to become Mexico, more than a decade of warfare ended in February 1821, when royalist General Agustín de Iturbide surprisingly switched sides, allying with guerrilla leader Vicente Guerrero, and proclaimed independence in his Plan de Iguala. By any assessment, this was a backroom deal. The creole upper class determined that independence was the best path, but they could not achieve their goal without the support of the popular classes, the castas and indios Guerrero represented. At the same time, the agreement had to assure conservative whites that no repetition of the excesses of the Hidalgo revolt, like the slaughter at the Alhondiga would occur. Iturbide proposed the creation of a constitutional monarchy and protection of the Catholic Church and the Spaniards who supported the pact. Spanish rule collapsed.

With independence from Spain won, the question then became what exactly that meant. The creoles in the big cities where they proclaimed their separation from Spain did not necessarily represent whole provinces, smaller cities, or villages. Many manifestos asserted independence, but these often meant independence from Buenos Aires or Mexico City, not Spain. The people of Quito in the former Kingdom of Quito, now Ecuador, proclaimed its independence, but they referred to independence from Lima and Bogotá. At the same time, the towns of the Ecuadorian highlands sought independence from Quito!

Compared to their counterparts in Spanish America, Brazilians attained their independence relatively peacefully, and Brazil remained united rather than split into many small nations. This does not mean, however, that conflict and preoccupation with local concerns were entirely absent from the Brazilian struggle for independence. As in the case of Spanish America, events in Europe triggered Brazilian independence.

Napoleon invaded the Iberian Peninsula in 1808 in order to sever Portugal's longstanding alliance with Great Britain. For decades, policymakers in Lisbon toyed with the idea of removing themselves from the vicissitudes of European power politics by making Brazil, rather than Portugal, the center of the empire. The rapid approach of French troops in November of 1807 persuaded the government to consider this radical proposal as a temporary expedient in the face of a national emergency. The Crown decided to move the court and its entourage, numbering perhaps 10,000 people, sailing with a British naval escort. Queen María and her son, the de facto ruler Prince Joao, arrived in Rio de Janeiro in 1808. King Joao VI continued to reside in Brazil after his mother's death in 1816.

The presence of the royal court brought dramatic changes to Portuguese America. Intellectual activity flourished with the long overdue introduction of printing presses at Rio de Janeiro and Salvador, the expansion of education at the primary level, and the establishment of two medical schools and a military academy to train officers for Brazil's new army. Rio de Janeiro thrived as never before, as local merchants found a market providing the court with its many needs. Most important, Brazilians took pride in their homeland, touting its greatness in new periodicals that circulated in major cities. As one young man from Bahia put it, "Brazil, proud now that it contains within it the Immortal Prince.,… is no longer to be a maritime Colony… but rather a powerful Empire." In 1815, Portuguese America became the Kingdom of Brazil, equal with the mother country.

Other changes proved less welcome, however. Brazilians shouldered new tax burdens to pay for the expanded bureaucracy and the costs of waging war against the French in Portugal. Willingly at first but with increasing reluctance as time passed, prominent citizens of Rio de Janeiro vacated their homes to accommodate the courtiers and bureaucrats who accompanied the king to Brazil. People in Bahia in the northeastern part of the country chafed under Rio de Janeiro's growing dominance. Although the government in exile officially encouraged trade with all nations, it also bound Brazil more closely than ever before to an economic dependence on Great Britain that stifled the growth of local manufacturing.

Some Brazilians dared to express their opposition to the adverse effects of the Portuguese occupation, and King Joao was no more sympathetic to their concerns than King Ferdinand was to the grievances of his American subjects. In March of 1817, a revolt began in Pernambuco in the northeast after royal authorities arrested a number of army officers and others suspected of harboring treasonous sentiments. The rebels destroyed images of the king and his coat of arms, proclaimed a republic, and trumpeted ideals voiced by their contemporaries in Spanish America, among them personal liberty, equality before the law, support for the Catholic religion, and devotion to their homeland, or patria. They also expressed their hatred toward the many Portuguese-born Europeans who settled in Brazil in the years since 1808, but vigorously denied rumors that they advocated an immediate end to African slavery, a mainstay of the Brazilian economy. The revolt spread throughout the northeastern part of Brazil, the area that most resented the heavy hand of the royal government based in Rio de Janeiro.

King Joao was aghast at what he called "a horrible attempt upon My Royal Sovereignty and Supreme Authority." His forces suppressed the rebellion within just two months and executed its leaders, but the king could no longer take his Brazilian subjects for granted. He brought new armies over from Portugal and stationed them in Rio de Janeiro, Salvador, and Recife.

Unrest rose in Portugal when the King did not return after the defeat of Napoleon. Discontent within the military sparked a revolt in August 1820 that strongly resembled the Spanish coup of that same year. The participants called for the convoking of a Cortes and the writing of a constitution modeled after the Spanish document of 1812. They also demanded that King Joao return to Lisbon, and he prudently acquiesced. Before embarking from Rio de Janeiro in April of 1821, he placed his 22-year-old son, Pedro, in charge as prince regent of the Kingdom of Brazil.

This was a period of important political change in Brazil. With the blessing of the Portuguese Cortes, many towns and cities formed juntas, asserting local autonomy rather than accepting the continued domination of the government in Rio de Janeiro, much as Spanish Americans of their time tried to free themselves from the control of capital cities. The Cortes also dismantled the superior tribunals created during King Joao's residency, and the local governing juntas refused to send tax revenues to Rio de Janeiro. The cumulative effect of these changes was to reduce Prince Pedro's authority. In effect, he functioned little more than as the governor of the capital city and its immediate surrounding area.

Meanwhile, delegates in the Cortes worried with considerable justification that those opposed to these constitutional changes might rally around Prince Pedro. The Cortes therefore commanded the prince regent to return to Portugal. In January of 1822, Pedro announced his decision to stay in Brazil. The final break came on September 7, 1822. Pedro I became the "constitutional emperor and perpetual defender" of Brazil, a position he held until 1831, when he abdicated in favor of his son, Pedro II, who in turn ruled until Brazil became a republic in 1889.

Results

As they went about setting up governments, leaders of the new nations of Latin America borrowed very selectively from the egalitarian rhetoric of the North American and French Revolutions. They eagerly invoked ideas of representation and freedom of expression when it came to claiming a voice for themselves in governing their homelands and they forged a new concept of citizenship, calling on all who lived within their orders to place loyalty to the nation above any ties to their church, family, or local community. The kind of equality proclaimed by the more radical factions of the French Revolution, and the specter of the bloody slave revolt that had brought independence to the former French colony of Haiti, terrified Latin American political elites. At the same time, fighters both for and against independence sought to enlist the lower classes on their side. Various insurgent leaders in Spanish America promised to abolish the tribute, a special tax on indigenous and blacks levied by on the colonial state. In Peru, the insurgents also ordered an end to the mita, a highly oppressive system of forced labor that had sent thousands of indigenous to work in silver mines and other enterprises. The tribute and the mita both symbolized the power of the colonial state the insurgents were anxious to destroy. Despite these reluctant, halting efforts to win them over, indigenous had few reasons to trust privileged creole patriots and often sided with the Spanish. In Peru and Bolivia, for example, indigenous comprised the bulk of the royalist armies. After independence, many leaders declared that the people formerly known as "Indians" were now citizens of the new national states. In practice, however, many forms of discrimination lingered long beyond the end of colonial rule. Royalist commanders throughout the hemisphere promised freedom to enslaved who helped them fight the rebel forces. Similar offers went out from insurgent camps as well, but sometimes creoles advised blacks that they would have to wait patiently for fulfillment of these promises. In 1812, for example, the revolutionary junta in Buenos Aires told the city's slaves that "longed for liberty cannot be decreed right away, as humanity and reason would wish, because unfortunately it stands in opposition to the sacred right of individual liberty." By "individual liberty," the Argentine patriots meant the property rights of slave owners. Even when the offers of freedom were genuine, creole leaders of the independence movement often showed extreme prejudice toward blacks even as they tried to recruit them, and, not surprisingly, many people of color cast their lot with the royalists. After independence, victorious creoles devised means to deny blacks access to the political process in their new nations. Only in places where slavery was no longer economically viable did they carry through with their wartime promises to abolish slavery.

Both sides in the independence struggle sought the support of women. Women accompanied soldiers into battle, preparing meals, nursing the wounded, and sometimes taking up arms themselves. In South America, Bolivar's companion Manuela Sáenz played a prominent role in the final battles for independence. Throughout the Americas, women served as spies for royalist and patriot armies alike. María Josefa Ortiz de Domínguez, wife of a royal official in the Bajío and nicknamed "La Corregidora," alerted Father Hidalgo and his coconspirators that the authorities discovered their plot. Women smuggled weapons, and, in one instance in Mexico, a printing press, to insurgents and persuaded soldiers in the royalist armies to desert. In Mexico City, however, a women's organization called the *Patriótas Marianas* drummed up support for the royalist cause. Despite the active involvement of many women in the independence movement, the new leaders of Latin America, like those who commanded the United States and all the nation states of nineteenth century Europe, included only males in their definition of who was entitled to play an active role in civic affairs.

Conclusion

In most of Latin America, the wars of independence were long drawn out, brutal contests. The Spaniards defeated the insurgencies in the first phase by 1815. Popular and creole movements (in New Spain and northern South

America, respectively) failed because of the deep-seated mutual distrust between the upper classes and indigenous and castas. Upper class fear of the indigenous and mixed population cut short Hidalgo's campaign, and the unwillingness of creoles to make concessions to the lower classes in New Granada ensured Bolívar's initial defeats. Undercurrents of class and race war added a vicious, murderous aspect to the fighting.

Beginning about 1817, the tide turned in favor of independence, in part because the creoles learned from past mistakes and reached temporary arrangements with the lower classes, such as the llaneros of Venezuela and Vicente Guerrero's guerrilla forces of southern Mexico. Politics in Europe also played a role in pushing the colonies toward the final break with the mother countries. Following his restoration to the Spanish throne, King Ferdinand VII paid little attention to colonial concerns, and the representative assemblies that reemerged in Spain and Portugal in 1820 proved intransigent on issues of vital concern to Latin Americans. Colonial upper classes finally felt confident they could declare independence and contain popular discontent without help from overseas. From 1817 to 1824, Spanish and Portuguese authority yielded to independent governments from Mexico to southern South America.

Soon after taking power, leaders of the new Latin American governments declared national holidays honoring the heroes of independence and their victories on the battlefield, but more than a decade of war left most Latin Americans with little to celebrate. Parts of the region were in ruins, and hundreds of thousands died. Many survivors, armed and mobile, had nothing to which they could return. Facing an uncertain future, those who did have resources hesitated to invest in new enterprises. It would take much of Latin America a century to recover economically from the wars of independence. Poverty in turn undermined the political stability of the new republics.

It was easy to create new symbols of nationhood, such as flags, monuments, and coinage. The task of forging new national identities, "imagined communities," in which racially and culturally disunited peoples who thought mostly in terms of their own towns and villages, could live together and come to see themselves as Mexicans or Peruvians or Brazilians, was far more difficult. The resulting tensions would undermine the stability of Latin American politics for a half century.

Timeline

1788	Charles IV takes the throne of Spain
1788	French Revolution
1791	Haitian Revolution
1807–1808	Napoleon's armies invade Portugal and Spain
1810	Hidalgo begins Mexican War of Independence
1812	New Spanish Constitution
1814	Restoration of Spanish monarchy
1821	Mexican independence
1822	Brazilian independence
1824	Battle of Ayacucho ends wars of independence

How Historians Understand

Were the Wars of Independence a Turning Point?

Periodization, the dividing of history into segments and identifying crucial turning points, is a major device historians use to explain and simplify the past. Traditionally, historians have considered the Latin American wars of independence between 1808 and 1825 as the crucial watershed in the region's history, and many Latin American history courses divide into terms focusing on the colonial and national periods. This interpretation inferred that Latin America abruptly ended its colonial era and entered into modern times with a sharp break from Spain and Portugal. We know, however, that while independence hastened many transformations already underway during the previous century, the colonial order did not disappear in the 1820s. Slavery and discrimination against indigenous peoples endured well past independence, and many laws and government procedures carried over from the colonial regimes to the new nation states. Puerto Rico and Cuba remained colonies of Spain until after 1898. The traditional division of eras obscured critical continuities and made it difficult to assess the effects of change.

During the 1960s, an alternative approach arose, viewing the independence era as part of a broader period stretching from approximately 1720 or 1750 to 1850. This "Middle Period" incorporated the transition from traditional to modern society and from colonial to independent politics. The newly configured century allowed historians to trace the evolution of the trends and forces that caused the independence movements and to evaluate the impact of the end of colonial rule.

Investigating the half-centuries before and after independence elucidated a number of new themes and hypotheses. First, traditional assumptions that the Spanish Empire was peaceful in the century before 1810 were incorrect. In the Mexican countryside, for example, there was constant unrest. Second, colonial rule was far from omnipotent. Historians long ago documented corruption and inefficiency, but recent explorations revealed the considerable extent of local autonomy. We only scratched the surface of understanding to what degree the innovations introduced by the Spanish Bourbon kings and their counterparts in Portugal not only disrupted accommodations reached earlier but also began processes of change that independent governments built on after 1830. The Iberian monarchs of the eighteenth century, for example, took steps to reduce the power and political influence of the Catholic Church in Latin America. Many independent governments in the nineteenth and twentieth centuries continued to pursue this objective. Economic development, especially of frontier regions, was a major concern of late colonial kings and independent governments alike.

While the inclusion of the wars of independence as part of a longer period and as part of longer historical processes provided much new knowledge and many new insights, the more traditional periodization has considerable advantages. First, the break with Spain and Portugal had an enormous political impact. It set off decades of conflict over who was to rule and how. Independent governments tried for a century to establish their legitimacy and control. Moreover, there is little doubt that the wars of independence were economically cataclysmic. The damage to property and people over the course of nearly two decades of fighting was massive. It required nearly the entire century to recover to the level of production and prosperity in 1800. Independent Latin America had broken significantly from the past and begun a new era.

Latin American Lives

Manuela Sáenz, 1797–1856, Liberator of South America

The life of Manuela Sáenz demonstrates how South Americans, and women in particular, experienced the transition from colony to independence. Manuela was born in Quito, the illegitimate daughter of a Spaniard who served on the city council and a woman from a prominent creole family. Her father provided for her upbringing in the largest and most affluent of Quito's convents, where she learned to read and write. In 1817, her father arranged for her to marry one of his business associates, the wealthy British merchant James Thorne, some 20 years her senior.

Manuela relocated to Lima with her husband and over the next few years helped manage his business affairs. Meanwhile, she became involved in Lima's political intrigues. She joined other women who supported Peruvian patriots' efforts to overthrow Spanish rule and actively helped recruit men to serve in José de San Martín's armies, even though both her husband and her father supported the royalist cause. In 1822, she paid a visit to her native Quito, in part because she wished to claim a portion of her mother's estate. She observed Simón Bolívar's triumphant arrival in the city on June 16, 1822, and shortly thereafter met him in person. The two soon began an intimate relationship that lasted the remaining eight years of Bolívar's life. She left Quito for Lima and from there accompanied Bolívar on his final campaigns against royalist forces in the Andes, serving as his personal archivist. After independence, she continued to support Bolívar against the many enemies who opposed his dominance of the newly emerging nations of northern South America. In 1828, when they were both living in Bogotá, she foiled an assassination attempt against her lover, winning for herself the title of the "Libertadora del Libertador."

Bolívar resigned the presidency of Gran Colombia in 1830 and died of tuberculosis later that same year. Manuela's subsequent years were difficult. Bolívar's political adversaries in Ecuador refused to let her return to Quito, citing her unbridled ambition, outspoken nature, and past sexual improprieties. In 1835, she settled in Paita, a small port on the northern coast of Peru, not far from the Ecuadorian border. There she lived in poverty for the remainder of her life, depending on proceeds from the sale of handicrafts, occasional remittances from property in Ecuador, and the generosity of friends. A debilitating hip injury eventually confined her to a wheel chair. Her involvement in politics continued, however. She connived with other exiles and provided intelligence to her longtime friend, Ecuadorian President Juan José Flores, alerting him to Peruvian plots afoot to seize Ecuadorian territory and topple him from power. Even after Flores left office in 1845, she continued to maintain ties with other prominent conservative politicians in Quito. Gabriel García Moreno, a future president of Ecuador, was a frequent guest at her home during his period of political exile in Peru.

While in Paita, Manuela corresponded with her estranged husband, whom she had not seen since her departure for Quito in 1822. Thorne was murdered in 1847 at his hacienda in Chancay province, some 500 miles to the south of Paita.

(continued)

(continued)

Manuela was devastated when she heard the news, dressing in black and demanding that authorities identify and punish the perpetrators of the crime. She corresponded with her attorney in Lima, hoping to claim the dowry she had brought to their marriage and a share of Thorne's assets. Her husband's executor dismissed her pretensions, citing her notorious affair with Simón Bolívar. She died in 1856, as a diphtheria epidemic swept through northern Peru.

Sáenz has long been a controversial figure in Latin American history, denounced in her own time and subsequently for transgressing societal norms of proper feminine conduct. She smoked cigars, rode horseback, sometimes wore men's military uniforms, and was exceptionally outspoken She was not alone, however, for many other literate and well-connected women, less flamboyant in their personal style than Manuela, participated in Latin American political life in the turbulent years surrounding national independence. Although Manuela and other women of her generation could neither vote nor hold office, their social networks proved vital for the emergence of new political ideas. They hosted political gatherings, and in the words of historian Sarah Chambers, "were active in social spaces between the public and private spheres, where philosophies were discussed, plots hatched, and alliances formed."

In recent years a novel by Colombian Nobel laureate Gabriel García Márquez, a film by Venezuelan director Diego Rísquez, and a carefully detailed biography by historian Pamela Murray have portrayed Manuela Sáenz as a strong, intelligent woman who made important contributions to the independence of Latin America. Feminists in her native Ecuador and elsewhere in Spanish America have seen her as a role model and a precursor of women's emancipation. She has also become a symbol of Ecuadorian patriotism. In 2007, Ecuador posthumously promoted her to the rank of general in the national army.

Slice of Life

The 16th of September: Independence Day in Mexico

The Leaders of Latin America's new nations not only had to set up governments and rebuild economies disrupted by the independence wars, but they also had to convince their people to pay allegiance to the nation. Historians sometimes speak of nation-states as "imagined communities" in which people who do not have face-to-face contact with one another and who may not have much in common all see themselves as citizens of the nation. In practical terms, forging new communities meant persuading people as diverse as pampered creole aristocrats in Mexico City, Zapotec-speaking indigenous in Oaxaca, far to the south, and farmers who eked out a living on the far northern frontier of New Mexico, to set aside their racial, economic, linguistic, and cultural differences and swear loyalty to the new republic of Mexico.

Most Latin Americans of the early nineteenth century, whatever their back—grounds, saw themselves as part of a universal community, that of the Catholic Church. Those who took command of the new national governments strove to convince their citizens to transfer their loyalties from the church to the nation, and they borrowed some of the tools the church had used for centuries to instill a sense of community among the faithful. Elite-invented national holidays now competed with religious ones. Heroes of the independence wars became examples of patriotism, much as saints had served as examples of Christian piety.

Leaders of Mexico lost little time in setting up a new ritual calendar intended to kindle a sense of nationalism from Oaxaca to New Mexico. Foremost among the days they chose to commemorate was September 16, the anniversary of Father Hidalgo's "Grito de Dolores" of 1810, the proclamation that ignited the first phase of Mexico's wars for independence. The initial celebration of September 16 took place in Mexico City in 1823. The festivities included the ringing of church bells, a splendid parade with music supplied by a military band, and speeches extolling the virtues of the new nation. The government brought remains of national hero José María Morelos to Mexico City for burial. Just as saints' days offered a variety of secular entertainments in addition to the religious observances, the independence celebrations of September 1823 featured music and theatrical presentations in the Alameda, the city's centrally located park. Fireworks shows at the *zócalo,* the main plaza facing the cathedral, lasted far into the night.

From 1825, a private, voluntary organization supervised the celebration in Mexico City. For 30 years, with only one exception, when U.S. troops occupied the city in 1847, *the Junta Patriótica* (patriotic committee) oversaw the events. Beginning on the night of September 15 and continuing throughout the next day, patriotic speeches, artillery salutes, music, theater, and fireworks entertained the people. The junta, the president of the republic, and other dignitaries marched through the city's streets on the morning of the 16th. Schoolchildren sang patriotic hymns specially commissioned for the occasion. The people of Mexico City turned out in droves dressed in their best. The junta also marked the day with charitable works such as cash payments to disabled or impoverished

(continued)

(continued)

veterans and to widows and orphans of rebels who died in the wars. In the 1820s, poor children received new clothes. Every prisoner in the Mexico City jails received a good meal, a packet of cigarettes, a bar of soap, and one *real* (a coin, worth one-eighth of a peso) on September 16. In the provinces, the holiday people celebrated with equal fervor, if not with equal splendor. In San Luis Potosí, for example, local dignitaries marched and tossed coins to the assembled crowds, who also enjoyed music and fireworks.

From the 1820s to the present, the timing, scale, and specific content of Mexico's independence festivities varied according to the political climate of the time. Sometimes, members of the nineteenth century upper class muted the celebrations because they feared rekindling of the same kind of popular unrest Hidalgo's proclamation unleashed. On some occasions, they suspended all observances except for a few speeches in Congress. In times when national governments felt more securely in control, they praised the revolutionary aspirations of Hidalgo and Morelos, hoping to win the allegiance of the lower classes. The first celebrations of Mexican independence commemorated Agustín de Iturbide's triumphant entry into Mexico City in September 1821, along with Hidalgo's Grito de Dolores, but later leaders chose to focus exclusively on the first phase of the movement, when Hidalgo and Morelos so forcefully articulated the grievances of the masses, even though Iturbide's actions secured Mexico's final independence from Spain. Iturbide's victory represented the consummation of upper class negotiations with insurgents—a backroom deal. Subsequent leaders of Mexico had more to gain politically if they claimed to be the heirs of Hidalgo and Morelos, although their outlook and their means of governance far more closely resembled those of the conservative Iturbide. Ironically, the symbol of the people's movement, Father Hidalgo, triumphed just as governments grew strong enough to encroach upon the local autonomy for which the people fought.

Nature's Way

The Mosquito Conquers All

Mosquito-borne diseases proved the decisive factor in the Haitian Revolution, the northern South America wars of Independence, and the Cuban war of independence and played an important role in the Mexican war with the United States and the construction of the Panama Canal. The best known of these are malaria and yellow fever, of course, but fifteen others exist, such as dengue, chikungunya, Marayo, West Nile, Zika, and various encephalitides. Not all are fatal. Many mosquitos (the Aedes, Anopheles, and Culex do) do not carry and transmit them. Yellow fever and malaria were and are the most lethal. Fatality rates for yellow fever varied depending on time and place, generally 25 percent, but often rising to 50 percent, and in some Caribbean locations as high as 85 percent. Although not as deadly, malaria, in the estimation of some scientists accounts for a substantial amount of the poverty, malnutrition, and underdevelopment in the world. The disease is debilitating physically and psychologically to humans. By some calculations, the mosquito was and is the single largest killer of humans in history, responsible for the deaths of almost half of all the people who ever lived on earth, perhaps 52 billion.

Until the late nineteenth century, no one understood that mosquitos transmitted yellow fever and malaria. Scientists discovered the means to prevent the diseases only at the beginning of the twentieth century. Nonetheless, government leaders and military clearly were aware that these diseases were deadly and they must avoid certain regions or suffer severe losses. Unfortunately, these same leaders sent their soldiers to their deaths anyway.

The Europeans brought the malaria carrying mosquitos with them in the sixteenth century, along with the other plagues. Mosquitos existed in the Americas prior to the arrival of the Europeans, but they did not carry the disease. Malaria was among the earliest killers of the indigenous peoples in the Caribbean and elsewhere, making Panama a "hell on earth" in the 1530s, perhaps doing away with as many as 40,000 Spaniards before 1550. It may be that Christopher Columbus had malaria during his fourth voyage. One aspect of the Columbian Exchange exacerbated the impact of the newly arrived diseases, the transformation of agriculture, in particular the construction of dams and commercialization of agriculture.

Against all odds, the enslaved people of Haiti rebelled against their French oppressors in 1791. Their ultimate extraordinary victory owed in part to mosquito-borne diseases. The French were at first taken up with their own homegrown revolution, but their long-time enemies and rivals in the Caribbean, the British, saw an opportunity in 1793 both to quash the slave revolt, worrisome to its own colonies, and to annex the lucrative sugar economy of Haiti. The British sent 23,000 soldiers to Haiti, of which 15,000 died of yellow fever and malaria. They gave up the expedition in 1798. The British also attempted to take over other islands in the Caribbean, but the same diseases defeated them again. The estimated losses were between 60,000 and 70,000 soldiers. According to historian J. R. McNeill, the British fought "to conquer a cemetery."

(continued)

(continued)

The French attempted to reconquer Haiti in 1801 with 40,000 troops. Haitian leader Toussaint Louverture conducted a guerrilla war, based in part on strategic use of yellow fever and malaria. Of the 65,000 soldiers Napoleon dispatched to Haiti, 55,000 died of these diseases. Haiti gained its independence. The French and British surrendered their ambitions to extend their domains in the Caribbean.

Some historians argue that not only did the mosquito (unknown as the cause of yellow fever and malaria) defeat the British and French, securing Haitian independence, but ensured the independence of Spanish America, as well. After a series of defeats, Simón Bolívar, the leader of the independence movement in New Granada, went into exile in Jamaica in 1814. The same year, Spain sent 14,000 troops to the region to shore up its rule. Later, Spain dispatched an additional 20,000. Ninety percent of all Spanish soldiers fell victim to yellow fever and malaria. Apparently, Bolívar visited Haiti on two occasions while in exile and learned to use the susceptibility of the Spaniards to these diseases as part of his strategy. The rebels returned and won the war by 1819.

Mosquito borne disease played a role in Mexico's wars against foreign invaders. They helped defeat the Spanish in 1829 and the French in 1837, when the armies of each landed at Veracruz, where the diseases were rampant. In 1846, however, against the United States the defense of Veracruz did not work as well. The U.S. commander General Winfield Scott was aware of the danger of disease in the port and moved quickly inland to avoid the slaughter. This success enabled Scott to march to Mexico City.

The same diseases helped determine Cuba's fate from the mid nineteenth century through the mid twentieth century. During the Cuban war for independence, Spanish forces suffered 45,000 casualties due to disease out of 155,000 and of those remaining 60 percent yellow fever and malaria incapacitated. Like the Haitians and the South Americans, the Cubans' most important ally was mosquito borne disease. When after the explosion onboard the USS Maine precipitated war between Spain and the United States in 1898, disease again took a crucial role. The United States invaders confronted what appeared a formidable army of 200,000. However, only a quarter of them were fit to fight. The so-called "Splendid Little War," though brief cost the United States over 5000 deaths, 4700 of them because of disease. It was quickly evident that the U.S. occupation was untenable without mitigation of the mosquito borne diseases. The U.S. occupation ended in 1902, as a result.

The discovery of mosquitos as the culprits in spreading yellow fever and malaria and the subsequent steps taken to mitigate the impact of the diseases enabled the United States to seize territory in Panama and build the Panama Canal from 1904 to 1914.

Recently, scholars brilliantly illuminated the crucial role of mosquito borne disease at various turning points in Latin American history. In doing so, they put the mosquito at the center of the narrative. We must remember, the mosquito was only but one factor in these stories. Individual will, historical trends, economic interests, and politics also arguably played even more important parts.

3

Politics and Economics, 1821–1880

The prospective leaders of the newly independent countries of Latin America confronted two enormous challenges: to persuade fellow inhabitants to render allegiance to the nation-state and to rebuild shattered economies following the widespread destruction caused by the prolonged wars of independence. Before they could undertake these efforts, they had to resolve endless, seemingly intractable, disputes over who was to rule and what type of government was most appropriate. Most important, those who sought to lead their new nations had to overcome the fact that the majority of people thought about politics in terms of their village, town, or province not in terms of nation. Their overwhelming concerns centered on how best to earn their livelihoods and maintain their local traditions, and for centuries, they had stubbornly resisted outsiders' attempts to meddle in their affairs. Regionalism shaped the independence struggle in many parts of Latin America, and it would continue to frustrate the efforts of nineteenth century politicians who sought to forge national communities.

Class and ethnic divisions also stymied nation building. Underlying all politics was the deep fear the white upper classes had for the lower classes—comprised of African Latin Americans, indigenous peoples, and mixed bloods—in part the result of a series of rebellions by indigenous and enslaved people during the half century before the end of colonial rule.

— people thought about gov in different ways.

disagreed
of gov

Competing visions about the form that governments should take dominated the first decades after independence, as well. Some called for monarchy
as the only way to guarantee stability, while others favored representative government. Among the advocates of democracy, some wanted a broad franchise,
while others preferred to limit political participation to a select few. Often,
charismatic strongmen, called *caudillos*, who were able to impose order by
either mediating or coercing the various rival groups, took the reins for long
periods.

Finally, for many Latin Americans the struggle for independence was just
the beginning of a cycle of intermittent and devastating warfare that lasted for
much of the nineteenth century. Civil conflicts, wars with neighboring Latin
American nations, and invasions launched by nations outside the region all
took an enormous toll in human lives, wreaked economic havoc, and undermined all efforts at achieving national political cohesion (Maps 3.1, 3.2, 3.3,
3.4 and 3.5).

Building strong economies proved equally daunting. The damage caused
by the wars of independence was extensive. The lack of continuity caused by
changes in the form of government and turnover in personnel made economic development difficult.

The Challenges of Nationhood

The new leaders of Latin America embarked upon nationhood with no clear
blueprint of the forms their national governments should take. Recent experience with kings was unfavorable. The principal model of republican government was the young United States, but elite political leaders were wary of
representative democracy. Like their neighbor to the north, the larger nations
grappled with the question of whether to create a strong central government
or to leave substantial power in the hands of state, provincial, or local governments. Given the profound attachment that many Latin Americans had to
their own regions and towns, this dilemma of centralism versus a loose confederation proved especially vexing. Latin Americans vociferously disagreed
about how much change their societies needed. What institutions and practices left over from the colonial period should they retain, and what colonial
legacies should they discard? In particular, they quarreled over the proper
role of the Catholic Church in their societies and how best to make their
economies more productive. Before they could address any of these questions, they had to settle the argument over who was to control the new
national governments.

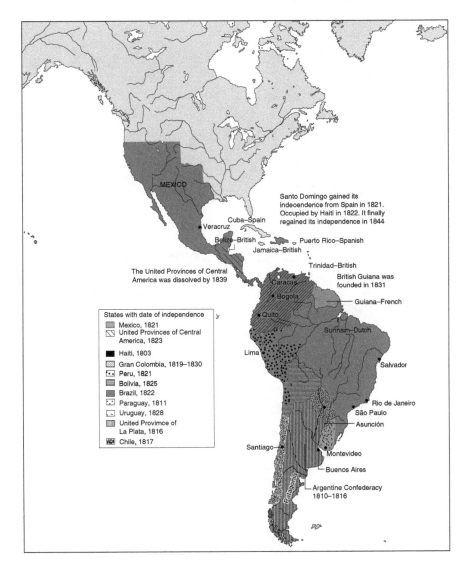

Map 3.1 Latin America in 1830

From Independence through the 1870s, four broad groups vied in the political arena. At the top were wealthy, influential whites, such as prosperous merchants, large landowners, mine owners, and church officials, who expected to rule their nations for their own benefit. The military, comprised of national armies, provincial militias, and locally based private forces, formed the second contender. Mostly, they allied with the interests of the upper class, but commonly had their own goals. The nineteenth century's many wars reinforced

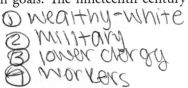

Map 3.2 Brazil, states and their capitals

their role. A small middle sector made up of professional bureaucrats, who allied with the upper classes and ran the everyday operations of government, lower level clergy, and merchants, also competed. Lastly, the lower classes, consisting of sharecroppers, tenant farmers, small-scale merchants, unskilled and skilled workers, artisans, street venders, and domestics, demanded a say in the political debates. Although the upper class dominated politics and commanded most of the economic resources, the lower class wielded influence at the local level. The upper class feared the lower classes but also needed

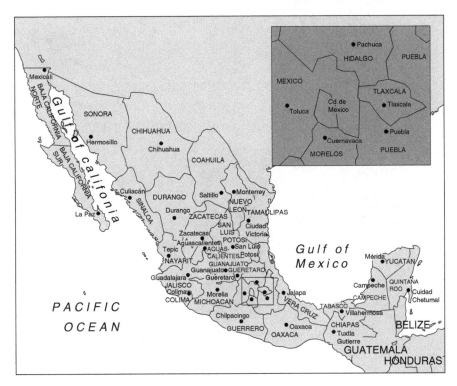

Map 3.3 Mexico and state capitals

their support, especially in times of internal conflicts or external war. The lower classes could negotiate, trading their assistance in return for local auton- NT omy or other concessions.

The type of government was also under discussion. Mexico and Brazil first adopted monarchies. In Mexico, Emperor Agustín I (Iturbide) lasted little more than a year (1821–1822). The Brazilian monarchy, however, endured for 67 years (1822–1889) and two emperors, Pedro I (1822–1829) and Pedro II (1839–1889). For the most part, Latin Americans chose the republican model of government with three branches, the executive, the legislature, and the judiciary, with political participation limited to literate male property owners. For much of the nineteenth century, dictators who did the bidding of the upper classes ruled.

Regionalism was at the core of the political discourse with the political ideologies of the times focused on the roles of government at the various levels. On one side were the federalists who advocated weak national governments and strong provincial (state) governments. On the other were the centralists who favored strong national governments and weak provincial

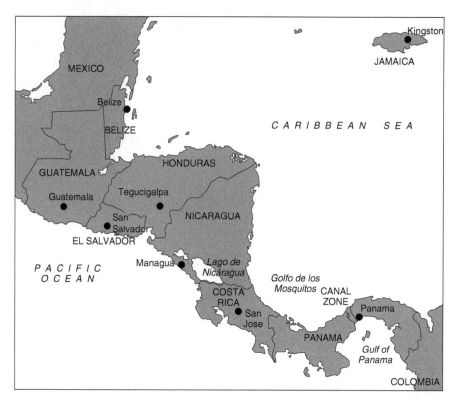

Map 3.4   Central America

governments. Each counted landowners among their ranks, but the centralists also included urban merchants, top-echelon government bureaucrats, military officers, and high clergy. No faction trusted the lower classes but nonetheless relied on their support, particularly at the local level.

During the middle decades of the nineteenth century, the political discourse expanded to include the role of the Roman Catholic Church in the economy and politics, the place of collective landholdings as practiced by indigenous and mestizo villages, and the relative merits of free trade and protectionism. Federalism subsumed in Liberalism (except in the Río de la Plata) and centralism in Conservatism. Each of these new factions for the most part incorporated the followers of their predecessors. The Liberals vehemently opposed the position of the Church as a large landowner, insisted on individual rather than collective property holding, and advocated free trade. They sought to create a nation of small farmers, practitioners of capitalism, who would form the backbone of the republic. Regional elites tended toward

—liberals opposed church ⟹ centralists
(free trade)

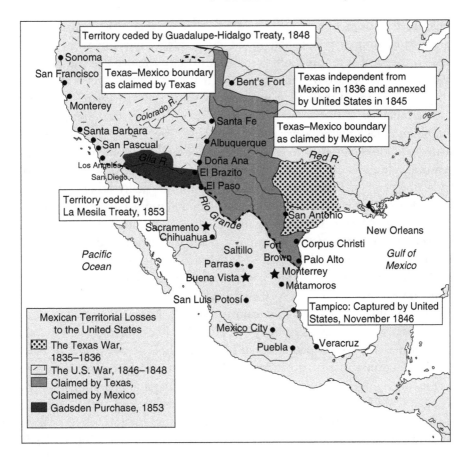

Map 3.5 The Wars for Northern Mexico

Liberalism, because it would maintain their traditional autonomy. Large scale merchants were Liberals because they favored deregulation of commerce. Ironically, the Liberals discovered by century's end that their goals for economic development were incompatible with federalism, so they became centralists. They found too that free trade did not foster modern industrial development. Conservatives fought most fiercely for the rights and privileges of the Church, which they believed served as the protector of social stability.

Whether Liberal or Conservatives, privileged groups distrusted, even despised, the lower classes, while at the same time they eagerly solicited their support. For most people in the countryside the struggles of everyday life remained paramount; access to good land and avoidance of oppressive taxation were at the center of their agenda. Keeping local community and

religious traditions free of outside interference were also of utmost importance. Most country people had joined independence movements in order to
reassert the local autonomy lost to the administrative reforms of the late colonial era. To them ideology meant far less than did control over local affairs.
They often changed their allegiances, establishing links to whatever regional
and national forces that seemed least likely to intrude on local prerogatives.

The histories of almost every nation in Latin America recount decades of
struggle to forge regions into larger entities and build national identities. The
centuries-old desire for local autonomy on the part of many lower class people
lay at the heart of Latin American regionalism, but many other factors also
worked against any quick achievement of national unity. Geography played a
decisive role. Mountains, deserts, and jungles often impeded easy overland
transportation and communication and made it difficult to determine clear
national and provincial boundaries. In Mexico, the lack of navigable rivers
further hindered contact among people across its vast territory that extended
from present day California to Central America. Linguistic differences and
racial antagonisms divided many countries as well. Although a small group of
upper class whites in each country by the 1810s had imagined nationhood,
the vast majority of the people owed loyalty to their home villages or cities.
Mexico, Central America, northern South America, and Argentina all required
a series of civil wars to create nations from regional conglomerations. Bolivia,
Paraguay, and Uruguay owed their status as separate nations to their efforts to
escape from the control of Argentina. Brazil avoided the ravages of civil war
but still experienced serious conflicts among its many regions. Only Chile did
not struggle to unify. It maintained orderly politics for 60 years, and Chilean
presidents succeeded one another at 10-year (two 5-year terms) intervals
until 1890.

Four areas, Argentina, Mexico, Colombia, and Central America, required a
series of civil wars to amalgamate nations from their disparate regions. The
rivalries between federalists and centralists and Liberals and Conservatives
were often bitter and brutal. Independent Argentina (originally the Viceroyalty
of Rio de la Plata) consisted of four regions: the city and environs of Buenos
Aires, the area along the coast north of Buenos Aires, the territory across the
river (present day Uruguay), and the interior (west of Buenos Aires to the
Andes mountains). From the outset of independence, the people of the Río de
la Plata struggled among themselves based on regional loyalties. Centralists,
primarily export oriented landowners and merchants in Buenos Aires, favored
a unified, secular nation with an economy based on free trade. They earned
their fortunes by exporting animal products, such as salted meat, to Europe.
They also sought to limit the influence of the church and advocated religious

freedom. Against them stood the regional bosses, usually landowners with armed cowboy (*gaucho*) followers, who objected to a strong central government and who supported the church, and fiercely fought to maintain their provincial autonomy.

The old Viceroyalty of Río de la Plata disintegrated as a political entity immediately after independence. It would take more than four decades to unite what is today Argentina. The northeast (Corrientes, Entre Rios, and Santa Fe provinces) sought to throw off the domination of Buenos Aires as early as 1810. Upper Peru (now Bolivia) broke away in 1810, followed by Paraguay in 1811. Montevideo (across the river in present day Uruguay) simultaneously rejected the rule of Buenos Aires. In 1819, several coastal and interior provinces declared themselves independent republics, each ruled by a local warlord.

The city of Buenos Aires, which was the strongest political and military entity in the Río de la Plata, led the struggle for centralization. Bernardino Rivadavia (1821–1827) and Juan Manuel de Rosas (1829–1852) established Buenos Aires's dominance until the provinces reasserted their autonomy, overthrowing Rosas in 1852. After nearly a decade of warfare, Buenos Aires finally defeated provincial forces in 1861 and imposed unification. Delegates from the provinces elected Bartolome Mitre (1862–1868), the victorious general, Argentina's first president in 1862. He then used war with Paraguay (1865–1870) to strengthen further the power of the national government at the expense of provincial autonomy. By the mid1870s, the government eliminated the last of the regional bosses. The achievement of a centralized nation-state was costly, however, requiring two civil wars and an external war.

Regionalism was also at the core of nineteenth century Mexican politics. In Mexico, centralists and federalists alternated in power through the 1850s. The experiment with monarchy immediately after independence was short lived. Emperor Agustín I, who, as Agustín de Iturbide, forged the negotiations between the upper classes and rebel guerrilla leaders, that obtained independence from Spain in 1821, failed to unite the country and fell to a federalist insurgency. Mexico's first elected president, Guadalupe Victoria (1824–1829), a hero of the guerrilla wars of independence, managed to balance the two factions. From 1829 until 1855, as the battle between federalism and centralism teetered back and forth, Antonio López de Santa Anna dominated the political landscape. Santa Anna began as a federalist, but quickly changed views when confronted with the fragmentation of his country. The centralists ruled for a decade from 1836 to 1846, lost out to the federalists from 1846 to 1853, and reasserted themselves in 1853. The loss of Texas in 1836 and defeat in the war with the United States (1846–1848) badly discredited the centralists led

Mex 1 pres. Guadalupe Victoria
—wars between centralists and federalists

by Santa Anna. The federalist-centralist struggle then subsumed in the new conflict between Liberals (who were federalists) and Conservatives (who were centralists). A terrible civil war erupted, which ended only in 1867 with the defeat of the centralists-Conservatives. Mexico began to come together under the presidency of Benito Juárez (1858–1872), a Liberal, who unified the nation through his heroic struggle against the French Intervention from 1862 to 1867. The Conservatives allied with the French and, as a result, suffered devastating defeat. Like Argentina, the emergence of Mexican nationhood had required a series of brutal civil wars and an external war in which there were hundreds of thousands of casualties.

Regionalism destroyed independence hero Simon Bolívar's grand dream of a unified northern South America. From 1821 to 1830, Bolívar, as president, built Gran Colombia out of Ecuador, New Granada (present day Colombia), and Venezuela. By 1830, despite his enormous efforts, the three nations separated and individually beset by centrifugal forces. In Ecuador, the height of its regional divisions occurred in 1859, when no fewer than four governments with capitals in four different cities claimed to rule. Six major regions divided Colombia, five with an important city at its center: Cauca (Popayán), Antioquena (Medellín), the coast (Cartagena), the Central Highlands (Bogotá), the northeast (Vélez), and the llanos (coastal plains). Francisco de Paula Santander, an important lieutenant of Bolívar, who was president from 1832 to 1837, maintained an unsteady peace. After he left office, federalists and centralists fought a series of bitter civil wars from 1839 until 1885. Venezuela, through the skills of José Antonio Paéz, another important lieutenant of Bolívar, resisted regional fragmentation into the 1850s. However, the nation erupted into the Federal Wars from 1859 to 1863, which resulted in a federalist victory. The triumph was short lived, however, because in 1870 Antonio Guzmán Blanco (1870–1877, 1879–1884, and 1886–1888) reestablished centralized rule. In neither Colombia nor Venezuela did civil wars settle the conflicts between federalism and centralism.

Central Americans struggled against each other for much of the nineteenth century. In 1821, they put their fates in the hands of Mexico, joining the newly independent empire of Agustín de Iturbide. With the fall of Iturbide, a Central American congress met to declare the independence of the United Provinces of Central America in 1823, but the government of the United Provinces never gained control as the region plunged into civil war. Although the central government continued, the individual states increasingly expanded their influence. By 1865, Guatemala, under the rule of José Rafael Carrera (1844–1848, 1851–1865), defeated unification once and for all. In Central

America, as in Argentina and Mexico, it took civil war to establish nation states. Nothing, however, could unite the regions.

Although Brazil experienced no widespread civil wars, it, too, suffered deep geographic divisions. Regional leaders never ceased their opposition to the nation's first ruler, Pedro I, and finally forced him to abdicate in 1831. Regional rebellions erupted during the 1830s, when a regent ruled during the minority of the heir to the throne. (Pedro I abdicated when his son was only 4 years old.) Brazil seemingly was on the verge of dissolution in 1840, when Pedro II became emperor at age 14. War with Paraguay (1864–1870) to some extent served to push some Brazilians to think in national terms. Pedro II kept Brazil together until he abdicated, when regional tensions overwhelmed the monarchy in 1889. Regionalism determined Brazil's political fate, though the nation did not pay as great a price in bloodshed as had Mexico and Colombia

Nations at War

War was the second major factor in the political instability in Latin America, as well as the primary reason for the lack of economic development. Hardly a year went by when there was not a war or some kind of military action somewhere in Latin America. Warfare inflicted enormous physical and economic damage; disrupted commerce, communications, and transportation; and drained governments of scarce financial resources. Political scientist Brian Loveman has identified four categories of wars in Latin America: transnational wars of political consolidation; international wars between Latin American nations; wars against foreign military intervention; and civil wars.

The best examples of wars of political consolidation were actually unsuccessful in unifying the contesting countries, leading instead to the dissolution of large confederations. Uruguay emerged as a separate nation from the war between the Argentine Confederation and Brazil from 1825 to 1828. One of the longer wars of political consolidation took place in Central America, where the struggle for unification dragged on from 1824 to 1838, ending in failure. Peru and Bolivia, once together as part of the Viceroyalty of Peru, also failed to unify, engaging in a fruitless war from 1836 to 1841.

The most important wars between Latin American nations were the War of the Triple Alliance (1864–1870) and the War of the Pacific (1879–1883). The War of the Triple Alliance, or Paraguayan War, in which Paraguay fought against the alliance of Argentina, Brazil, and Uruguay over disputed borders, was the most prolonged and destructive. The war devastated Paraguay, which lost between 8 and 18 percent of its population and over one-third its territory. After the peace, alliance troops occupied parts of Paraguay for 8 years. All of the progress of the previous half-century toward a self-sufficient, relatively economically egalitarian society ended. Political instability followed for the next six decades.

The War of the Pacific was damaging to its losers. Chile fought Peru and Bolivia over access to nitrate fields. Chile and Bolivia had a longstanding disagreement over the territory—located in an area in northern Chile, southern Peru, and western Bolivia—while Peru and Chile disputed control over the taxes on nitrate deposits. Chile won a drawn-out struggle; its army occupied Peru from 1881 to 1883. Peace brought a substantial victory for Chile, for it acquired the nitrate fields and a monopoly on the world's supply of this fertilizer. Bolivia lost its access to the Pacific Ocean, which was a serious hindrance to its future economic development (Map 3.6).

The most devastating war with a nation outside the region was the Mexican War with the United States (1846–1848). Mexico previously in 1836 lost its northern province of Texas to North American settlers, who revolted against

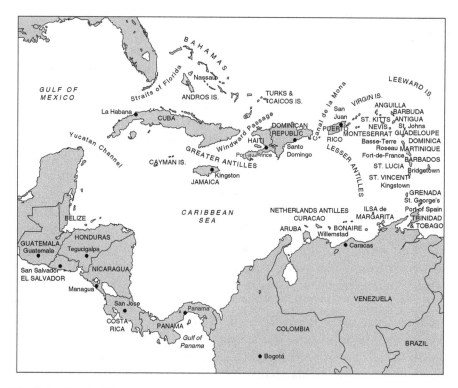

Map 3.6 The Caribbean

Mex lost ½ territory

centralist rule. Mexico never recognized the independence of the Republic of Texas. In late 1845, the United States, ignoring Mexico's protests, annexed Texas. A few months later, a clash between Mexican and U.S. forces in south Texas led to war. The U.S. army eventually captured the major cities Monterrey, Veracruz, and ultimately Mexico City. Mexico lost half its national territory, including present day Texas, Arizona, New Mexico, and California.

In addition to the actual wars themselves, the potential for war with neighbors over boundaries and other issues was continuous. Argentina and Chile disputed each other's rights to Tierra del Fuego. Peru and Ecuador were at odds over their Amazonian territories. The threat of foreign intervention was constant. For a decade after independence, Mexico feared Spain would attempt to reconquer it. It also anticipated invasion by the United States for almost a century after the two ended their war in 1848. Central America and the Caribbean lived in the shadow of United States intervention from the 1850s.

NT

The small civil wars that plagued Latin America in the nineteenth century were innumerable. There were 11 "national level rebellions" in nineteenth century Colombia alone. From 1831 to 1837, Brazil endured continuous rebellions in Maranhao, Bahia, Minas Gerais, Mato Grosso, and Rio Grande do Sul. Thirteen military uprisings occurred in Peru in the months between June and October 1840. From 1852 to 1862, there were 117 uprisings of one type or another in the Río de la Plata.

The struggles between Liberals and Conservatives in some countries, Mexico and Colombia for instance, erupted in brutal warfare during the middle decades of the century, as the conflicts over the place of the church in society, politics, economy, and over collective landholding intensified. These were emotional issues, for at stake was the very essence of day-to-day life: control over one's religion and livelihood.

destroyed LA

The effects of warfare were politically and economically profound. Wars militarized society, gave political prominence to military leaders, undermined democracy, widened ethnic divisions, diminished daily life, killed tens of thousands of people, destroyed property, transportation, and communications, and squandered scarce resources. They made economic development nearly impossible and thus prevented any substantial improvement in living conditions for most Latin Americans.

Constant warfare militarized society as formal national and informal regional armed forces proliferated. Regular armies were supposed to defend the nation against external threats, but instead often they overthrew national governments. In addition, local militias formed the power bases of regional

conflict between Con and Lib caused problems

NT

bosses who challenged national unity and authority. It seemed at times that everyone was armed.

Military

Warfare spawned countless military leaders who dominated high government office in many countries. Six civilians and 16 generals served as president of Mexico between 1821 and 1851. Three of the civilian presidents lasted just a few days. Two generals, Antonio López de Santa Anna and Anastasio Bustamante (1830–1832, 1837–1841), dominated Mexican politics for the first half of the nineteenth century. The men who overshadowed all others in the politics of the Río de la Plata were in the military. Juan Manuel de Rosas was a noted military commander. Bartolomé Mitre (1862–1868) won fame for winning the decisive battle for Argentine unification in 1861. Military officers ruled Chile despite its reputation as perhaps the most stable of the continent's republics through its initial three decades.

Democracy suffered because of militarization. The presence of so many military figures gave politics an authoritarian air. In times of war, governments often suspended civil liberties, such as freedom of the press and freedom of speech. National legislatures, when confronted with war emergencies, regularly chose to suspend the rule of law temporarily in order to bestow extraordinary powers on the president.

Economically, wars were devastating. The mining sector was initially hardest hit. It took decades for production in the mines of Bolivia, Peru, and Mexico to regain their colonial levels. The destruction of mine shafts by flooding, scavenging of equipment, and deteriorating roads impeded redevelopment. The human cost of war in terms of casualties was catastrophic, as in the case of Paraguay in the War of the Triple Alliance. In Yucatán, in Mexico's southeast, more than 100,000 people lost their lives in the vicious rebellion during the late 1840s. Perhaps 300,000 people died in Mexico's War of the Reform a decade later. The tremendous losses among young males profoundly altered family structures and gender relations.

Wars and military preparedness bankrupted national governments. Armies drained scarce, precious financial resources better spent on roads and schools. The cost of the military was nowhere more evident than in Mexico. In 1836, the Mexican military expended 600,000 pesos a month, while government revenues totaled only 430,000 pesos. These figures did not include the cost of the Texas War (1836), which added another 200,000 pesos a month! Dictator Rosas of Buenos Aires maintained a standing army of 20,000 and a militia of 15,000, the cost of which accounted for one-half to three-quarters of his annual budgets. War left no money for other functions of government.

money spent

Because armies regularly expanded and shrank in size, a substantial number of out-of-work soldiers, who were unwilling to return to their former homes to toil as tenants or peons on a hacienda or the communal holdings of their villages, became bandits. Lawlessness followed. From the 1820s to the 1860s, it was virtually impossible to travel between Veracruz, Mexico's major port, located on the Gulf of Mexico, and Mexico City without enduring a hold-up. Some stagecoaches experienced several robberies over the course of a single trip. It was common for passengers to arrive at their destination wrapped in newspapers, having been relieved of all their worldly possessions in route. This disorder greatly discouraged commerce and impeded economic development.

Not all of the effects of war were adverse. The military provided unparalleled upward social mobility. Indigenous, mulattos, and mestizos obtained unprecedented opportunities for economic and social advancement through war. NT Many of the national leaders who emerged from the wars of independence and subsequent conflicts had lower class origins. Notable among them was Porfirio Diaz, who was dictator of Mexico in the last quarter of the century. Mobilization in Brazil during the Paraguayan War conscripted mostly black and mulatto troops. The war probably assured the end of slavery as an institution, for slaves earned their freedom through military service. Returning soldiers were not the docile workforce they had been when they went to war. Some veterans received money bonuses and land grants. Others who had received nothing for their service refused to return to the status quo before the war.

Constant warfare undoubtedly eroded the fabric of everyday life and politics. Ironically, a few international wars probably contributed to the creation of nationalist sentiment and helped forge a sense of nationhood. Its two wars against Peru and Bolivia unquestionably helped consolidate sparsely populated Chile. These clear victories boosted popular association with the nation. The War of the Triple Alliance, which came only three years after unification, promoted a sense of Argentine national identity. The valiant fight of Benito Juárez against the French Intervention in Mexico also produced the first extensive sense of nation and Mexican-ness.

Popular Participation

Regional fragmentation, divisions among the upper classes, and war provided unusual opportunities for lower class participation in political affairs during the first five decades after independence. Local and regional bosses required regular retainers recruited from their areas. While personal loyalties were sometimes sufficient to secure followers, lower class supporters demanded not only personal gain, such as wages, war booty, and promotions, but more importantly, maintenance of local autonomy for villages and protection from laws against collective landownership and taxes.

The struggle to maintain control over their daily existence in the countryside manifested itself in the vast conflict over local autonomy, which translated into the national conflict between federalism and centralism. This in turn led the lower classes into broader political participation. In search of supporters, national leaders courted the concerns of everyday people, who comprised the armies of various competing factions.

In the cities, local issues revolved around food prices and employment. Riots were important expressions of political involvement in urban settings. Protests erupted in Latin American cities because of the high cost of corn and beans. For example, in 1831, the populace of Recife, Brazil, attacked Portuguese merchants believed to have been price gouging.

In a number of instances, the urban lower classes played crucial roles in national politics. Mexico City's lower classes formed the backbone of Iturbide's support during his last days. However, he was unwilling to use their support to maintain power, so strong was his sense of solidarity with the upper class and his fear of the lower classes. Mexico City dwellers erupted again in 1828 in the Parián Riot (see Slice of Life: The Parián Riot) in support of Vicente Guerrero, the hero of the war of independence, in his campaign for president. Mobs in the streets of Rio de Janeiro helped to force Pedro I to abdicate in 1831.

The lower classes also influenced national politics in some instances when they were willing to fight foreign invaders long after the upper classes, who, while looking after their own self-interests, surrendered to or collaborated with the enemy. After the United States army defeated Santa Anna's army in a series of battles on the outskirts of Mexico City in 1847, the general withdrew from the capital. The population of the city continued to fight, however, sniping and throwing debris from the rooftops at the North American troops. During the War of the Pacific (1879–1883), after the total defeat of the Peruvian army, the civilian country people of the central sierras and the south of Peru continued to fight under the leadership of General Andrés Caceres against the invading Chileans. Upper class Peruvians collaborated with the invaders. In both Mexico and Peru, the upper classes signed disadvantageous peace treaties at least in part because they feared the expansion of popular upheavals.

Throughout the nineteenth century, the upper classes faced a decided dilemma. They needed support from the lower classes, but they were not always pleased with their allies, for the masses were not easy to control. The upper class lost control of the 1831 revolt in Recife, Brazil, when slaves joined in, hoping to obtain their freedom. In 1835, outraged blacks and indigenous in Belem, Brazil, joined and then overwhelmed an upper class led revolt seeking independence for their province, engaging in widespread destruction of property and attacking wealthy whites. It took the government five years to quash the rebels. The death toll for this bloody uprising reached 30,000, approximately one-fifth of the provincial population.

The new rulers of Latin America were more successful at re-imposing traditional gender roles in politics. Females were crucial participants in the wars of independence on both sides. This, of course, upset long-held views that women's place was in the home in the private sphere. The male casualties endured during the decades of war in some areas, however, created demographic imbalances that threatened male domination. In Argentina, females were in the majority until midcentury. The upper classes realized that in times of war and disruption, families rather than governments held society together. They therefore insisted on the model of a male dominated family. In order to maintain stability, the upper classes sought to maintain long established gender roles.

Leadership

Strong leaders, known as caudillos, often emerged to bridge the gap between the upper and lower classes and temporarily bring order to disrupted politics. The term *caudillo* refers to a leader whose notoriety and authority arose from the local level, where he attained a reputation for bravery. The caudillos of the nineteenth century, who first emerged from the wars of independence, often obtained their economic and popular bases as hacendados. A caudillo's army comprised of the workers on his hacienda, and a web of patron-client relations (informal and personal exchanges of resources between parties of unequal status) served as the base of his support. Typically, landowners expected labor, deference, loyalty, and obedience, while the employees, in turn, received a basic level of protection and subsistence. Many caudillos sought support among the lower classes and earned their fierce loyalty.

Juan Manuel de Rosas, who dominated Buenos Aires and allied provinces from 1829 to 1852, embodied the qualities of the nineteenth century Latin American leader. He was rough, brave, ruthless, tyrannical, and a sharp political strategist. Rosas was a military leader with a common touch. Growing up on a large cattle estate (*estancia*) he shared the austere life and learned the ways and language of the people who inhabited the vast plains of the Pampas. Although he became a large landowner, Rosas presented himself as one of the people. He adhered to their "code" of honesty and discipline. Legend has it that he once ordered his servant to give him twenty lashes for being a bad gaucho, and when, unsurprisingly, the servant balked, Rosas threatened him with 500 lashes if he did not comply with the order. Virtually unchallenged through the 1840s, Rosas succumbed to his provincial opponents in 1852. Rosas's crucial base of support was in the popular classes, especially among indigenous and blacks. He organized a personal retinue from the poor of Buenos Aires and had a wide following among the gauchos of the Pampas. The lower classes regarded Rosas as the protector of their way of life. Rosas negotiated fairly with the indigenous of the plains, thereby gaining their respect.

Rosas turned Afro-Argentines into a pillar of his regime, relying on them for his war machine. Through his wife, Encarnación, he worked with African mutual aid societies. Rosas lifted the previous bans on African street dances that reached the pinnacle of their popularity during his rule. His daughter Manuela defied creole norms, when she attended dances and danced with black men. Once when the provincial government was strapped for money, forty-two black nations (mutual societies) made special contributions to it. Rosas named his urban home after the black saint Benito de Palermo. His propagandists wrote in African Argentine dialects. By 1836, Buenos Aires ended the forced draft for freed slaves and in 1839 ended the slave trade. Rosas promoted blacks to high military rank and took others as personal retainers. His large military force provided jobs for the chronically underemployed lower classes. He distributed land to the poor who were willing to live on the frontier and rewarded loyal soldiers with land.

Heroism and charisma were no guarantees for a long or successful political career. Several of the foremost figures of the wars of independence suffered tragic fates. Bernardo O'Higgins won independence for Chile, but as ruler, he lasted only until 1822. Antonio José de Sucre, one of Bolívar's best generals, was the first president of Bolivia (1825–1828), but he failed in his efforts to end the oppression of the indigenous population.

Economic Recovery

Regionalism and war adversely affected Latin American economic development. Regionalism created an uncertain political environment, which frightened investors, while war unproductively consumed vast human, material, and financial resources.

During the years from 1810 to 1870, Latin American economies, with a few exceptions, stagnated due to the inability or unwillingness of the upper classes to establish governments that could create stable environments for commerce and industry. Institutional obstacles left from the colonial period, the widespread damages and disruptions caused by the wars of independence and subsequent upheavals, and the lack of capital further stifled economic growth. In Mexico and Bolivia, the loss of territory deprived the nation of valuable resources. After 1850, the situation slowly began to change, as booming markets for Latin American agricultural staples and minerals, along with European capital investment in mining and transportation, brought renewed economic growth. From 1850 until World War I (1914), most nations in the region attached their economic fortunes to the burgeoning export markets in Western Europe and the United States. Still, economic development of Latin America faced substantial obstacles.

In many regions, geography was a major obstacle to development. Most of Latin America lacked inexpensive transportation and easy communications. The lack of transportation greatly limited the establishment of national and regional markets. The cost of moving products to market was prohibitive. The Spanish colonial government never invested much in roads, and the wars of independence left existing roads in disrepair. With the exception of the Río de la Plata, few major waterways ran through population centers. Coastal trade was not important in the nineteenth century.

Laws, attitudes, and institutions inherited from the colonial period further hindered growth after independence. These included local and regional autonomy; overregulation and under-enforcement of rules; indifference to long-term planning and preference for short-term benefits; concentration on the export of precious minerals; state monopolies of commodities such as liquor and tobacco; strict limitations on international trade (including with neighboring nations); widespread corruption; a tradition of smuggling; and failure to invest in roads and ports. Three-hundred-year-old colonial habits and tendencies were not easy to break.

Considerable institutional constraints stymied economic enterprise. Laws were often arbitrary and capricious, changing from regime to regime, and easily subverted through corruption. Laws often differed from region to region within the same nation. Each region also imposed its own taxes. Perhaps most important was the lack of modern systems of banking. The lack of credit handicapped both industry and agriculture. The shortage of capital prevented the repair and maintenance of mines and haciendas. The church, which had acted as a major source of credit during the colonial era, lost its primary base of income when the new governments abolished the tithe (an annual tax of 10 percent on all income collected by the colonial government from individuals for the church). The church's funds were still considerable, but invested in illiquid landholdings and virtually unredeemable loans to landowners. Europeans, with the exception of a few brief (mad) years in the 1820s, were unable or unwilling to invest in Latin America. Governments also experienced chronic revenue shortages because the newly independent states did away with many royal taxes and, because of their incompetence, were unable to collect those taxes that remained. The flight of Spaniards with their capital in the aftermath of the independence wars drained Latin America of potentially crucial investment funds.

The new nations sought to make up for the lack of capital during the 1820s by borrowing funds abroad in the form of government loans. Several of the founders, like Bolívar, obtained loans from British investors, which he used to buy arms. From 1822 to 1825, seven Latin American nations (Brazil, Buenos Aires, Central America, Chile, Colombia, Mexico, and Peru) contracted for more than 20 million (British) pounds debt. Not surprisingly, economic difficulties prevented repayment. All the Latin American nations except Brazil remained in default of these debts for a quarter century. This foreclosed the possibility of attracting external capital to the region. After 1850, Europeans were attracted once again with the upturn of Latin American agricultural and mineral exports.

Although the general trend for the region as a whole was bleak for much of the first half of the nineteenth century, as continuous war and periodic political disruptions impeded economic growth, several nations prospered because of increasing demand for agricultural commodities. Buenos Aires became one of the remarkable economic success stories of nineteenth century Latin America. Even when fighting raged, its foreign trade expanded. Markets for hides and cattle byproducts flourished. A new industry arose to process hides and salt meat. The Río de la Plata provided the slaves of Brazil and the working class of Europe with their food. Entrepreneurial landowners raised sheep to provide cheap wool for the carpet factories of New England and Great Britain. Buenos Aires evolved into a complex of stockyards, slaughterhouses, and warehouses. The vast plains around Buenos Aires, the Pampas, became an enormous, efficient producer of agricultural products. In a more modest example, Venezuela experienced a coffee boom that brought two decades of prosperity from the 1830s through the 1840s.

After midcentury, European markets expanded rapidly. The increasing affluence of a growing population in Europe, a crucial aspect of which was the transfer of people from agriculture to industry, created a demand for Latin American products. Because most European nations were self-sufficient in basic agricultural staples, at first demand centered on luxury and semi-luxury commodities such as sugar, tobacco, cacao, coffee, and (later) bananas. Salted and dried beef also became a preferred part of the European diet. As industrialization in Europe accelerated, so too did the demand for raw materials. Cotton production grew rapidly during this period to meet the demand for inexpensive clothing. As the population continued to grow in Europe, less land was available for raising livestock, and Europeans looked abroad for their tallow, hides, and meat. As Europe required more and more efficient agricultural production, the demand for fertilizers rose. Latin America had the natural resources to fill these demands. Sugar was a commodity much in demand. The Haitian revolution of 1791 destroyed the island of Hispaniola as the major sugar-producing region, creating opportunity for Cuba and Brazil. Brazil, which as a colony was the world's largest producer of sugar, competed again for new markets. Production doubled in the 1820s and nearly doubled again the following decade. Perhaps the most spectacular case of the rise and fall of an export economy occurred in Peru. The demand for fertilizers in Europe created an enormous demand for the natural fertilizer guano (bird excrement) found on Peru's offshore islands. Beginning in 1841, export shipments of guano rose sharply. The Peruvian government used the prospects of future revenues from guano to borrow huge sums abroad. It also used guano funds to build the country's major railroad lines. By the early 1880s, however, guano deposits were nearly exhausted, and nitrate came on to the market as an alternative fertilizer. The guano boom ended, leaving Peru with huge debts to foreign companies and no possibility of repaying, because the revenues from guano ceased.

A pattern of boom and bust cycles emerged. Latin America's national economies reacted to market forces using their competitive advantages in the production of agricultural and mineral commodities. Before 1850, when the market demanded agricultural products domestic entrepreneurs responded. Later in the century, however, when the demand was for minerals, foreign investors played an increasing role. Latin American nations became increasingly dependent on foreign capital and vulnerable to fluctuations in world markets as the nineteenth century closed. Economic recovery from a century of war and political upheaval rested on an extremely precarious base.

Conclusion

The nineteenth century was a difficult time for governments and ordinary people in Latin America, but some progress occurred nonetheless. Once established, nations displayed remarkable continuity and cohesion in the face of strong regional forces. Despite the high turnover among high officeholders and the occurrence of civil wars, elements of stability in Latin American politics existed. Not infrequently, one or two figures dominated for a decade or more, though not continuously occupying the presidency. For example, Mexico had 49 national administrations between 1824 and 1857, and only one president, Guadalupe Victoria (1824–1829) finished his term. However, five chief executives held office on three or more separate occasions. Two, Anastasio Bustamante and Antonio López de Santa Anna, headed the nation for approximately half this period.

The high turnover was deceptive elsewhere as well. Though at times upheavals beset its politics, four men dominated Venezuela, José Antonio Paéz (1831–1835, 1839–1843, 1861–1863), the Monagas brothers (José Tadeo and José Gregorio, 1847–1858), and José Guzmán Blanco (1870–1877,1879–1884, 1886–1888). Pedro I (1822–1831) and Pedro II (1831–1889) ruled Brazil for more than six decades. Chilean presidents followed successively by election from 1831 to 1891. Rosas ruled the Río de la Plata from 1829 to 1852. Argentina's presidents followed one another by election from 1862 to 1930. Three dictators ruled Paraguay from 1815 to 1870.

Peru was perhaps the worst case of unstable politics. From its independence in 1821 to 1845, there were 24 major regime changes and more than 30 presidents. Strongman Agustín Gamarra (president 1829–1833 and 1839–1841) established some measure of order, interrupted only by Bolivian caudillo Andrés Santa Cruz's attempt to conquer Peru and establish the Peru-Bolivia Confederation from 1836 to 1838. During the early 1840s, Peru came apart. Finally, General Ramón Castilla reestablished order from 1845 to 1862 (as president 1845–1851 and 1855–1862), despite fighting a vicious civil war in 1854 and 1855.

Stability was more evident at the regional and local levels of politics. In Mexico, state (regional) politics were mostly in the hands of locally prominent merchant and landowning families who ruled for generations through control of municipalities and courts. In the Río de la Plata, provincial leaders like Estanislao López in Santa Fe ruled for decades. In Brazil, local bosses, known as *colonels*, and their families ran roughshod for generations.

One could argue that this era was in some ways the most democratic period in Latin America until nations introduced unlimited universal suffrage and mass voting after World War II. The lower classes not only participated in government, particularly on the local level, but also took part indirectly in national politics and helped shape the political debates. It was also the time of the most extensive economic equity in Latin American history. In some areas, large landholdings suffered from disruptions and uncertainties. War and the expansion of the armed forces provided opportunities for upward mobility for the lower classes, including people of color.

Post-independence Latin America, as we will see in the succeeding chapter, was by no means the Garden of Eden, but common people had control over their everyday lives, a role in national politics, and often a chance to get ahead. The next 50 years were not to be as kind.

Timeline

1814–1840	Dr. Francia rules Paraguay
1822–1831	Pedro I
1828	Gran Colombia fails
1828–1852	Juan Manuel de Rosas dominates the Río de la Plata
1836–1838	Peru-Bolivian Confederation
1846–1848	Mexico War with the United States
1857–1860	Mexico War of the Reform
1862	Argentine Confederation
	French Intervention in Mexico
1866–1870	Paraguayan War/War of the Triple Alliance
1879–1883	War of the Pacific

How Historians Understand

Benito Juárez—The Making of a Myth

Benito Juárez was president of Mexico from 1858 to 1872. Mexico's first indigenous head of state led the nation through its bloodiest civil war, the War of the Reform (1858–1860), and its longest foreign war, the French Intervention (1861–1867). During his distinguished career, Juárez served at every level of government in both elected offices and the courts: from city councilor, to state legislator, national congress member, state governor, cabinet minister, and president, and from district judge to chief justice of the Supreme Court of the nation. Almost singlehandedly, by force of his own determination, Juárez assured the triumph of Liberalism as the dominant political ideology and began the process of creating Mexico as a nation from the conglomeration of regions that had emerged from independence. Despite his obvious importance in nineteenth century Mexican history, the myth of Benito Juárez has changed over time to reflect its creators' needs at the time. In the words of historian Charles Weeks: "...what Mexicans say about Juárez represents what they want to believe about themselves, as individuals and as a nation."

Because his career bridged and overlapped the careers of the two most vilified figures of nineteenth century Mexican history, Antonio López de Santa Anna, who dominated politics from 1828 to 1855, and Porfirio Díaz, the dictator from 1876 to 1911, Juárez should have attained the status of the nation's greatest hero, but mythical status came hard. In the fragmented politics of the era, his leadership never went uncontested. Two rivals vied for the presidency against him in 1861. He faced opposition to his continuation as president, during a time when the nation was at war, after his term ended in 1865. Two opponents confronted him in the elections of 1868 and 1872. (In the latter year, he died shortly after his reelection.) Despite having defeated the French and their figurehead, the emperor Maximilian, Juárez found himself demonized by his enemies as a dictator.

For the first 15 years after his death, Mexicans forgot Juárez. His successor, Porfirio Diaz, tried twice to overthrow him by force, and the two men ended as enemies. As president, Díaz initially sought to get out from under Juárez's shadow. A radical change in attitude toward Juárez took place in 1887, when Díaz sought reelection for the first time. Díaz served as president from 1877–1880, sat out for a term, and ran for election again in 1884 and in 1888. Díaz placed himself as the heir to Juárez of the mantle of Liberal leadership, and since Juárez too ran for reelection in a time of national crisis, a positive view of him legitimized Díaz. The opposition to Porfirio Díaz supported the myth of Juárez, as well. They saw him as the champion of anticlericalism (anti-Roman Catholic Church), a strong legislative branch of government, and individualism. The celebration of Juárez the hero peaked in 1906 with the centennial of his birth.

Juárez then became a symbol of the radical opponents of Díaz, who sought to revive his program—democracy, and anticlericalism—that the dictator betrayed. The major opposition to Díaz, which arose in 1910, led by Francisco I. Madero, named its political clubs after Juárez. Ironically, they called themselves antireelectionists. Madero deeply admired Benito Juárez as the epitome of legality. Madero's followers called him the modern day Juárez. During the Revolution (1910–1920), Juárez emerged in yet another reincarnation as the model of a strong president. Amid the chaos and civil strife, Juárez stood for strength and law. Revolutionary leaders eventually constructed a centralized state and raised Juárez to hero status in order to legitimize strong presidential rule.

Latin American Lives

Francisco Solano López

Some historians of Latin American have labeled the nineteenth century the "Age of the Caudillos," when these often charismatic leaders imposed order through either negotiations or violence. The most notable examples, such as Antonio López de Santa Anna in Mexico and Juan Manuel de Rosas in the Río de la Plata (Argentina), dominated the histories of their nations, especially during the first decades after independence. In every instance, the caudillos were controversial. This was particularly true in the case of Paraguay, whose three successive leaders—Dr. José Gaspar Rodríguez de Francia (1811–1840), Carlos Antonio López (1844–1862), and Francisco Solano López (1862–1870)—determined their nation's fate for 60 years. Historians have gone so far as to call two of them, Dr. Francia and Francisco Solano López, mad men. To others both were national heroes.

At independence, Paraguay carved itself out of the Spanish Viceroyalty of Río de la Plata (which also included current day Argentina and Uruguay). Its first caudillo, Dr. Francia, isolated the nation. The scrupulously honest dictator established a highly efficient government and a relatively egalitarian society, carefully curtailing the wealthy landowning class. He operated unusually successful educational programs and profitable state enterprises. He also created a strong military, ever in fear of larger neighbors Argentina and Brazil. His successor Carlos Antonio López for the most part continued his policies. López, in addition, broadened the rights of the nation's indigenous people, the Guaraní, expanded export agriculture, and developed independent military industry. His son Francisco Solano López took over after Carlos Antonio's death in 1862.

Francisco Solano López (1826–1870) was the material from which writers make great novels. Brought up as the privileged eldest son of a powerful dictator, to whom no one ever said no, the young López was a brigadier general at 18 and his father's chief advisor while barely in his twenties. Carlos Antonio sent him to Europe to be his chief procurement agent in 1853 and 1854. The experience yielded a close-up view of balance of power diplomacy and an Irish mistress, Elisa Alicia Lynch, who eventually bore him five sons. Many observers thought the beautiful Lynch the dark power behind the dictator; she was well-hated by the local elite. López's mercurial temperament added to the drama.

Shortly into his 10-year term as president, López involved himself in the complicated politics of civil wars in both Argentina and Uruguay. As a result, Paraguay plunged into a 5-year long, catastrophic war against the Triple Alliance of Argentina, Brazil, and Uruguay. Uruguay was the 1828 creation of diplomatic compromise between Argentina and Brazil, both of which claimed its territory. At stake was access to the Río de la Plata-Paraná-Paraguay river system. After more than a quarter century, during which each nation turned inward, civil wars in Argentina that eventually resulted in its unification under the leadership of Buenos Aires, and in Uruguay restarted the rivalry between Argentina and Brazil over influence in the region. López worried that one or the other of his larger neighbors would upset the balance of power in the Río de la Plata, endangering Paraguay. He attacked Brazil in late 1864 to prevent it from interfering in Uruguayan politics. In April 1865, he invaded an Argentine province, setting off war with his second neighbor. Although they had overwhelming advantages in population and resources, neither Argentina nor Brazil succeeded in taking advantage. López held them off until he died in battle in 1870.

(continued)

(continued)

López to this day is a controversial figure. The victors vilified him. Paraguayans proclaimed him a national hero. Recent scholarship more judiciously analyzed López's strengths and weaknesses, concluding on one hand that his motives for war were sound—his fear of his neighbors was reasonable. He also clearly commanded the loyalty of his people, who stayed with him to near extinction. On the other hand, he could have ended the war in 1866, but refused because the terms of the peace included his resignation; and as the war continued and his desperation intensified, he resorted to brutal methods to maintain discipline.

The result for Paraguay was, however, indisputably a catastrophe from which the nation never recovered. Although recent demographic studies debated how many Paraguayans died in the tragic war, there is ample evidence that perhaps half the total population was lost and a much higher percentage of the male population. The nation also ceded tens of thousands of miles of territory to Argentina and Brazil. Brazilian troops occupied the country until 1878. Perhaps the most prosperous, stable, and egalitarian nation on the continent in 1865, Paraguay never came back from the debacle. Whether a mad man or sound strategist, Francisco Solano López had led his homeland to ruin.

Slice of Life

The Parián Riot in Mexico City, 1828

In the nineteenth century Latin America, common folk struggled constantly both to sustain themselves—furnishing sufficient food, adequate shelter, and safety for their families—and to maintain some measure of control over their everyday lives. During the first five or six decades after independence, the lower classes exercised a degree of political influence because the upper classes were divided, and in some places, periodically at war among themselves. Urban and rural working class folk participated in the politics of the time in several ways: as voters in local elections, soldiers in civil wars and revolts, allies of upper class factions, and perpetrators of specific, directed incidents of urban violence. Upper class Latin Americans needed the lower classes to fight their battles and as allies. Nonetheless, the wealthy and powerful were wary, often fearful, of the lower classes, knowing full well that to arm the masses risked unleashing the dangerous forces of centuries of pent-up resentment. The Parián riot, which occurred in Mexico City in 1828, was an instance in which the lower classes took part in political events, leading to a tumultuous episode that shook the Mexican upper classes to their very core.

As in most history, the upper classes defined the riot, slanting the actual events of the day in a way unfavorable to the masses. On the early afternoon of Thursday, December 4, 1828, simultaneous to and probably in association with a popular revolt that broke out against President Guadalupe Victoria (1824–1829), a crowd of 5000 assaulted and looted the luxurious shops located in the Parián Building in Mexico City's Zócalo. It ended sometime the same evening. Upper class chroniclers depicted the riot in graphic terms, such as "savage invasion," "murders in cold blood," and a "stain on the pages of our history." We know that the rioters were people of the lower classes and some soldiers, probably part of the troop sent to bring the tumult under control.

Two murders occurred, neither committed by the lower classes (but by the upper class), and rioters inflicted considerable damage to stores and houses around the Zócalo, although most of the heavy destruction actually resulted from three days of street fighting that preceded the riot. Considerable disorder followed.

The revolt against President Victoria began on November 30. The lower classes rushed to support the upheaval led by Vicente Guerrero, a hero of the long guerrilla war that led to independence. One observer estimated that 30,000 to 40,000 people, 20 to 25 percent of the population of the capital, fought on the side of the rebels. Most soldiers abandoned the government and joined the rebellion.

Upper class Mexicans disdained Guerrero, an uneducated, dark skinned casta. Guerrero advocated two policies especially popular among the capital's poor. He propounded protective tariffs for the native textile industry, where many lower class and artisan city dwellers earned their living. He also proposed to expel the remaining Spaniards. The lower classes deeply resented the Spaniards, many of whom were wealthy at a time when the Mexican economy was in dire condition. It may have been that some rioters shouted "Death to the Spaniards" as they stormed the Parián. Many of the merchants in the building were Spaniards.

(continued)

(continued)

The Parián riot was indicative of the politics of lower class mobilization in the first decades after Independence. Mexican upper classes both in the cities and in the countryside needed popular support, but this came at a price—sometimes mobilization got out of control. In the countryside, lower classes demanded local autonomy for their villages and delay in the implementation of many of the modernizing policies so dear to upper class hearts. By mid-century, it was clear to the Mexican upper class that the price of lower class cooperation was too high. The Parián riot remained an indelible memory for Mexico's rich and powerful. Their fear of the masses was justified, to their mind.

Nature's Way

Natural Disasters

Given the geological composition of the region, and our scientific knowledge, it is more than likely that Latin America endured innumerable disasters resulting from earthquakes and their accompanying phenomena, such as tsunamis, long before known documentation recorded them. Archaeologists discovered circumstantial evidence of two, major earthquakes between 1438 and 1491 C.E. at Machu Picchu, the extraordinary Incan retreat in the Peruvian Andes. They found 140 examples of damage to buildings. They also concluded that the Incas altered their construction techniques to accommodate for the possibility of more such events. Nahuatl annals describe earthquakes in the former realm of the Aztecs in 1568 and 1575. At least ten other earthquakes struck Latin America during the colonial era, all at a magnitude above 7.0 on the Richter scale. The most destructive were in Lima, Peru in 1687 with 5,000 dead and 1746 with 4,000–5,000 deaths; and Quito, Ecuador and Cuzco, Peru in 1797, with 6,000–40,000 dead. We have documentation of another half dozen earthquakes during the nineteenth century. In 1812, two successive earthquakes destroyed Caracas and Mérida, Venezuela, killing 15,000–20,000 people. Another earthquake in 1868 in Arica, Peru (now Chile) had 25,000 dead.

Northern South America (Colombia and Venezuela) experienced at least 10 hurricanes between 1500 and 1900 and 19 more during the twentieth century. Cuba, situated in hurricane alley, endured 15 such storms in the twentieth century. The hurricanes that hit the rest of the Caribbean are too many to list here. After 1950, the damages caused by these storms escalated exponentially. Beulah in 1967 caused $US 208 million, Allen in 1980, $US 1.24 billion, and Gilbert in 1988, $US 7 billion.

The Inter-American Development Bank estimates that 972 natural disasters, including hurricanes, floods, earthquakes, and volcanic eruptions, befell Latin America between 1970 and 2000, causing 226,000 fatalities, costing about $US 29 billion in direct damages and $US 21 billion in indirect damages. That amounted to an average of 32.4 disasters and 7,500 deaths a year. In the 1990s alone, these events caused 2.5 million people to become homeless. The two most well-known disasters were the Mexico City earthquake in 1985, which killed 10,000–20,000, caused $US 6 billion in destruction, destroyed thousands of buildings, and left countless people without shelter, and the 2010 Haitian earthquake which brought about the deaths of 300,000 people and wiped out the entire infrastructure of Port-au-Prince. Many other calamities struck. Earthquakes in Peru in 1970 killed 66,000 and in Guatemala in 1976 killed 23,000. Floods and mudslides in Venezuela in 1976 caused 30,000 to die. The earthquake in Valdivia, Chile, in 1960, magnitude 9.5, was the strongest in recorded world history.

In the years 2000 to 2019, according to the United Nations, Latin America and the Caribbean endured the second most disasters of any area in the world with 1,205, affecting an estimated 152 million people. Seventy-five earthquakes rocked the region, 20 were of 7.0 magnitude or more. Seventy-four droughts struck, of particular severity in El Salvador, Honduras, and Nicaragua. In addition, the region suffered 548 floods, 12 of which caused more than $US 1 billion damages; 330 storms, averaging 17 hurricanes a year; 66 landslides; 38 volcanic events; and 24 wildfires.

(continued)

(continued)

Catastrophes such as these reveal the strengths and weaknesses of politics and society. They peel away the layers that often obscure the true relations of power. At times disasters brought down despots. They vividly show up incompetence and greed. Several sets of issues come to the fore. The first involves pre-event conditions. Since many disasters were not the first of their kind where they took place, questions arise, in some instances, as to why people reside where they do and as to what precautions governments adopted to mitigate any threats. For example, if an area was a known flood zone, why do people build there or why do governments permit them to live there? If an area is an earthquake zone, do governments enforce strict construction codes that assure that buildings withstand the earthquakes? The second concerns warning and evacuation. Did the infrastructure exist to give fair warning to residents of impending threats and to assist in their leaving the area to avoid harm? The third and perhaps the most important politically is about how governments assist victimized residents and how they plan and carry out the reconstruction. How do governments feed and shelter the affected population? How do governments rebuild? Far too often Latin American governments at all levels failed in all three concerns.

The starkest example of a regime's venality occurred in 1972, when an earthquake destroyed Managua, Nicaragua, the country's capital and largest city. The Somoza family, with the support of the National Guard, ruled the nation for over three decades. In the aftermath of the disaster, the Somozas stole relief supplies and sold them for their own profit. Their inefficiency and corruption, revealed to all, lost them the backing of Nicaragua's middle class, which in turn resulted in the overthrow of the family in 1979.

Another example of government failure was after a disaster occurred in Peru in 2017. The inhabitants of Barba Blanca, a village just northeast of Lima, in the Andes in March barely escaped with their lives when mudslides, the result of torrential rains, destroyed their village. Miraculously, no one perished, but the village longer existed. At the same time, elsewhere in Peru mudslides buried 100 people, destroyed 14,000 homes, and left 150,000 homeless. In Ecuador and Colombia, the rains brought equal destruction. Mocoa, Colombia suffered 293 deaths.

According to the latest reports in 2019, reconstruction of Barba Blanca was a promise not kept. No one laid a stone. No government rebuilt the road that connected the village to the outside world. The government provided 12 square meter modules for families, but no basic services. Those who remained worried that the rains would come again. Perhaps, bad luck intervened. The Peruvian government was in flux. Scandal forced Pedro Pablo Kuczynski, president at the time of the mudslide, to resign in 2018. His successor Martín Vizcarra was hardly in his seat before he dissolved Congress. The scandals rendered the national government useless.

Natural disasters reveal the weaknesses of and divisions in politics and society. They especially lay bare the inefficiencies or incompetence of governments and their leaders. They reveal the unfairness of society in starkest terms. These terrible events also bring people together, showing them at their best. They help each other. They sometimes join in protest. Whatever the case, natural disasters are integral to the region's history.

4

Everyday Life in an Uncertain Age, 1821–1880

IN LATIN AMERICA during the 60 years after independence, the uncertain political environment and frequent warfare adversely affected the material wellbeing of a large number of people of all social classes. The absence of consistent rules and regulations, the widespread lawlessness, and the loss of life and physical damage to property resulting from armed conflict often made day-to-day living quite difficult. It also substantially transformed important aspects of society, most importantly gender relations. Much changed profoundly over the course of the nineteenth century, but as much—good and bad—stayed the same. Despite these oft times troubled conditions, ordinary folk continued to earn their living and conduct their private lives much like their ancestors for decades, even centuries. Ordinary people and to some extent their wealthier neighbors, particularly in the countryside, resisted the transformations sought by modernizers.

The vast majority of Latin Americans during the nineteenth century lived in rural areas either as residents of large estates or villages with collective or small individual landholdings. Only a minority of country dwellers owned their own lands, though many were tenants or sharecroppers. In Brazil, most people in the countryside were enslaved, forcibly brought in large numbers from Africa until 1850, when the trade in slaves from Africa ended as the result of enormous pressure put on the Brazilian government by Great Britain. A significant minority of Latin Americans lived in large cities, such as Mexico City, Buenos Aires, Lima, Rio de Janeiro, and Sao Paulo. Wherever they resided, most common folk lived in poverty, often barely surviving. Work was never easy, whether one toiled on a large estate, on one's own plot of land, in the mines, or as a domestic in a wealthier family's home in the city. Latin

© The Author(s), under exclusive license to Springer Nature Switzerland AG 2022
M. Wasserman, *Modern Latin America Since 1800*,
https://doi.org/10.1007/978-3-030-96185-5_4

Americans toiled long and hard for their sustenance. However difficult their labor, they took pride in their jobs and did them well (no matter how much their bosses complained about them). Latin Americans, no matter how poor they were, mostly enjoyed their lives with *fiestas* (festivals) and other entertainments, the comfort of one's family, and the pageantry and solace of the Catholic Church.

The contrasts between rich and poor were enormous. Wealthy landowners often lived in palatial splendor in the cities, while only blocks away workers struggled in filth and squalor. Moreover, the well-to-do often had little sympathy for those less fortunate.

Let us turn, now, to the lives and work of Latin Americans, rich and poor.

Who were the people who populated the newly independent nations? Latin America emerged from the colonial era with an ethnically diverse population, which, during the eighteenth century, recovered from the horrific losses suffered in the sixteenth century, when the number of people fell by as much as 90 percent, mostly because of epidemic diseases brought by the Europeans. The vast majority of Latin Americans were indigenous, Africans, or castas. Typical of Mexico at the turn of the nineteenth century, the population of the state of Puebla was 75 percent indigenous, 10 percent white, and 15 percent castas. Less than one-third of Brazil's population was white, the rest black or mulatto. More than 30 percent were enslaved. In the early 1820s, out of 1.5 million Peruvians the white population counted only about 150,000. Mestizos numbered between 290,000 and 333,000. The population of enslaved Africans was an estimated 50,000. The remaining million were indigenous peoples. Approximately 65 percent of the people of Central America were indigenous, 31 percent *ladino* (mestizo and mulatto), and 4 percent white.

The disruptions that followed independence slowed demographic growth and the region's economies stagnated. Mexico's population grew only at an average annual rate of 1 percent. Its population increased from 6 million in 1820 to 7.6 million inhabitants in 1850. Brazil's population rose from between 4 and 5 million inhabitants at independence (1822) to 7.5 million by the early 1850s. Unlike the other new nations, Argentina experienced rapid population growth, as its half million people in the 1820s increased to 1.8 million by 1869. Latin America experienced growth after 1850, as Mexico's population rose to 15 million and Brazil's to 22 million by 1910 (Table 4.1).

In contrast, during the first half of the nineteenth century the population of the United States rose from less than that of Mexico in 1800—just over 5 million—to 92 million in 1910. The United Kingdom grew from 11 million to 45 million during the same period. These differences in population growth accounted for a large portion of comparable difference in economic progress

Table 4.1 The Population of Latin America in the Nineteenth Century

Nation	1820	1850	1880
Argentina	500,000+	1,800,000 (1869)	
Bolivia		1,378,896 (1846)	
Brazil	45,000,000	7,500,000	
Chile	1,000,000 (1835)		2,100,000 (1875)
Colombia			
Ecuador	496,846 (1825)		1,271,761 (1889)
Mexico	6,000,000	7,600,000	
Paraguay			
Peru	2,488,000	2,001,203	2,651,840
Uruguay			
Venezuela	760,000	1,660,000 (1860)	2,080,000
Costa Rica	63,000	101,000	137,000 (1870)
El Salvador	248,000	366,000	493,000 (1870)
Guatemala	595,000	847,000	1,080,000 (1870)
Honduras	135,000	203,000	265,000 (1870)
Nicaragua	186,000	274,000	337,000 (1870)

between Latin America and these industrial leaders. While Latin America failed to grow economically, the United States and the United Kingdom's economies expanded exponentially. Latin America never made up for these 50 or so years of economic and demographic stagnation.

The colonial heritage of large, dominant cities continued in post-independence Latin America. Mexico City's population fluctuated between 150,000 and 200,000. Rio de Janeiro experienced growth from 100,000 inhabitants in the 1820s to 275,000 in the 1850s. Buenos Aires blossomed from 50,000 inhabitants in 1810 to 189,000 by 1869. The expansion of the cities outpaced governments' ability to provide a healthy and prosperous environment for their residents.

Land and Work in the Countryside

Most Latin Americans earned their living on the land, planting, maintaining, and harvesting crops and tending to the livestock of their wealthier neighbors. Other Latin Americans toiled on lands owned either collectively by the residents of their home villages or individually by themselves and their families. Some worked as both employees and owners. Whichever the circumstances, the land was a way of life and it was difficult. Sometimes, as in the case of enslaved, conditions were oppressive and cruel. Even those worst off, including enslaved, made lives for themselves with humor, love, and grace.

A large number of Latin Americans resided on large estates (known as *haciendas, estancias,* or *fazendas* in Mexico, Argentina, and Brazil, respectively), where they worked for the landowner or leased land as tenants or sharecroppers. In rural areas, the owners of these large properties (known as *hacendados, estancieros,* and *fazendeiros)* controlled much of the land. Conditions on these large estates varied widely according to era, region, property size, and crops under cultivation.

At the top of hacienda society in Mexico was the owner, the hacendado, and his family. Beneath him were the supervisors and administrators, headed by the chief administrator or *mayordomo.* Usually males headed haciendas, but occasionally a widow operated a large property. Mayordomos in the Río de la Plata managed the larger estancias, directing employees, keeping records, and communicating with the owner about all estate-related matters. The mayordomo controlled his workers through foremen *(capataces).* On smaller ranches, the foreman took the role of the mayordomo. The living conditions of the capataces were hardly better than the workers. The mayordomo, however, was well paid.

Estate employees worked long, hard hours. On the Mexican haciendas, there were two types of employees: permanent and temporary laborers. Permanent labor included resident peons (unskilled laborers), tenants, and sharecroppers. A hacienda's temporary labor came from neighboring villages, whose residents supplemented their incomes from communally held land or family plots by working seasonally at planting and harvest. Commonly, the hacienda's sharecroppers and tenants earned extra money by working for the landowner.

While some hacendados farmed their own land with their own employees, the most common arrangement was for owners to combine farming their lands with sharecropper or tenant-cultivated lands. Tenants paid their rent to the hacendado in the form of cash or a portion of the harvest. Although most tenants leased small plots, a few leased entire haciendas. Sharecroppers paid the landowners with a preset part of the harvest, usually 50 percent. A typical arrangement in the central region of Mexico included resident peons earning wages and rations of corn to feed their families and receiving the use of small plots of land for cultivation. Tenants received a hut, firewood, seeds, and some pasturage, along with their plots, in return for half their crop. Occasionally, tenants worked for the hacendado and earned additional cash. For peons, the crucial part of the arrangement was the corn ration. Custom obligated hacendados in some areas to provide peons with the ration, regardless of the market price of corn. Because corn comprised 75 percent of a peon family's diet, this arrangement ensured the peon's most important staple, even in periods of drought and crop failure, and partially insulated him and his family from the effects of inflation, which resulted from shortages of staples arising from crop failures. Tenants and sharecroppers had no such security, so their wellbeing depended on the vagaries of the weather. A good-size plot with oxen and plenty of rain might turn a profit, but there were no guarantees.

Conditions on the haciendas varied according to region. A relatively dense population, concentrated in mestizo or indigenous villages, as in central Mexico, meant a large pool of potential workers and, therefore, low wages and less favorable terms for tenants and sharecroppers. Labor shortages, as in the far north and the far south, produced one of two outcomes: heavy competition for workers, which raised wages and added benefits, such as advances on wages; or intensified coercion to retain employees.

Debt peonage was the most notorious aspect of hacienda labor relations. In this system, peons went into debt to the hacienda in order to pay church taxes and fees; expenses for rites of passage such as marriage, baptism, and burial; or for ordinary purchases at the hacienda store. Peons then were obligated to work until they repaid the debt—but, of course, they often could not repay it. In some regions, debts tied multiple generations to the hacienda, custom (and perhaps coercion) dictated that children repay their parents' debts. Debt peonage in a few areas was nearly indistinguishable from slavery. On one of the great estates of northern Mexico, the owner dispatched armed retainers to hunt peons who tried to escape their obligations. Some historians observed, however, that debt was not always to the disadvantage of the debtor, for in some areas debt served as a kind of cash advance or bonus, attracting peons to work on a particular hacienda. In these instances, both debtor and creditor understood that the debtor did not have to repay. Debt, in these situations, became a device to attract and keep workers.

The Hacienda del Maguey, a grain and livestock estate in central Mexico, provides us with an example of relatively benign living and working conditions. The normal workday on this hacienda lasted from 6 A.M. to 6 P.M. There were breaks for breakfast and a traditional midday dinner followed by a resting period, or *siesta*, which lasted for 2 to 3 hours. The complete workday was 8 to 9 hours long, which was not arduous when compared to the contemporary industrial workforce in the United States and Western Europe. The workload was heaviest at planting, weeding, and harvest times.

Peons on the Hacienda del Maguey, according to the calculations of historian Harry Cross, were relatively well treated. The average peon laboring in the fields probably needed 2150 calories a day. His family, two adults and two children, required 9000 calories. The ration of com provided by his employer contained 75 percent of this caloric need. The rest of the diet consisted of *frijoles* (beans), chili peppers, lard, salt, and meat. The peon added to these staples wheat flour, rice, and sugar, which he bought at the hacienda store. (Usually, there were no other stores in the area. Sometimes employers allowed employees to purchase goods only at the hacienda stores.) The typical family also gathered herbs, spices, and cacti from the countryside at no cost. Workers consumed alcoholic beverages, particularly *pulque*— the fermented juice of the maguey plant--- in large quantities, providing vitamins. The combination of beans and corn produced most of the diet's protein.

Not all haciendas treated their peons so well. A passerby noted the conditions for resident peons on the Sánchez Navarro estate in northern Mexico in 1846: "The poor peon lives in a miserable mud hovel or reed hut (sometimes built of cornstalks, thatched with grass). He is allowed a peck of corn a week for his subsistence, and a small monthly pay for his clothes … Peons generally earned 2 or 3 pesos a month and 1 or 2 pecks (a peck equals a quarter bushel or 8 quarts) of corn a week. The Sánchez Navarro family paid their highly valued shepherds and cowboys (*vaqueros*) a bit more, 5 pesos a month and 2 pecks of corn a week salary. These modest wages hardly covered an average family's necessities.

The Hacienda de Bocas, located 35 miles north of San Luis Potosí, also in central Mexico, for which we have extensive records for the 1850s, illuminates another example of hacienda life. Bocas had between 350 and 400 permanent workers. The better off minority of these had free title to land they used for a house, corral, and farming. The best-treated permanent workers also received a corn ration. A resident earned 6 pesos a month, slightly less than $1.50 a week, with a corn ration of 15 liters a week. Because this was not enough to feed his family—1 liter a day per adult was necessary for sustenance— he purchased on account another 7 or 8 liters a week for 0.125 pesos each, leaving him with roughly 50 centavos a week to cover all the family's other expenses. The worker received a plot of 3000 square meters for which he paid no rent. He bought seed for planting from the hacienda. Other purchases during the year included food, sandals *(huaraches),* leather pants, and a burial. His expenditures totaled just over 72 pesos for the year, approximately the same amount as his annual salary. The circumstances for temporary workers on the Hacienda de Bocas were not quite as favorable as for permanent workers. Despite earning 10 pesos a month (if they labored 30 days), versus permanent workers' 6 pesos, temporary employees were not guaranteed subsistence rations. Regardless of employee status, however, few of the 794 tenants and 200 sharecroppers at Bocas in 1852 made ends meet without supplementing their incomes with temporary work for the hacienda.

Work was equally hard in the Río de la Plata, where most of the employees on the estancias were wage labor called in for cattle branding and horse breaking. A few permanent workers tended cattle or sheep and rode the perimeter looking for strays. Each of these workers maintained a hut and a corral in his area. Their routine work was tending to the herds and rounding them up every morning. Shepherds' chores were to wash and shear, brand, and slaughter, as well as to tend the herd. Cowboys earned wages, while shepherds shared in the profits. Some owners gave shepherds one-third to one-half the increase in their flocks per year. Other sheepherders earned up to one-half of the sale of wool, grease, and sheepskins. Cowhands, in addition to their flat wage, received rations of salt, tobacco, *yerba mate*, and beef, and perhaps a small garden plot.

The estancias employed Europeans, mixed bloods, and both free and enslaved blacks. Part-time workers came from the interior of Argentina and Paraguay. Native-born mestizos and mulattos, migrants from the interior, tended cattle, while immigrants raised sheep, farmed, and traded. Labor for the cattle roundup and sheep shearing came from nearby rural communities. When labor was scarce, temporary workers earned more. Estancieros paid high wages to skilled workers, such as sheep shearers, who could demand as much as 40 to 50 pesos a day plus food. A native-born laborer, with his own string of horses, could hire himself out at 20 to 25 pesos a day in cattle branding season. Some estancieros offered advances and credit at the ranch store to attract laborers. Estancieros often paid irregularly or in scrip at assigned stores. Agricultural wages remained relatively high until the late 1880s, when immigration and improved stock raising methods ended the labor shortage.

The differences between the affluent and the poor were particularly evident in the conduct of their everyday lives. Daily routines for upper class women and men focused on work and meals. Wealthy women on the hacienda began their day around nine and spent much of the morning doing needlework together in the drawing room in "virtuous silence." After the midday meal, each female family member carried out chores before retiring for a nap (siesta). During the midafternoon, the women gathered again to continue their needlework. Males and females joined at eight in the evening to say prayers and eat the evening meal. Afterward, the women put in another hour of needlework, while one of the men read aloud to the family.

Women administered the domestic sphere and acted as heads of family, when their husbands were away. Girls stayed at home while boys went to school. Young women learned needlework and enough reading skills to enable them to read the Bible and carry out religious observances. A curious relationship existed between wealthy families and their household servants, who simultaneously were part of and separate from the family. A hacienda's rich and poor children grew up together, even shared confidences, but real friendship was never possible, because the social barriers between classes were too great.

Enslaved Brazilians lived perhaps the hardest lives of all the Latin American poor. About two thirds of them worked in agriculture and of these, the largest group, one third, worked on coffee plantations in the environs of Rio de Janeiro or Sao Paulo. Others toiled on sugar plantations in the northeast. On plantations, particularly in the south, masters practiced swift, brutal discipline. They regarded their enslaved as "by nature the enemy of all regular work." Planters lived in constant fear that their enslaved workers would rebel.

At the beginning of the nineteenth century, Brazil had 1 million enslaved and during the next 50 years imported another million. Perhaps surprisingly, their life expectancy was not much different from that of the rest of the population: 23 to 27 years. The crucial difference, however, was the odds of a child born into slavery surviving infancy. One third of all enslaved male babies died before the age of 1, and a little less than one half died before the age of 5. If an enslaved male reached the age of 1, he was likely to live until he was 33.5. If the enslaved child survived until age 5, then he could expect to live more than 43 years. Twenty-seven percent of enslaved female children died before reaching the age of 1, and 43 percent died before age 5. If the female lasted until age 1, she could expect to live until 25.5, and if she endured to age 5, she would likely reach 39 years.

Enslaved people born in Africa had difficulty in adapting to the new climatic and biological environments of Brazil, and, as a result, their mortality rate was high. In the northeast, the climate was very humid and hot, but sudden drops in temperature were common.

Many Africans, unaccustomed to such swings in temperature, suffered chills, which, in turn, often resulted in pulmonary illness. Diseases such as tuberculosis, scurvy, malaria, dysentery, and typhus were endemic. Enslaved workers and their families lived in unhygienic conditions and medical care was crude or unavailable. The number of deaths of the enslaved in Brazil always exceeded that of births, and only the continual importation of newly enslaved people from Africa permitted their population to increase.

The flow of enslaved Africans to Brazil ended in 1850, a decision made because of pressure from the British. This brought about a massive transfer of enslaved workers from the cities and towns to the countryside and from regions where markets for export crops were in decline to those areas where exports flourished. Regardless of an enslaved person's age, the dynamics underlying the relationship with his or her fazendeiro were coercion and violence. Owners required them to be loyal, obedient, and humble. In return, enslaved people might expect to be part of the patron's family, with all the accompanying benefits and protections: enslaved Africans who attained "family" status could become skilled artisans and attain positions as overseers.

Most enslaved workers toiled in the fields in regimented gangs closely supervised by overseers. Corporal punishment, such as whipping or locking in stocks, was common. The workday lasted 16 to 17 hours. Overnight work was rare, except when sugar had to be milled and coffee dried. Surprisingly, they did get breaks during the day. While everyday work was always hard, it may have been truly unbearable only for short periods during harvest.

Many enslaved workers had occupations other than field hands. Owners gave a few men skilled positions repairing equipment, constructing buildings, and sewing clothing. Planters sometimes rented the services of enslaved artisans to other landowners. As a result, fewer enslaved male and more women planted, weeded, and harvested. Enslaved men and women were also domestic servants. Those who worked in the masters' houses or as artisans experienced better living conditions than those in the fields.

In the nineteenth century, most enslaved worked in the Sao Paulo coffee region. The typical fazenda had 70 to 100 enslaved, though the largest employed as many as 400. The average enslaved adult cared for more than 3000 coffee trees and produced approximately 1000 kilograms of coffee.

Their daily routine began before dawn with breakfast, which consisted of coffee, molasses, and boiled corn. They then said prayers and divided into work teams, led by supervisors who were themselves enslaved. At 10 A.M., they ate a meal of corn porridge, black beans, pieces of lard covered with a thick layer of manioc flour, and on occasion highly seasoned sweet potatoes, cabbage, or turnips and then at 1 P.M., another break for coffee and a corn muffin. They ate dinner at 4 P.M. Work went on, often, until well after dark, as late as 10 or 11 P.M. Finally, before retiring, workers received a ration of corn, a piece of dried meat, and some manioc meal.

Their living quarters usually consisted of a single unpleasant building. Some had the use of a plot of land to raise coffee or vegetables and allowed to sell these crops and keep the proceeds. Coffee planters did not give their enslaved workers Sundays off because they feared that religious or social gatherings of the entire enslaved population would lead to trouble. Instead, to prevent the possibility of any kind of unified revolt, they assigned rotated groups different afternoons off during the week.

Within the larger plantations, enslaved Africans established their own communities, resembling small villages. They established families and forged a new culture adapting African ways with those of the Americas. Almost all enslaved native born married. Although they were not usually married by the church, the fazendas commonly recognized the marriages. Maintaining a family was difficult, however, for the possibility always existed that the fazendero would sell one or more family members, permanently separating the family. The reality of high mortality rates among enslaved people was a perpetual threat to family stability, as well. On the plantations, enslaved women were subordinate in marriage to their husbands (like their free counterparts). As with every aspect of their existence, their family and social lives were both separate from and intimately attached to the world of their masters.

Like marriage and family, religion played an important part in plantation enslaved communities. Enslaved people practiced god-parenthood *(compadrazgo)*, in which close friends of the parents of a child became godparents, which meant that they were obligated to care for the child if its parents died. They also synthesized their African religions with Catholicism, producing a folk Catholicism and religious cults, such as *candomble, voudoun,* and *santeria.* In these hybrid spiritual practices, African deities often took on the guise of Catholic saints.

Ultimately, however, resistance to their conditions consisted of slowing the work pace, working shoddily, or refusing to do work that did not fit their described assignment (i.e., work that was not in their "job descriptions"). Cooks would not do housework, for example. Occasionally, they struck back violently at their masters. More commonly, enslaved people tried to gain their freedom by running away. Those who fled sometimes found haven in isolated communities, known as *quilombos.* Whatever the approach—harsh or paternalistic—taken by the planters, few were entirely successful in controlling their enslaved workers. The enslaved refused to surrender either their cultural heritage or their dignity.

The majority of the rural population in Mexico and Peru consisted of indigenous peoples, who continued to live in relatively autonomous villages, as they had during colonial times. The small, individual plot of land used for family subsistence farming was the basis of rural life. Villages had simultaneously symbiotic and conflicting relationships with haciendas: Villagers relied on the estates for work to supplement earnings garnered from farming their own lands. Haciendas, in turn, depended on village residents for temporary labor and tenants. Nonetheless, haciendas and pueblos frequently clashed over land and water rights. The relationship was, perhaps, most equal in the years from 1821 to the mid1880s, a period when war and uncertain political conditions badly weakened the haciendas economically. Warring political elites desperately needed allies. Villages traded their political support for increased local autonomy and protection of their lands.

It is important not to idealize rural life, particularly in the villages. In Mexico, the *pueblos* (villages) had their own forms of social stratification, with local bosses *(caciques),* municipal officeholders, and lay leaders of religious organizations comprising the upper level. Small traders, muleteers, and some of the larger tenants (in terms of the amount of land they rented) at times entered the top group. At the bottom were poorer residents who worked permanently or temporarily as hacienda peons and tenants.

Generally, village leadership came from elder males, who nominated people for local offices, made decisions in times of crisis, and oversaw all dealings by local officeholders with the wider society. Elders attained their elevated status through hard work on the community's behalf or, perhaps, through economic achievement. As the century wore on, the ability of the elders to act justly and to reach community consensus lessened, as state or provincial and national governments intruded on their autonomy.

Politically, village residents concerned themselves primarily with protecting their individual and collective landholdings, minimizing taxes (both of which required local autonomy), as well as maintaining the right to govern their everyday affairs without interference from state or national governments. Throughout the nineteenth century, taxes were a never-ending source of friction between pueblo residents and the various levels of government. Country people also bitterly opposed coerced military service. It was common for the armies of various factions to raid villages in order to drag off their young men, the loss of whom badly disrupted the local economy and society.

A considerable measure of competition, petty bickering, and serious disputes often existed among villagers. In many places, such as Oaxaca in southeastern Mexico, inter-village conflict was endemic, as rival pueblos fought perpetually over land and water.

For most rural dwellers in Mexico and elsewhere, life revolved around their land and their families. Country people lived in two worlds: the first was the traditional subsistence economy, which retained ancient practices, and the second was the modern money and wage economy, the incursion of which country people carefully limited. Indigenous people, such as the Maya of the Yucatán peninsula of Mexico, fiercely resisted the discipline and values of the plantation and the industrial workplace. North American John Lloyd Stephens, who traveled extensively in the peninsula in the 1840s, reported: "The Indians worked as if they had a lifetime for the job." Working slowly, though, was only one strategy for resisting the demands of overbearing employers. Unlike Brazil's enslaved, however, passive resistance was not the only tactic available to rural folk: They met attempts to alter existing custom or wages with strikes or mass migrations.

In many parts of rural Latin America, the family was an economic unit, both on small plots and on the large estates. Families worked together in the fields, especially during planting and harvest. The men worked their 8 to 9 hour days at the hacienda or, perhaps, even longer on their own land or in helping neighbors at planting and harvest times.

Families' small fields were ever on the brink of ruin, watered only by erratic rainfall. When the rains did not come, crops failed, and people either starved or went deeper into debt to the hacendados in order to purchase food. Often, farmers cultivated their plots with the slash and burn method, clearing the field of forest or scrub, burning the debris to create ash fertilizer, and tilling the land with a wooden digging stick. Crops quickly exhausted such lands' nutrients after only 2 or 3 years, whereupon the farmer abandoned it. Usually, it took 7 years for the land to restore itself for cultivation.

In Argentina, small, family landowners comprised the most common productive unit on the vast plains of the Río de la Plata. Most farmers lived in comparative modesty on land they worked with family members and a few hired hands. In one sector of Buenos Aires province, almost 70 percent of the landholdings were smaller than 5000 hectares in 1890. The typical rural residential unit was a farm or small ranch with six to eight persons: a man, his wife, their children, a peon, an orphan, and perhaps a enslaved or *liberto* (a enslaved born after 1813 who was to remain a enslaved until age 21).

In the Brazilian northeast, small farmers eked out a living raising the region's staple crop, cassava. To plant cassava, farmers cleared the land with an iron axe and set fire to the brush, then, the farmers' slaves used hoes to heap the earth into small mounds. These prevented the cassava roots from becoming waterlogged and rotting during the winter rainy season. Two or three pieces of stalk cut from growing plants went into each little mound. In the rows between the mounds, farmers planted corn or beans. In about 2 weeks, the cuttings took root and poked through the soil. For several months, enslaved workers guarded the crops from weeds and other natural enemies, such as ants, caterpillars, and livestock. After 9 to 18 months, the central stalks sprouted small branches. Below ground, each plant put down five to ten bulbous roots, which the farmer harvested.

Enslaved workers then prepared the cassava for processing into coarse flour (*farinha*). Most important was to eliminate poisonous prussic acid from the roots, which involved scraping, washing, grating, pressing, sifting, and toasting. They first scraped the roots with blunt knives and washed them. Then they grated or shredded the roots with a grating wheel. The pulp fell through the wheel and dried overnight to remove the prussic acid. The fine white sediment that collected at the bottom of the trough, when dried, washed, and sifted, became tapioca. They sifted the grated pulp of the cassava root into a coarse grain with the texture of moist sand. They placed the sifted cassava on a large griddle made of glazed clay or copper and then lightly toasted it over an open hearth, stirring often to prevent burning. Toasting made it taste better and removed the last of the prussic acid. Cassava was a crop planted or harvested at any time. Harvesting, moreover, could delay for a year before the roots would spoil.

Regardless of where they lived, non-enslaved women's workdays and responsibilities went far beyond those of men. Mexican women rose well before dawn to prepare the family's food. The backbreaking work of making tortillas took hours, and because men took breakfast and lunch with them to the fields, women prepared enough food for both meals early in the day. Women drew the water, gathered wood for the fire, cared for the children, prepared three meals for their households, did the wash, spun thread and wove cloth, and made clothing. They also made pottery and then hauled it to the Sunday market. When men hired on to a hacienda, the women commonly accompanied them as field hands, or as domestics in the hacienda house—work for which they received no pay. Not all was drudgery, however: The weekly market day provided a welcome respite from the dull daily routine, giving the women vendors the opportunity to meet, gossip, and laugh with friends. Despite the enormous amount of work done by pueblo women, employment opportunities for women in rural areas were very limited. Consequently, a large number of young women migrated to the cities, where, for the most part, they entered domestic service.

Religion occupied a central place in rural Latin American life, and permeated popular culture. The influence of Catholicism was everywhere. Almost every small town had at least one chapel, and many had several churches. Perhaps the most important religious institutions in the countryside were the *cofradías,* the village organizations that maintained the church and funded religious celebrations. Much of a village's social life revolved around these celebrations and rites of passage. Priests often lived only in the larger villages or towns, and so traveled periodically through the villages in their districts to perform masses (Catholic religious services) and sacraments (baptism, marriage, and burial). Though clergy were among the most important figures in Latin American society, most country people rarely encountered a priest. As a result, the folk Catholicism practiced in the countryside retained many indigenous customs from pre-Christian times. The characteristics of Christian saints were often indistinguishable from those of gods worshipped by pre-Columbian peoples. Religion was a daily presence in the lives of all villages, rich and poor. The literate wealthy, for example, read primarily devotional literature, and adorned their houses with religious artwork. Poor families decorated their huts with corner altars bearing candles, flowers, and the likenesses of saints.

In the Cities

During the nineteenth century, most of Latin America may have been rural, but the region's cities rivaled any in the world in size. These cosmopolitan centers were at once splendiferous and horrifying. Often situated in physically beautiful settings with impressive colonial architecture, they also were unsanitary and dangerous, filled to overflowing with poverty-stricken people. The cities were crucibles of change, for it was in the urban areas that modernization most directly confronted tradition—especially in the realm of gender roles and relations. It was in the cities that the transformation of the role of women was most dramatic.

Mexico City was the largest city in the Western Hemisphere and the fifth largest city in the Western world during the early nineteenth century: Its population was 168,846 by 1811. Half its people were of Spanish descent, with the rest comprised of indigenous, mixed bloods, and African Mexicans. During the next three decades, through the 1850s, the city fluctuated between 160,000 and 205,000 residents, because of periodic epidemics. Migration from the countryside, rather than natural increase, accounted for the net growth. At the beginning of the nineteenth century, Rio de Janeiro had between 50,000 and 60,000 residents and the count rose to 425,000 in 1890. The city's population included immigrants from Portugal, Spain, and Italy, free blacks and mulattos, and white Brazilians from the hinterlands. Buenos Aires was the fastest growing large city in Latin America during the second half of the century, becoming the largest city in the region by 1890. In 1914, in all the Americas, only New York exceeded it in number of inhabitants. Half of Buenos Aires' population was foreign-born.

The physical spaces of the cities were impressive, but their beautiful buildings and picturesque settings hid the dismaying conditions of most of their inhabitants. Mexico City was a grid with an enormous central plaza, the Zócalo, the great cathedral at the north end, the palace of government on the east, and the offices of the municipality on the south. Five causeways furnished access to the city over the lakebeds that surrounded it. A legacy from Aztec times, the city divided into distinct sections, known as barrios. The poor occupied outer margins of the city, while the affluent lived in the central area.

Rio de Janeiro was located in a setting of overwhelming physical beauty but was just as shabby and disease ridden as Mexico City. With narrow, stinking streets and crowded tenements, it teemed with poor people. In contrast, Buenos Aires at midcentury was little more than a large village, possessing none of Rio de Janeiro's topographical beauty or Mexico City's impressive architecture. One Scottish traveler remarked that the houses had "filthy, dilapidated look." Pastureland, adorned with grazing livestock, lay 20 blocks from the central plaza.

All these cities were unsanitary and unhealthy. The Spaniards had built Mexico City on the ruins of the great Aztec capital Tenochtitlan and surrounding dry lakebeds. During rainy season, these beds flooded, frequently transforming the outlying districts into lakes, dumping mud, garbage, and human feces into the houses, and leaving the central plaza knee-deep in stagnant water. Buenos Aires also had poor drainage, making even paved streets difficult to pass when rains were heavy. Built on filled-in swampland, Rio de Janeiro suffered similar problems.

Mexico City never had enough water for any purpose or sufficient waste disposal (nor does it today). Walking its thoroughfares was dangerous to one's health. The air smelled horribly from the sewage and piles of garbage. The city dumped trash into Lake Texcoco, which, unfortunately, was one of the primary sources of municipal drinking water. These unsanitary conditions had an enormous cost. Diseases such as smallpox, scarlet fever, measles, typhoid, and cholera were endemic. In 1840, smallpox killed more than 2000 children, while cholera killed almost 6000 in 1833 and 9000 in 1850. Cholera killed 15,000 in Buenos Aires in 1870. These diseases and others, such as diarrhea and dysentery, were closely associated with the wretched living conditions. Rio de Janeiro also was chronically short of water. In the 1860s, the city built a new system of reservoirs to hold water from mountain streams, but this did not solve the problem.

Governments wasted minimal resources to finance their armies and were simply unable to provide the public works necessary to make the cities healthy and safe.

Life in the cities in early nineteenth century Latin America differed in many respects from that in the countryside, but many of the societal dynamics were much the same in urban settings as in rural ones. The social structure was equally as stratified in the cities as in the country, the work was equally hard and as badly paid, and the gap between rich and poor was comparably wide. The vast migration of the populace from the countryside to the city made these conditions worse, especially during the last half of the century, when migration intensified.

Society in Mexico City divided into very small upper and middle classes separated by vast differences in wealth and status from the majority of people, who were tremendously poor. The upper classes comprised of high civil government and ecclesiastical officials, merchants, and wealthy mine owners and landowners. Professionals, such as doctors, lawyers, prosperous merchants, civil servants, industrialists, and other business people formed the next layer of the strata, the upper middle class. This group closely associated in circumstance and outlook with the uppermost class. The "true" middle sectors consisted of small shopkeepers, tradesmen, artisans, and the better off skilled workers. At the bottom lived 80 percent of the city's population: the unskilled workers, peddlers, artisans of low prestige trades, and others who lived at the margins of society, such as prostitutes and beggars (*leperos*). Most urban dwellers lived on barely subsistence wages. Steady employment was insufficient with only 30 percent of those employed fulltime. Only 1.4 percent of city residents owned property.

A large number of tiny businesses supplied consumer goods; many of these merchants conducted their commerce on dirty blankets in the filthy main market. The most common occupations, much like on the haciendas and in the pueblos, were domestic service, manual labor, and artisanship. Shoemakers, carpenters, and tailors were the most common types of skilled workers, while bricklayers, domestics, and street peddlers made up the majority of unskilled laborers. The average daily salary was .50 to 1.0 peso per day for skilled workers and .25 to .50 for unskilled, while the cost of subsistence was .75 to 1.0 peso per day. (Until late in the century, the Mexican peso was equal in value to the U.S. dollar.) The region's stagnant economy and a labor surplus ensured that wages did not rise much, if at all, through the 1830s.

The nineteenth century migration from rural to urban life transformed the situation of women. These brave, determined women, many of whom were single and aged 15 to 29, left their rural birthplaces in search of a better life. They often came to urban areas without a father or a husband and suddenly found themselves having to lead self- reliant lives of unprecedented, even undreamed of, independence. Now, they had to function in public spaces (such as factories and markets), make their own living, and even act as head of their own household.

Women made up between 57 and 59 percent of the inhabitants of Mexico City and the majority of the migrants from the countryside throughout the first half of the nineteenth century. As with the men, almost all were castas or indigenous who came from the densely populated regions around the capital.

A quarter of all women in Mexico City worked, accounting for one-third of the total work force in the capital. More than a third of casta women and almost half of indigenous women worked. Sixty percent of women worked as domestic servants; 20 percent sold food from their homes, on the street, or in the markets. Other occupations varied in skills. Compensation and employment conditions of women were no better than that of the men. Work was hard to come by and wages were paltry. Even those who found employment were underemployed. Worse still, women were limited to the lowest paying occupations. The jobs most easily obtained, in domestic service, they regarded as humiliating. Some servants received good treatment, but all owed their employers "submission, obedience, and respect." They were on call 24 hours a day and often received no more than their room and board. Because so many young women were available for domestic service, the labor market precluded any improvement in these conditions. Although they considered factory work more respectable than domestic service, the pay was no better, and conditions in the textile and tobacco industries, large employers of women, deteriorated considerably over the course of the 1820s and 1830s. Social norms did not allow women into the clergy, the military, or government bureaucracy—which were, of course, the main paths to upward mobility in Mexico.

In Rio de Janeiro in 1870, 63 percent of free women and 88 percent of slave women worked. Only a very few, however, were professionals, such as midwives, nuns, teachers, or artisans. Society prohibited women from holding jobs in the government bureaucracy and in law and medicine. Women found work in commerce only as street vendors or market sellers because employers preferred to hire men as clerks and cashiers. More often women found jobs in the textile and shoe industries. By far and away the most common occupation for women in Rio de Janeiro was, as in Mexico City, domestic service. More than 60 percent of free, working women and almost 90 percent of urban enslaved women were servants.

Circumstances often separated urban women from their families and they became necessarily independent and desperately poor. Not surprisingly, then, many women did not conform to the traditions of their male dominated society. In Mexico City, slightly less than half were married. Eighty percent of females married at some point, either in formal or informal unions. Nonetheless, most spent only a small portion of their lives married. If they migrated from the countryside, they delayed marrying. Because of the higher mortality rate among men, widowhood was likely. One-third of adult women were single or widowed at the time of the censuses (1811 and 1848). Seventy percent of married women between 45 and 54 outlived their husbands. Rich or poor, women spent much of their lives on their own.

An average woman in the Mexican capital bore five children. With infant mortality (death before age 3) estimated at 27 percent, it was likely that she would outlive at least one of them. Although two thirds of adult women bore children, less than half of these women had children at home.

For much of their lives, therefore, a substantial proportion of Mexico City's women headed their own households as widows. Widowhood afforded wealthy women a degree of independence, although in many wealthy families, an adult son or son-in-law controlled the finances and negotiated with the outside world for the woman. Half of white women headed their own households in 1811, while only a third of casta or indigenous women did so. Wealthy widows benefited from inheritance laws, which forced the division of an estate among spouse and children. The wife would always have at least some control over the estate. Because affluent males commonly married late, the number of offspring was often limited, thus keeping the widow's share of the estate larger. These kinds of calculations, of course, were of no consequence to the poor. Poor women barely subsisted. They had few alternatives other than to turn to men for support. Even then, survival was uncertain. Children were such women's only old age insurance; the hope was that children would care for and support their parents in their old age.

Marriage and motherhood did not end a woman's work outside the home. Poor women worked out of necessity, because families could not subsist on men's incomes without the addition of women's earnings. Poor women, whether married or not, worked. Marriage probably changed a woman's occupation. Domestic service, for instance, was not possible for a married woman because it required that she live apart from her husband, in the residence of her employer. Self-employment, on the other hand, allowed women to care for their children while generating income. They could prepare food for sale, sew, operate small retail establishments, or peddle various wares. The result was that women dominated the markets.

Marriage, an entirely patriarchal institution, was an unequal relationship for women. A husband expected his wife to be submissive and to "obey him in everything reasonable." Domestic violence was common. Sexuality was another arena defined by double standards: It was perfectly acceptable for men to engage in extramarital relations, but unacceptable for women to do so.

Daily Life

For most Latin Americans the fabric of everyday life—the food they ate, the housing that sheltered them, and the clothes that covered them—remained much the same throughout the tumultuous decades of the nineteenth century. Nowhere were disparities between social classes as clear as in these three basic aspects of daily existence.

The staples of the Brazilian diet were black beans, dried meat, and manioc flour, occasionally augmented by game, fruit, molasses, and fish. The average Mexican's diet consisted of maize, beans, squash, and *chiles,* with small amounts of eggs, pork, meat, and cheese, with the corn tortilla as an essential staple. To make tortillas, women shucked corn and soaked the kernels in water with small bits of limestone, which loosened the sheath of the corn, imbued it with calcium, and increased its amino acid content. The latter created proteins from the mix of corn and beans, crucial in a diet that lacked meat. Next, the women beat the corn in the grinding bowl for hours. Finally, the women worked the small pieces of the resulting dough between their hands—tossed, patted, and flattened—until they were no thicker than a knife blade, after which they threw them on a steaming hot griddle *(comal)*. The combination of maize tortillas and beans (tucked inside the folded tortilla) was not only delicious, but also provided almost all of the eater's required daily protein. (The more prosperous could afford to obtain more of their protein from meat, mostly pork.) Squash, which is 90 percent water, supplied badly needed liquid in an arid land and filler (fiber) to make meals more satisfying. Women added chiles to the beans as the source of crucial vitamins A, B, and C. The capsaicins, the chemical elements that make chiles "hot," killed bacteria that caused intestinal disorders. Water or pulque were preferred beverages with the meal, and lump sugar provided a sweet. The urban poor took few meals at home for there was no place in their crowded rooms for cooking appliances. Instead, they purchased inexpensive food from vendors and ate it on the street.

The diet of the middle class, while also modest, was more varied and nutritious. In a respectable house in Rio de Janeiro, residents woke to a cup of strong coffee. Later in the morning, they ate bread and fruit. The afternoon meal consisted of hot soup, then a main course of fish, black beans sprinkled with manioc flour, rice, and perhaps vegetables and, on occasion, well-cooked meat or stewed or roasted chicken. Two favorite dishes that took hours of preparation were *feijoada,* which required black beans soaked overnight and then cooked for a long time with fatty pork and cod *(bacala)*, which was soaked for 20 hours and then baked. Desserts were sweets, such as fruit glazed with a paste made from guavas and sugar, or candy made from egg yolks, egg whites, and sugar, accompanied by highly sweetened strong coffee.

In Mexico City, breakfast started with a hot drink—chocolate for the adults or corn gruel *(atole)* for the children—and then toast, biscuits, or pastries with coffee and milk. At 11 A.M., people drank chocolate or atole again, but this time flavored with anisette. The large meal, served in midafternoon, consisted of bread, soup, a roast, egg in chili, vegetables, and beans flavored with pickled onion, cheese, and sauce. Dessert was honey with grated orange on a toasted tortilla. A light dinner in the evening consisted of a spicy sauce *{mole)*, stewed meat, and a lettuce salad. A small staff served the meals.

For wealthy Mexicans, food was plentiful, varied, and rich, and meals were leisurely. At 8 A.M., the well-to-do partook of a small cup of chocolate with sweets. Two hours later, they ate a hearty breakfast of roasted or stewed meat, eggs, and beans (boiled soft and then fried with fat and onions). Dinner took place at 3 P.M. It began with a cup of clear broth, followed by highly seasoned rice or some other starch; a meat course consisting of beef, mutton, pork, fowl, or sausages; various vegetables and fruits; and dessert. After such repast, a siesta was in order. At 6 P.M., families enjoyed a warm drink of chocolate during the cooler months or a cold, sweet beverage in summer. Cigars and conversation or a walk followed. Wealthy families ate a "light" supper at 10 P.M. consisting of roasted meat, salad, beans, and sweets. Domestics served all meals on elegant china and silverware with tablecloths and napkins.

Differences in dress between the affluent and poor were as striking as the differences in their diets. Rich urban women conformed to the latest fashions from France, often adding traditional Spanish garb, such as the *mantilla* (a shawl, usually made of lace, worn over the head). European diplomat Brantz Mayer described one woman in church in Mexico in the 1840s: "She wore a purple velvet robe embroidered with white silk, white satin shoes, and silk stockings; a mantilla of the richest white blond lace fell over her head and shoulders, and her ears, neck, and fingers were blazing with diamonds." The dandies who frequented the fashionable spots in Mexico City might wear a "French cutaway suit, American patent leather shoes and an English stovepipe hat." The more sedate wore broadcloth suits and silk hats.

Few Mexicans, of course, could afford rich silk and woolen apparel. Travel writer Frederick Ober described mestizo dress in the early 1880s: "In the warmer regions he wears (on Sundays) a carefully plaited white shirt, wide trousers of white or colored drilling, fastened round the hips by a gay girdle, brown leather gaiters, and broad felt hat, with silver cord or fur band about it." Ranchers wore "open trousers of leather ornamented with silver, with white drawers showing through, a colored silk handkerchief about the neck, and a *serape*—the blanket shawl with a slit in the centre ...." The women "seldom wear stockings, though ... feet are often encased in satin slippers; they have loose, embroidered chemises, a woolen or calico skirt, while the *rebozo*— a narrow but long shawl—is drawn over the head, and covers the otherwise exposed arms and breast."

Poor Mexicans dressed in simple, practical clothes. They went barefoot or wore sandals (*huaraches*) made simply from rawhide or plaited fibers. Despite the laws that demanded they wear pants and hats in public, indigenous men usually wore only a breechcloth. Other rural Mexicans wore cotton shirts without collars and buttons and pants with long legs that covered their feet. Belts were strips of rawhide or cloth. The serape, a brightly covered woolen blanket, was an all-purpose garment that protected its wearer from the elements. The one common luxury among poor men was a straw hat. Rural women's apparel was no fancier than that of men. Indigenous women often wore only a few yards of cloth wrapped around their bodies. They used *rebozos* similarly to serapes, protecting women from the elements and providing modesty. They also used the rebozo, when folded the right way, to carry small children. Other women wore a scarf bound at the hips with a girdle that extended to the feet, accompanied by a broad mantle that covered the upper part of the body. This wool garment, often ornamented with colorful embroidery, had openings at the head and arms. Wealthier indigenous women wore a white petticoat with embroidery and ribbons. Some girls wore simple white cotton dresses with the head, neck, shoulders, and legs below the knees left bare. Women also wore heavy earrings and necklaces of cut glass. Their feet bore the same sandals worn by men or nothing. For the most part, women went without head coverings. Both men and women often carried rosary beads.

As in the case of diet and clothing, housing, too, sharply differentiated the classes. The wealthy lived in opulence. In larger cities, houses of the affluent often had two stories. The ground floor in these buildings was for shops or other businesses, while the second floor was the family home. The house of Vicente Riva Palacio, well-known soldier-statesman, had 50 rooms. One entered through an impressive stairway leading to the living quarters. The stairs and the floors of the corridors were made of the finest Italian marble. Tropical plants decorated the halls, and singing birds filled an aviary. Of the numerous rooms, there were three parlors, a grand salon, two smaller salons, and an impressive private chapel adorned with luxurious drapes and beautiful religious ornaments. Mirrors and massive sideboards took up the walls of the dining room, measuring 100 by 50 feet. On these shelves were thousands of pieces of china, crystal, and silver. The brass beds in each of 30 bedrooms each bore an elegant bedspread of velvet, silk, lace, and crochet; hand-stitched linens; and canopies. The large living room, whose ceilings were 30 feet high, contained furniture decorated with gold trim, fabulous mirrors and chandeliers, and rich carpets. The family had its own 200-seat theater. Maintaining this remarkable establishment required 35 servants.

Guillermo Prieto, a noted social critic, described the typical middleclass home in Mexico City, which was considerably more modest:

A steep stairway led to a corridor paved with red varnished millstones. (The middle class usually lived on the second floor ... because of the flooding that periodically afflicted the city, and the servants occupied rooms on the first floor.) The corridor was embellished with cages filled with stuffed birds, squirrels, wind chimes, and earthen crocks packed with stored foods and vegetables. Landscapes ... adorned the walls. Comfortable chairs and couches ... furnished the principal chamber....

In the bedroom were a large bed of fine wood, easy chairs, and wardrobes. The small children of the family slept in the halls. Those of a small family slept with their parents in curtained compartments of the main bedroom. The dining room contained a washstand holding towels, soap, straw, and a scouring stone for scrubbing. Colored vegetables, pots and pans, and jars lined the kitchen walls ... with strips of garlic and pepper for a festive air.

In contrast to the domestic comfort enjoyed by the urban well-to-do, housing for farmers in the countryside was little more than a hut. Because wood for construction or fuel was prohibitively expensive in deforested or arid areas, neither lumber nor bricks were practical building materials. (Wood was too costly to use in ovens to bake bricks.) Consequently, in temperate climates, country people constructed their huts with adobe made from sunbaked straw and mud blocks. In the highlands, where wood was more plentiful and affordable, houses consisted of brick (or stones plastered with mud rather than mortar) walls and a flat roof of beams laid close together and covered with finely washed, carefully stamped clay. In the tropics, farmers built their huts with saplings and leaves held together with mud. Occupants drove hewn logs into the ground to support the beams and roof and used bamboo sticks for the walls. The normal hut measured 20 by 15 feet and contained one room with no windows and a floor of packed earth mixed with ashes. Doorways (without doors) provided ventilation and light. Roofs were thatch or rows of poles across the tops of walls covered with 1 or 2 feet of dirt and a layer of pine boards. Where it was colder, shingles covered the roofs. Native vegetation, such as palm leaves or straw, served as roofing material in the tropics.

The kitchen area, where a fire burned continuously, was outside or in a separate, smaller building. The metate for tortillas was beside the fire. Huts had no furniture. Mats known as *petates* served as sleeping pallets. Better off rural dwellers might have a bed consisting of four mounds of clay crossed with rough boards. No one could afford bedding or mattresses. Men and women slept in their clothes, wrapped in serapes and rebozos in cold weather. Because most people owned only the clothes they wore, there was no need for chests or closets. Pottery and baskets stored food and whatever other possessions the family owned. The only decoration in the hut was a picture of the Virgin of Guadalupe or a saint. Most regions were warm enough that homes did not require heating—and even if they needed heat, no one could afford it. The more prosperous rancheros lived in slightly less simple abodes. They might have a few pieces of furniture, such as a bench, a table (perhaps with low stools for seating), and board beds with mats and skins for pillows.

Poor people in Mexico City lived in rooms rented in crowded tenements (*vecindades*). Because the city endured periodic flooding, ground floor rooms were continually damp. Badly ventilated, filthy, and crowded, the vecindades were breeding grounds for disease. Apartments lacked cooking facilities, which meant most of the poor took all their meals from street vendors. Not everyone was fortunate to have a roof over his or her head. Joel Poinsett, the United States Minister in 1824, estimated that 20,000 people slept on the streets. In Buenos Aires, most of the poor lived in small, ugly houses on the outskirts of the city. About a quarter of the residents in 1887 lived in tenements *{conventillos*), where they and their many children inhabited tiny rooms piled high with garbage and filth. In Rio de Janeiro, many of the new immigrants and internal migrants lived in crowded slums known as *corticos*. As in Mexico City the fashionable suburbs sprang up on the periphery, while the core of the city became the ever more crowded home of the poor.

Statistics and anecdotal evidence depict everyday life in nineteenth century Latin America as being unpleasant or even miserable (if one were poor or a enslaved), but people found ways to enjoy themselves. The church, family, drinking, and gambling provided the most common entertainment for people of all classes. Solemn church masses were great spectacles, offering the best entertainment of the time, a theater of rites and rituals, resplendent priests, and majestic music. While no parish in the capital or anywhere else duplicated the magnificence of the great cathedral in Mexico City, many churches elsewhere stirred and inspired the people. Even in a modest village chapel, a visiting clergyman might put on a good show despite the lack of an opulent setting.

Religious fiestas took up a large number of days; in Aguascalientes, Mexico, for example, in the 1860s, there were 40 per year. These occasions provided both solemn consideration and joyous fun. Cities, towns, and villages prepared carefully for these celebrations by repairing and cleaning the streets, so that the processions that marked the special days were fit for the event. The Palm Sunday march represented Jesus' entrance into Jerusalem. On Good Friday, the crucifixion procession took place. Repentant sinners paraded through the roads half-naked and wearing crowns of thorns.

Mexico City celebrated Corpus Christi in unusual splendor. The archbishop conducted mass in the great cathedral in the Zócalo after which he led a grand parade from the church through adjacent streets, walking under a canopy of white linen, decorated with a red border. Everyone who was any-one—presidents, generals, cabinet ministers— appeared in full regalia. The procession was a time to show off. The wealthy displayed their fine clothes, perhaps imported from Paris. A vast crowd of costumed people of different races and colors watched as the spectacle passed before them. Owners decked out the surrounding homes with carpets, flowers, flags, and streamers.

The Day of the Dead, celebrated in late October and early November, was one of the most important holidays in Mexico. The celebrants burned massive numbers of candles and consumed large quantities of food. Poor indigenous expended years of earnings in remembrance of departed loved ones. The night of the last day of October, families decorated their homes with flowers and candles and set out a colorful mat on which they lay a feast to lure dead children back. The next day, the family repeated the ritual, adding dishes too hot for children, such as turkey mole and tamales. On this day, they also offered liquor. The Day of the Dead celebrations indicated that Mexicans knew death well and did not fear it.

Drinking was an important aspect of religious celebrations and, perhaps, for many, a crucial method of alleviating the pain of daily life. Alcoholism was a serious problem among the poor, as the alienation of urban life and industrialized working conditions became widespread at century's end. Pulque was the alcoholic beverage of choice. The *maguey* (agave) cactus has leaves of up to 10 feet in length, 1 foot wide, and 8 inches thick. After some years, it sends a giant flower stalk 20 to 30 feet high, on which grow greenish yellow flowers. The plant dies after it blooms. Just before it is about to emit its stalk, the indigenous folks cut into the plant to extract the central portion of the stem. The incision leaves only the thick outside rind, forming a natural basin 2 feet deep and a foot and a half in diameter. The sap that would feed the stem, called *aguamiel* (honey water), oozes into the core and a small amount taken to ferment for 10 to 15 days. This becomes the *madre pulque,* which acts as a leaven inducing fermentation in the aguamiel. Within 24 hours it is pulque. As one draws off the pulque, one adds aguamiel to the mix. A good maguey yields 8 to 16 liters of aguamiel a day for as long as 3 months. Although the pulque has a lumpy consistency, tastes something like stale buttermilk, and smells like rotted meat, it is quite nutritious, and many believe it helps digestion.

Another popular diversion was gambling, which many observers of the time believed was a Mexican obsession. Cockfighting was a passionate outlet for gamblers and necessitated considerable preparations. Handlers bred and selected the cocks (roosters) carefully, fed them strictly, and trained them assiduously. The event required an arena 6 feet in diameter fenced in by 3-foot boards with benches around it. From the gallery, spectators urged on and bet on their favorites. The spectacle of the birds was bloody and brutal. The brave cocks exhausted themselves, but would not quit until one of the two contestants lay dead. Money then changed hands.

Of the different types of entertainment available in Mexico during this period, bullfighting was the most famous. Thousands frequented the Sunday afternoon spectacles in Mexico City. Although it was a sport shared by all classes, seating made one's status clear. The wealthy sat in the shade, while the masses suffered the searing sun. The spectacle proceeded in traditional stages: The bull entered to have *picadors* and *matadors* goad and tease him with lances and red cloaks. These men had to be agile to avoid death on the animal's horns. Then, amid trumpet sounds, the bull's tormentors stuck small lances into his neck. The bull, snorting, thundering to no avail, attacked anyone and anything. Finally, the chief matador emerged, accompanied again by trumpets, to do battle armed with his red cloak and long blade. After some flourishing, the matador plunged his weapon between the bull's shoulder blades and into its heart, putting the animal out of its misery.

Conclusion

Life in Latin America during the first seven decades of the nineteenth century was enormously difficult for all but the wealthiest classes. The huge majority of Latin Americans struggled in poverty. Most people resided and worked in the countryside, either on large estates, in communal villages, or on small farms. A small percentage found employment in mining camps. As the century progressed, growing numbers of the populace migrated to the great cities in hopes of creating a better future for themselves. Inept and corrupt governments, war and banditry, and stagnant economies tormented nearly everyone, most profoundly, of course, the poor.

In the face of such dauntingly difficult lives, Latin Americans sought to preserve their customs and traditions. The best means at their disposal was to defend local governance. Political and economic instability ironically allowed the lower classes to maintain their autonomy, at least in the countryside, for several decades after independence. Political centralization and economic development during the latter half of the century, however, undermined local prerogatives and eroded the practices of everyday life sustained for centuries. New forms of work emerged, and modernization made life worse, rather than better, for most of the population.

How Historians Understand

The Construction of Racism

Racism was the basis of the upper classes' fear of the lower classes that so impeded political developments in Latin America during the nineteenth century. White descendants of European colonials widely disdained, if not hated, Africans and indigenous as people of color. Historians of this era, many of whom were prominent intellectuals and politicians, were the generators and pillars of this attitude and ideology.

By midcentury, pervasive racism overwhelmed Argentina. In their desire to modernize, Argentines firmly believed that European immigration was the only path to "civilizing" their nation. Juan Alberdi, one of Argentina's leading intellectuals and author of the Constitution of 1853, disdained nonwhites, writing that to populate the Pampas with Chinese, Asian Indians, and Africans was "to brutalize" the region's culture. Domingo Sarmiento, another notable Argentine intellectual and later president of the nation from 1868 to 1874, also advocated the benefits of European immigration, because he believed that Africans and people of mixed blood were inferior. These men and others thought that Argentina in the 1850s was a mestizo country and that it would not progress unless Europeanized. Part of the consequent "whitening" campaign was having Argentine historians and government bureaucrats erase Afro-Argentines from the country's history and exclude them from its census. Similarly, Chileans saw to it that Africans disappeared from their history. They, too, firmly believed that development would come only with the Europeanization of local culture.

In Peru, intellectuals retained their hostility to Afro-Peruvians long after that country's abolition of slavery in 1861; one even insisted "the Negro [is] a robber from the moment he is born ...." Another thinker decried that "in South America, civilization depends on the ... triumph of the white man over the mulatto, the Negro, and the Indian."

The failure of Latin American governments to abolish African slavery at independence was not only an indication of the powerful political influence of planters, but also of the underlying contempt and fear the white upper classes had for Africans.

Abolition of Slavery			
Country	Year	Country	Year
Argentina	1861	El Salvador	1825
Bolivia	1831	Honduras	1825
Brazil	1888	Mexico	1829
Chile	1823	Nicaragua	1825
Colombia	1850	Paraguay	1870
Costa Rica	1825	Peru	1854
Cuba	1886	Uruguay	1846
Ecuador	1852	Venezuela	1854

(continued)

(continued)

Free and enslaved Africans were not the only victims of racism. In Argentina, Mexico, and Chile, governments conducted campaigns of extermination against nomadic indigenous peoples, who white officials believed also stood in the way of progress. Latin Americans of European descent perceived them as barbarians and obstacles to the betterment of society. These indigenous peoples fought back fiercely. In the north of Mexico, for example, the Apaches, Yaquis, Comanches, Mayos, and Tarahumara resisted incursions until the end of the century. In Yucatán the Maya Indians came close to eliminating whites from their peninsula in a bloody rebellion that began in 1847. (Historians did not confirm stories of this resistance until the late twentieth century, however.) Mexican historians of the era, such as Lucas Alamán and Carlos María Bustamante, had a predictably low regard for the nation's indigenous peoples, even though by virtue of Mexico's first Constitution (1824) all Mexicans were equal before the law. Alamán once said that "it would be dangerous to enable the Indians to read the papers."

How could these historians legitimate such inaccurate and destructive beliefs? Historians, like everyone, are products of their times: Nineteenth century historians such as Alamán, mostly from upper class origins, shared the same prejudices and fears of the others of their status.

Latin American Lives

The Gaucho

THE HISTORY OF the *gauchos* (cowboys) of the Argentine plains, known as the Pampas, reflects the evolution of the region's politics and economy in the post-independence era. Gauchos were the symbol of regionalism, fierce local independence, the crucial role of the lower classes in politics, and the importance of the export economy. Originally, a product of the vast growth of wild herds of horses and cattle on the Pampas during colonial times, gauchos were skilled horse men who roamed widely, taking the livestock that they needed to survive. Viceroy Arredondo, in 1790, considered them "vagabonds" who "live by stealing cattle from the estancias and selling the hides ... to the shopkeepers ...." Like other members of Latin America's working classes, cowboys in the Río de la Plata and Venezuela were important participants in the wars of independence and the uncertain politics and warfare of the early nineteenth century. During the wars, gauchos were among the rebels' best troops. After the wars, they comprised the local private armies of the numerous regional chiefs who ruled in the Río de la Plata. As the Argentine economy grew by exporting hides, tallow, and dried salted beef, gauchos worked on the expanding estancias. During the first half of the nineteenth century, their services were in such demand, both as soldiers and as ranch hands, that they escaped worker discipline.

To many upper class Argentines, however, the mixed blood gauchos were a symbol of backwardness. Domingo F. Sarmiento, in his famous polemic *(Life in the Argentine Republic in the Days of the Tyrants)* against Juan Manuel de Rosas, the notorious gaucho leader who ruled Buenos Aires from 1829 to 1852, defined the gauchos as representatives of "barbarism." He saw them as impediments to Argentine development.

Dressed in little other than a poncho, mounted on horseback, armed with rope and knife, the gaucho was a formidable sight. He subsisted on meat, a bit of tobacco, and *yerba mate* (a strong, tea-like beverage) and lived in simple huts roofed with straw and possessing neither doors nor windows: "The walls were sticks driven vertically into the ground, and the chinks were filled with clay ...." Furniture in a gaucho's hut consisted of perhaps "a barrel for carrying water, a horn out of which to drink it, a wooden spit for the roast, and a pot in which to heat the water for mate," with no chairs or tables or beds. Cutlery consisted of a knife, for gauchos ate only meat. To cook and keep warm, gauchos burned dung, bones, and fat. Their clothing, shelter, and food made the gaucho no different from other Latin Americans who struggled to make their living in the nineteenth century.

(continued)

(continued)

Compared to most Latin American workers, however, gauchos retained a relatively high degree of freedom, because Argentina's growing economy increased demand for their services. For example, gauchos attained the right to enjoy leisure time on the numerous fiesta days. Often, cowboys worked for a few months, asked for their pay, and moved on. Offering higher wages only delayed the inevitable. Somewhere another job existed for a gaucho to fill. However, time was against the gauchos, and their glory days did not last long. The export economy demanded their subordination, and the undisciplined gauchos, who were enthusiastic brawlers, and loved to sing, gamble, and drink, were not acceptable employees in the modern economy. In addition, technology, in the form of barbed wire, and a glut of immigrant agricultural labor in Buenos Aires province---they were no longer indispensable--- also worked to end their independence. The history of the Argentine gaucho parallels that of many other lower class Latin Americans, who defended their local prerogatives, customs, and traditions in an ever more difficult struggle against government centralization and economic modernization.

Slice of Life

Urban Enslaved

MANY ENSLAVED PEOPLE WORKED in the plantation fields, a few toiled in their master's home, and others had skilled occupations processing sugar and coffee. A surprising number of enslaved people worked in the cities, primarily as domestic servants, but also as artisans and in other jobs.

Enslaved people comprised 11 percent of the Brazilian industrial workforce in 1872. Approximately 13,000 of them worked in textile factories. They also made up 15 percent of construction workers. enslaved women represented 8 percent of seamstresses. Many of these lived in the cities, numbering some 118,000 in total, or roughly 15 percent of the population.

Enslaved urban people usually found themselves in one of three working situations (or some combination thereof): the traditional relationship with a master; a largely traditional relationship with a master but which included being rented out to a third party; or self-employment (the latter arranged housing for themselves). Self-employed enslaved generated considerable income for their masters. Such enslaved worked as bakers, barbers, carpenters, masons, porters, and prostitutes. It is likely that urban enslaved people in the cities had more control over their everyday lives than on the plantations. Nonetheless, enslaved urban dwellers were no less subject to abuse or the other hazards of survival. Thomas Ewbank, a traveler from the United States, observed at midcentury: "Slaves are the beasts of draught as well as of burden. The loads they drag … are enough to kill both mules and horses."

In Rio de Janeiro, the constant demand for domestic servants arose from the need for services later supplied by urban utilities and public works. As late as 1860, homes in the city had neither piped water nor a sewerage system. Residents also had no refrigeration, and perishable food could not be stored, because it spoiled easily in the tropical climate. Servants carried water, shopped, and did laundry. Most indoor chores centered in the kitchen, where enslaved workers were skilled cooks. Other enslaved household workers saw to the considerable volume of cleaning required in the dusty, dirty city in houses chockful of furniture and other objects. Still other servants emptied chamber pots and wet-nursed babies. Wealthy families trusted servants to an extent that parents sometimes passed such workers down to their children to ensure that the younger generation had a reliable staff when it established households of its own.

While a significant minority of enslaved people worked independently in the cities or held relatively privileged positions in their owners' households, they, nonetheless, remained in bondage. Their master still controlled their fate.

Nature's Way

The Cholera Epidemic of 1833 in Mexico

Six cholera pandemics worldwide occurred in the nineteenth century, three of which affected Latin America and the Caribbean, 1826-1837, 1846-1860, and 1881-1896. Two struck Mexico, the first in 1833 and the second in 1850. It is likely that the wartime conditions that existed during these years facilitated the spread of the dreadful disease.

Cholera is a brutal illness. Sharp stomach pains, with vomiting and diarrhea, convulsions and massive dehydration kill the victim often within hours. It is a bacterial disease spread by human feces contaminated water.

The dreaded disease arrived in Mexico in 1833, probably from Europe, where the pandemic began seven years earlier. The disrupted condition of the country facilitated its spread. An uprising toppled the government in 1833. Soldiers moving through the north central region spread it.

The mining town of Guanajuato, situated in the Bajío region, the breadbasket of the nation, provides an illuminating example of the impact of the disease. General Santa Anna's army brought it to the area. Interestingly, it appears that Guanajuato's leaders took preventative measures the year before its arrival. The municipal government adopted strict hygiene codes for markets, slaughterhouses, baths, and burials. They, of course, did not know the cause of cholera at the time, but, undoubtedly, these new practices alleviated the misery to come. In Guanajuato 2,487 suffered the disease with 1,244 or half dying. The disease revisited in 1849 and 1850.

Historian Donald Fithian Stevens reveals another aspect of the impact of the disease. Because no one understood the cause of cholera, this "left many people with only questions, doubts, and fears." As a result, many people changed their behavior. One segment of the population of Mexico City sought to "make things right with God." Evidently, according to Carlos María de Bustamante, enemies healed their differences and husbands and wives reconciled, all because they feared sudden death and the need to face judgment.

One bizarre aspect of the pandemic discovered by Stevens was that some hysteria existed over the possibility of premature burial. In the last stages of cholera when body temperature, respiration, and pulse fell precipitously, patients appeared to die, even though they were actually alive. Numerous instances occurred when victims showed life just before interment. Municipal government adopted rules that required a twenty-four hour waiting period before burial.

Another unusual effect was the change the pandemic caused in Catholic Church practices. First, the government in Mexico City forbade the ringing of bells, especially, those that preceded funeral processions. Officials worried that the endless ringing would terrorize residents. Some doctors believed that fear caused cholera. Whatever the proclaimed good intentions of the authorities, Mexican Conservatives took the prohibition as an attack on the Church. Given the times, and the recent Liberal rebellion, and the consistent liberal campaign to limit the Church, Conservatives had some reason to be suspicious. As Stevens points out, ironically while the municipal leaders worried about mitigating fear, conservative clergy fostered it. These priests argued that the disease was punishment for immoral behavior. The epidemic was God's wrath. Penance was the obvious need.

5

Economic Modernization, Society, and Politics, 1880–1920

new things created need for people

The period from 1880 to 1920 was a time of momentous changes in the world economy. Railroads, steamships, telegraphs, and telephones made it possible for people, goods, ideas, and money to move rapidly across oceans and international boundaries. In Western Europe and the United States, most people now lived in cities and earned their livelihoods in industry rather than agriculture. The population of these areas grew in both numbers and affluence, creating demand for a wide range of agricultural products, such as beef and grains for consumption and cotton and wool for wear. New industries required minerals, such as copper for electric wire, and other commodities, such as petroleum for internal combustion engines. Large corporations emerged to provide the capital, technology, and administrative knowhow in a global process of economic modernization.

These transformations had especially profound economic, political, and social consequences in Latin America. Beginning in the 1870s and continuing to the 1920s, Latin America experienced an extraordinary export boom. The construction of thousands of miles of railroads and the refurbishment of seaports eased the flow of products from Latin American mines and fields to waiting North Atlantic markets. Europe and the United States not only provided expanding markets but also new technologies and capital to facilitate the extraction of agricultural and mineral resources. Economic growth brought a measure of prosperity, but it was unequally distributed. Workers in the region's mines and nascent industries experienced harsh working conditions and often received scant compensation for their contributions to the growing economies. Poor farmers, usually indigenous peoples who still held their land communally, often lost their property to large estates that sought to

- many people lost jobs.
- depression caused conflict
- needed more people - immigration

increase their acreage in order to produce more agricultural commodities for export. Aided and abetted by national governments, which looked unfavorably on collective landholding as an impediment to progress, land expropriations created a large class of landless rural people, whose customs and mores for centuries revolved around collective and individual landownership. Meanwhile, as the region more closely linked to the world economy, it became exceptionally vulnerable to fluctuations in overseas markets. The resulting boom and bust cycles wreaked havoc in many countries. Major depressions in the world economy in the 1890s and again in 1907 sparked political conflict in various Latin American countries. political stability

Export-led modernization brought enormous political and social changes to Latin America. Emerging from the violent decades that followed independence, many nations experienced long periods of political stability, dominated by land-based upper classes ruling through rigged elections or dictatorships. This political stability was vital to the modernization process, but economic development generated forces that disrupted the status quo. The export boom created two new, crucial social classes—an urban middle class and an urban industrial working class—whose demands for equality and equity eventually brought an end to the rule of the large landowners. The export economy expanded the size and role of governments, which needed a growing number of white-collar workers who obtained middleclass status. These workers formed one component of the new middle class. Economic opportunities in boom times created an entrepreneurial group of small-scale businesspeople, who also joined the ranks of the middle class. This middle sector commonly formed the foundation of rising political parties.

new classes

Meanwhile, railroads, mining, food processing, and other new industries stimulated by the export economy required growing numbers of workers. In some countries, massive immigration—made possible by rapid development of railroads and steamship lines—helped fill the demand. The new export economies needed large numbers of unskilled workers, but the new technology also required many workers with specialized skills. Workers of all ranks, but particularly those who were highly skilled, organized labor unions and joined political parties in search of improved living and employment conditions.

Workers' grievances joined with those of dispossessed farmers to form an increasingly volatile political climate. The crisis, known in some countries as the "Social Question," intensified after 1900. Those who ruled struggled to maintain their position. Some upper classes grudgingly made concessions to the middle and lower classes, while others stubbornly refused. During the first two decades of the twentieth century, many cities and mining regions experienced violent protests against upper class oppression, but only in Mexico did these protests lead to revolution. Almost everywhere, however, the rule of large landowners ended.

Export-led development brought with it not only profound economic and political dislocations, but wrenching social changes as well. The old ruling classes faced the erosion of the patriarchal norms that underlay their positions of power. The urbanization, industrialization, and migration that accompanied export-led development undermined traditional gender roles and family structures that cast fathers and husbands as the heads of families and men as the sole actors in the political sphere. Women's positions in the family, the workplace, and the public arena changed. Feminism rose to demand recognition of women's important contributions to the construction of modern nations. Women sought equality under the law, both inside and outside the family. Not only was the public rule of the upper classes under attack, but the private basis of their position as well.

Economic change notwithstanding, the core of the political struggle remained control over everyday life. Urbanization and industrialization merely shifted the locations, altered some of the methods employed, and broadened some of the goals. In the countryside, struggle continued much the same as it had before against the intrusions of central authority. To country people, modernization and centralization meant a widespread assault against their culture and traditions.

After nearly a half-century of stagnation with interludes of export boom, much of Latin America entered into a period of economic growth from the 1880s through World War I, resulting from the influx of new technologies and capital, mostly from abroad, and the advent of domestic peace. Massive new railroad networks were both the products of modernization and the engines of further economic development. They also facilitated national consolidation in ways unimaginable before 1880.

The development of export agriculture and industry was at the core of the economic, social, and political transformations of the era. The export boom displayed several notable characteristics. First, most nations concentrated on one or two export commodities. Second, the booms were not sustainable, for the most part, for more than a decade or two at a time. International markets for primary products were cyclical, and busts inevitably followed booms. Third, the question of who actually benefited from the expansion of exports is subject to unending debate. Finally, linkages between the export economy and domestic sectors of the Latin American economies were not consistent. As a result, the growth of exports did not necessarily stimulate overall economic development.

economic growth 1880's

The industrialized nations of the North Atlantic (Great Britain, France, Germany, and the United States) greatly increased their population and general prosperity after 1850. Annual income per capita doubled. The market demand for agricultural staples, such as grain, meat, and wool, exceeded locally available supplies, while increased affluence stimulated demand for more "exotic" products, such as coffee, cacao, sugar, and bananas. Simultaneously, technological advancements in agriculture and industry created additional demands for primary materials. New farming techniques required fertilizers, for example. Intensifying industrialization created a need for mineral ores such as lead, silver, gold, tin, zinc, and copper. The invention and widespread use of the internal combustion engine expanded demand for petroleum. Technological improvements in metallurgy and mining made it possible to extract minerals from previously unusable sources and cut down on the bulk and cost of ore shipments. New railroads and communications and the introduction of steamships facilitated the transportation of raw materials. The new ships reduced the Buenos Aires to Europe route to weeks. Refrigerated shipping made it possible to send fresh meat and other delicate commodities across the ocean.

Latin American nations possessed the natural resources to help satisfy the North Atlantic market for food and minerals. The industrialized nations supplied capital, technological expertise, and administrative organization to extract and transport these commodities. A vast inflow of foreign investment stimulated the expansion of exports. The largest sectors of investment were in railroads, government obligations (bonds), mining, and public utilities.

Great Britain accounted for the largest share of foreign investment in Latin America. Between 1900 and 1914, the British doubled their holdings in the region. The British were a notable presence in Chilean nitrate mining and Mexican petroleum. U.S. capital was second in importance to the British and concentrated in Mexican railroads and mining, Cuban sugar production, and Central American plantations and railways. Between 1900 and 1914, U.S. investment in Latin America quintupled. Mexico received the most capital. U.S. investors mostly sought export industries. Before 1914, the third largest source of foreign investment was Germany. Germans invested heavily in Argentina, Brazil, and Mexico (more than $100 million in each). World War I, however, broke most of Latin America's commercial and financial ties with Germany.

Growing demand in the North Atlantic economies, transportation improvements, and massive foreign investment all combined to increase Latin American exports enormously. Some of this growth began as early as the mid nineteenth century, but the pace accelerated greatly after 1880. Between 1853 and 1873, Argentine exports grew sevenfold. By 1893, they had doubled again. Brazilian coffee exports more than doubled in the years between 1844 and 1874 and quadrupled between 1874 and 1905. Colombian, Costa Rican, and Venezuelan coffee exports also increased spectacularly. Total Mexican exports rose nearly 700 percent from 1878 to 1911. Bolivian tin exports jumped by 1200 percent from 1897 to 1913. The burgeoning export economy had important positive effects. In 1916, Argentina's per capita national wealth stood at approximately 10 percent less than that of the United States, but 62 percent higher than that of France. By 1914, Argentina's per capita income exceeded that of Spain, Italy, Switzerland, and Sweden and compared with that of Germany, Belgium, and the Netherlands.

Despite overall growth, export-led modernization proved a mixed blessing for Latin Americans. The rise in per capita income was statistically impressive, but the numbers masked the fact that this wealth was not equitably distributed. Wealthy landowners became fabulously rich, while the situation of the rest of the population remained the same or deteriorated.

[margin annotation: unequal distribution of money]

Moreover, few Latin American nations were able to sustain steady high growth. The other nations had spurts of growth followed by long periods of stagnation. By World War I exports seemed to reach a ceiling, because either the products of these nations dominated the world market to such an extent that little room for growth remained or severe competition had arisen and market share inevitably fell.

Most nations' continued reliance on a limited number of export commodities exacerbated Latin America's vulnerability to world market fluctuations. In the first decade of the twentieth century, a number of efforts to diversify from the model of one or two raw material exports took place, but concentration of exports persisted. In thirteen Latin American nations, one commodity accounted for more than fifty percent of exports (Bolivia, Chile, Cuba, El Salvador, Guatemala, Brazil, Ecuador, Haiti, Nicaragua, Panama, Costa Rica, Venezuela, and Honduras) in 1913. The most diversified export nations were Argentina, Colombia, and Peru. Argentina was the most successful at diversification, exporting grains (wheat, linseed, rye, barley, and maize) and livestock (chilled and frozen beef, lamb, wool, and hides).

Most Latin American export economies depended on a handful of consuming nations and therefore found themselves vulnerable to economic fluctuations in those countries. Four markets, the United States, Great Britain, Germany, and France, together accounted for 90 percent of the exports in 10 countries and more than 70 percent in 18. Only Argentina avoided this heavy dependence on the four markets.

The foundation of Latin American trade was the shipment of primary commodities in return for manufactured goods. Historians have long debated the equity of this system. Some have maintained the terms of trade were unfair because manufactured goods constantly rose in price while commodity prices declined. This is difficult to determine conclusively, however, because the statistics for trade and prices are not very reliable and those that are available do not show firm trends. The advantage, however, was not always with the industrialized nations.

Historians and economists also argue heatedly about the impact of export-oriented development. Advocates claim that these strategies stimulated the other sectors of the economy. Some export commodities require processing, such as butchering and chilling meat, tanning hides, and milling flour. Sugar production is as much an industrial as an agricultural enterprise. Industrialization, however, was not necessarily a result of increased primary exports. Exports drove the construction of railroads and other transportation. At the same time, export commodities often drained the nation of resources, leaving little or nothing for other economic activities. In nations where capital was chronically scarce, precious few resources trickled from the export machine. Some export economies, notably petroleum drilling, operated in enclaves without enhancing the overall economy. In general, the nations with the most varied export product base were the most likely to develop. Those economies that relied on one product were the least likely to develop.

Finally, export booms inevitably ended. Agricultural commodities wore out the soil, causing production to decline gradually, as was the case for coffee in Central America, Venezuela, and Haiti around 1900. Bananas were vulnerable to disease and natural disasters. More important, world market demand was fickle. For example, demand for Brazilian rubber skyrocketed at the turn of the century, creating fabulous fortunes, only to fall precipitously when competitors from Southeast Asia flooded the market and, later, chemists invented a substitute. railroads

Railroads were, perhaps, the greatest technological agents of change during the nineteenth century. They provide a good illustration of the benefits and drawbacks of modernization, for they were the "backbone" of the export economy, bringing unparalleled prosperity to some regions and but also unmitigated misery elsewhere. The expansion of the railways was spectacular. (See Table 5.1.) The railroad system of Argentina increased from 1600 miles in 1880 to 21,200 miles in 1914. Mexico had less than 400 miles of railroads in 1880, but by 1910, it had constructed nearly 15,000 miles of track.

Railroads provided inexpensive transportation for agricultural commodities, minerals, and people. The rail networks opened up new lands for cultivation. In Argentina, they made it possible to cultivate grains on the rich soil of the Pampas and to push livestock raising farther and farther south into the

Table 5.1 Railways in Latin America, 1880–1920 (number of miles)

	1880	1900	1920
Argentina	1600	10,400	21,200
Brazil	2100	9500	17,700
Chile	700	8300	13,000
Peru	1100	2700	5100
Latin America	7200	34,500	62,900

Source: Copyright © 2000 Frederick Stirton Weaver. Reprinted by permission of Westview Press, a member of the Perseus Books Group

semiarid region of Patagonia. Brazilian planters spread coffee cultivation to the vast interior of Sao Paulo. Railroad transportation facilitated the recovery of the Mexican mining industry.

The new transportation systems brought together nations torn by regionalism. They enabled governments to exert their authority in previously autonomous areas. What once were months-long journeys for armies now took only days, and former day trips now took only hours. Railroads enabled people to travel farther and at less cost than ever before.

Walking to the mines of northern Mexico from the center of the nation was an impossible dream, but the railroad carried passengers to potentially better lives for minimal expenditure. It also created truly national markets for the first time.

Despite the obvious benefits they generated, railroads also were a symbol of unwanted modernization, one that people frequently resisted. In Mexico during the last quarter of the nineteenth century, there was violence in almost every region where tracks appeared for the first time. Protesters often threw rocks at the train cars as they passed, so hated were the engines of progress. gov. The railroads disrupted old patterns of landholding. Their presence raised the forced value of land. In areas where indigenous people owned lands collectively and people individually and grew subsistence staple crops, government officials and large off of landowners forced them off their properties. The greedy landowners then their converted production to commercial crops, which they sent to urban and property international markets by means of the railroads. This process created a large, landless class of poor rural people, and thus a pool of inexpensive labor, and cut the total production of staple crops, which in turn caused the prices of basic foodstuffs to rise. The subsequent inflation undermined the living standards of both the middle and working classes.

The economic and technological transformations described in the preceding section triggered great changes in Latin American society. First, improved diets and medical care, coupled in many countries with a steady stream of immigrants, brought a substantial increase in population, most particularly in

urban areas. Second, new social classes arose, complicating the social hierarchy and political agendas for the region. Third, discontent mounted in the
countryside. Finally, people were on the move—from rural areas to cities and
mining camps, from overseas to Latin America, from one country to another.
All these changes had a profound impact on the daily lives of men, women,
and children throughout Latin America.

Warfare pervaded the first decades after independence throughout Latin
America. These conflicts cost many lives, and the population growth that
many areas had experienced in the late colonial period halted. By the 1880s,
however, the populations of Latin American nations grew once more. The
population of Argentina doubled between 1895 and 1914, from 3.9 to
7.8 million. Brazil's population went from 10.1 million in 1872 to 30.6 million in 1920. Cities exploded. The population of Buenos Aires went from
178,000 in 1869 to nearly million in 1914. Other than Hamburg, Germany,
it was the fastest growing city in the Western world. Lima, which because of
the War of the Pacific and subsequent civil wars, did not begin to grow until
the 1890s, jumped from 104,000 in 1891 to 224,000 in 1920. Guayaquil,
Ecuador, grew from 12,000 to 90,000 between 1870 and 1920.

The increase in population and the development of industry created both a
bigger, more complex middle sector and an industrial working class, while at
the same time providing opportunities for women. Each of these groups
would in turn seek to add their voices the political discourse begun in the
decades after independence.

From colonial times, a *gente decente* (decent folk) existed that comprised
light-skinned people who did not work with their hands. In great part, their
status depended on their race. Few indigenous, blacks, or mulattos found
acceptance into the middle class (although there were, of course, exceptions).
To the contrary, the new, middle class that arose from the export boom and
industrialization was more diverse in its make-up. In Buenos Aires, the mostly
immigrant middle class operated small businesses, such as bakeries, breweries,
print shops, and retail shops. The number of small-scale manufacturers doubled from 1853 to 1914. These remained vulnerable to the fluctuations in
economic conditions. The depression of 1907, for example, devastated small-
scale entrepreneurs in northern Mexico, erasing a decade of gains. Oftentimes
the middle class depended on the goodwill and good fortune of their bosses,
not necessarily their own merits. Proprietors of small businesses rarely had any
other assets other than their own skills. In the cities, few middleclass people
owned property.

White-collar employees occupied the most complicated and difficult position among the middle classes. Not always earning income sufficient for

full-fledged middle class status, they, nonetheless, sought respectability. They lived precariously on the edge of ruin, fearing above all the prospect of falling back into poverty. They had no family connections, earned poor pay for long hours, and lacked job security. Their highest realistic expectation was to "receive a steady paycheck and to wear a clean shirt. "

The rapidly emerging industrial working class was also quite diverse. In mining, its members ranged from unskilled peons, who carried 200-pound sacks of ore up rickety ladders from deep tunnels to the surface, to experts in explosives. On the railroads, common pick-and-shovel men toiled with loco-motive engineers. In meat packing there were unskilled meat carriers and skilled butchers. Although in Argentina meatpacking plants were large enter-prises, thousands of small workshops manufactured an enormous variety of products. European immigrants comprised from one-half to two-thirds of the workers. Women and children comprised one-fifth of the working class employed.

Expanding literacy rates among the middle classes and some sectors of the working classes gave these groups greater access to information about national affairs and emboldened them to demand a voice in political debates. In Brazil, to cite one example, only 19.1 percent of all Brazilian men and 10.4 percent of all women were literate in 1890. By 1920, literacy had improved to 28.9 percent for men and 19.9 percent for women. Literacy was much higher in the cities. By 1920, 65.8 percent of the men and 54.5 percent of the women in Sao Paulo and Rio de Janeiro had learned how to read and write.

The emergence of these new middleclass and working class groups added new voices to the political debates in Latin America by the early twentieth century. A growing number of these voices were female. Although women comprised a tiny percentage of white-collar employees, they entered the urban workforce and gained access to at least a rudimentary education in unprece-dented numbers. As factory workers, operators of small businesses, and heads of households, they acted independently of traditional family ties and increas-ingly sought equal treatment in both private and public spheres. Feminists among them asserted their equality with men, while insisting on their differ-ences as well. They used the regard society had for them as females to establish their role in the public sphere and their position as working women to cam-paign for societal reforms. Feminism called for a redefinition of the traditional notions of the home as women's space and the street as forbidden. At stake were the long-held values of honor and the double standard. They challenged the basic structure of the family, seeking to end the legal subordination of women and the illegality of divorce. Ultimately, women sought to obtain suf-frage. Initially, however, they focused on securing equality under the law and better health care for women and children. Their active voices changed the nature of political discourse in the modernizing nations of Latin America.

Although the emergence of middle and industrial working classes had limited impact in rural areas, other disruptive trends affected people living in the countryside. Generally, conditions for rural working people deteriorated. In central Mexico, for example, wages stagnated while purchasing power declined. In Mexico, land expropriations by politicians and large landowners left landless many rural dwellers, who toiled for small remuneration on the great estates or abandoned their villages to labor in the mines and cities or across the U.S. border. The ownership of land was concentrated among the upper classes. At the same time, in some areas, such as northern Mexico and the Argentine Pampas, the number of owners of small farms increased. In the Mexican north, small holders were a vocal and prosperous group that deeply resented unfairly high taxes and government centralization.

In Argentina, rural conditions for farm tenants, gauchos, shepherds, and seasonal laborers varied. Landowners no longer recognized any traditional, patriarchal obligations to look after the welfare of their employees, in return for which they had received both labor and loyalty. As in Mexico, there was a sector of small farmers, mostly tenants, who increased their numbers and prospered. By the 1910s, however, many tenants, chronically in debt to suppliers, lived in desperate conditions.

In both rural Argentina and Mexico, the onslaught of centralization grew more intrusive, because landowners and governments sought not only to extend their control to local governance but also to modernize owner-labor relations. This meant that the ruling classes attempted to transform age-old customs and traditions that lay at the core of rural society. Regional autonomy remained strong in Argentina, but rural society changed to suit the needs of the estancieros. In Mexico, however, where the traditional village structure remained strong despite unending assaults by the national government, rural protests led to revolution in 1910.

Latin American leaders, even before independence, had dreamed of populating their vast nations with immigrants from Europe as part of their effort to modernize their economies. For the upper class and intellectuals, disdainful of their indigenous and mestizo brethren, an influx of Europeans was the way to "get rid of the primitive element of our popular masses." Domingo Sarmiento, the liberal ideologue who was president of Argentina (1868–1874), claimed that only mass immigration could "drown in waves of industry the Creole rabble, inept, uncivil, and coarse that stops our attempt to civilize the nation." Despite the fervent wishes of upper classes almost everywhere, few

They wanted European immigrants

Table 5.2 Destination of European Emigrants to Latin America, c. 1820–1932

Country	Number of immigrants
Argentina	6,501,000
Brazil	4,361,000
Cuba	1,394,000
Uruguay	713,000
Mexico	270,000
Chile	90,000
Venezuela	70,000
Peru	30,000
Paraguay	21,000

Source: Copyright © 1998, The Regents of the University of California

Latin American countries attracted many immigrants. Five nations, Argentina, Brazil, Uruguay, Cuba, and Mexico, drew the preponderance of the new arrivals.

From 1860 to 1920, 45 million people left Europe to go to the Western Hemisphere (see Table 5.2). Massive immigration occurred in Argentina, Brazil, and Cuba. From 1904 to 1914, on average, 100,000 immigrants a year found their way from Italy and Spain to Argentina. Much of the new middle and working classes derived from the immigrant and migrant population. The export economies demanded labor and, consequently, Peruvian cotton and sugar industries brought in Chinese coolies, the construction of the Panama Canal drew British West Indians, and the Dominican Republic exploited Haitian workers for plantations. By the beginning of the twentieth century, then, an increasingly diverse population demanded a say in the affairs of Latin American nations.

An equally impressive degree of political stability that stood in marked contrast to the recurring political upheavals during the first few decades after independence accompanied the spectacular growth in Latin America's national economies in the late nineteenth and early twentieth centuries. Political stability fostered economic growth by guaranteeing a safe climate for domestic and foreign investment. Economic growth, in turn, gave the ruling classes the tools they needed to maintain order—professionalized and better equipped armies to repress dissidents and sometimes act as arbiters of political disputes, railroads to carry troops quickly to the scene of any potential disorder, and jobs to keep the middle classes happy. The philosophy of positivism was the ideological underpinning of the ruling classes during this era. Developed by Frenchman Auguste Comte (1798–1857) and infused with social Darwinism by Herbert Spencer (1820–1902), positivism emphasized reason, science, order, and progress, which fit nicely into the efforts of the Latin American upper classes to modernize their nations.

The political stability of the age of modernization assumed a variety of forms. In Argentina and Brazil, ranchers and planters played a dominant role in national politics. Chile demonstrated a fair degree of democracy, while in Peru an "Aristocratic Republic" held sway. The long dictatorships of Porfirio Díaz (1876–1911) in Mexico and Antonio Guzmán Blanco (1870–1888) in Venezuela brought a measure of peace and prosperity at least for those who enjoyed the favor of the regime in power.

The rise of the new middle and urban working classes and the widespread encroachments on traditional rural politics and society undermined this stability. In 1910, Mexico burst into revolution that tore it apart for nearly a decade. In other countries, political parties representing the new classes and labor unions formed to contest upper class rule. By the first decade of the twentieth century, the challenges to the ruling classes were profound.

military

Latin American military establishments reflected the transformations of the times. In Argentina, Brazil, Chile, and Peru, upper classes sought to modernize and professionalize the armed services. Latin American governments imported European consultants to update and professionalize their militaries. These foreign missions inculcated a sense of separateness, nationalism, and impatience, which reconstructed the military in a way that ultimately made it the major threat to democracy in the region. The military was a crucial ally of the upper classes, for the two groups envisioned similar futures of order and economic development. As the social pressures from below increased, self-proclaimed professional, apolitical, incorruptible military officers came to despise civilian politicians. Concurrently, middle class people entered the armed services as a route toward upward mobility. As a result, Latin American militaries were integral participants to the struggles over the "Social Question."

The revamped militaries recreated their officer corps through education at special military academies and a career system based on merit. The new career routes supposedly kept the young officers away from politics. Technology changed the military, as it did society as a whole. Railroads, cannons, rifles, machine guns, and telegraphs altered warfare. Ironically, professionalization took place when the region was at peace. After the War of the Pacific, there were no more external wars until the Chaco War between Paraguay and Bolivia in the 1930s. Nonetheless, militaries expanded their role in society and politics.

Isolated and confident (though untested in most cases), Latin American militaries set themselves up as arbitrators and saviors of their fatherlands. One Argentine army officer wrote in 1911, "The army is the nation. It is the external armor that guarantees the cohesive operation of its parts and pre-serves it from shocks and falls." No constitutional guarantees, moreover, could dissuade the military from its duty to ensure that governments responded to the needs of the nation. The military, like the upper classes, was not of single mind, for one faction wanted to crush all dissidents and another was willing to compromise with the new urban classes. In Chap. 6 we will see how these disagreements evolved as the militaries asserted more power and influence.

A pattern emerged across Latin America in which export-dominated economies experienced successive booms and busts, with the downturns leading to political unrest and sometimes rebellion. This pattern was evident in Argentina and Brazil during the depression of the 1890s, though none of the resulting rebellions overthrew the existing order. The large landowners of Buenos Aires and the Pampas and the coffee planters of Brazil who dominated politics in their respective nations from the mid nineteenth century until the 1920s were willing to concede very little, if anything, to the new groups. In Argentina, the large landowners accommodated only the middle classes, while harshly repressing the urban working class. The Brazilian upper class stubbornly refused any compromise, although, eventually, splitting over tactics toward the new classes.

General Julio A. Roca dominated Argentine politics at the end of the century, first through puppets from 1892 to 1898 and then as president from 1898 to 1904, using a combination of patronage and force. He advocated economic growth financed through foreign investment in the export sector. Eventually his support base among landowners split into two factions, one that supported him and his hard line toward the lower classes and the other that sought progressive reform. Fortunately, for the upper classes, the new classes also divided. The middle class took refuge in the Radical Party (Unión Cívica Radical), while the working class divided its allegiance among various leftist parties centered in Buenos Aires.

The Radical Party challenged the rule of the landowners, staging two revolts during the 1890s. In response, the upper classes consented to expand voting rights to all males through the Sáenz Pena Law of 1912. The Radicals changed their violent tactics and triumphed in the presidential election of 1916 with Hipólito Yrigoyen (1916–1922, 1928–1930).

The Buenos Aires working class divided into anarchists and socialists. The anarchists sought to obtain better conditions for workers by means of the general strike. In 1910, a government crackdown against threatened demonstrations at the nation's centennial broke the movement. Argentine socialists were moderates, who supported democracy and sought primarily to raise living standards by raising wages and lowering prices. They also advocated women's suffrage. Neither anarchists nor socialists made more than a passing mark on Argentine electoral politics. Nonetheless, they frightened enough of those in power into making some concessions to the lower classes.

Yrigoyen proved a masterful politician, building a formidable political machine founded on patronage. However, the Radicals, never in control of both houses of Congress, were neither able nor inclined to implement extensive reforms. Yrigoyen confronted his greatest crisis in 1919, when strikes in Buenos Aires led to widespread violence. The Radicals sided with the upper classes and crushed the unions during the Tragic Week (*Semana Trágica*). This instance of the middle class siding with the upper class in confrontation with workers set the pattern for the next century of politics in Latin America.

In Brazil, the emergent classes were weaker and the upper classes stronger than in Argentina. Regionalism remained a major force, with state governments more influential than the national government. In the 1880s, Brazil experienced two enormous political and economic shocks. First, the monarchy proclaimed the abolition of slavery on May 13, 1888. Then, on November 15, 1889, the army overthrew the Empire, thus beginning the First Republic (1889–1930). Thereafter, a fragile alliance of state upper classes ruled Brazil until this arrangement broke down in 1930 at the outset of the Great Depression.

At first, the military ruled. The Republic's first two presidents were military officers. Large landowners then took the reins of power, sharing control with state level alliances of local political bosses, known as colonels, who presided over the rural hinterlands through a strict system of patron-client relations, in which the colonels' clients obligated themselves to vote as ordered in return for patronage and protection.

An alliance of Sao Paulo coffee planters and Minas Gerais cattle barons controlled the national government. By agreement, the major states, Minas Gerais and Sao Paulo, alternated their representatives in the presidency. (This agreement was known as the *cafe com leche* alliance.) Of 11 presidents during the First Republic, 6 came from Sao Paulo and 3 from Minas Gerais. A third state, Rio Grande do Sul, muscled its way into the mix after the turn of the century. Brazilian states exercised control over their own finances and militaries. The State of Sao Paulo had a well-equipped state militia with as many as 14,000 men. State governments could even contract foreign loans. The coffee planters openly used government for their own economic gain, relying on the national and state governments to buy their surplus crops. Brazil's slower industrialization delayed the development of pressure from below for a decade or two after other Latin American nations confronted the social question.

The Chilean landed upper class ruled until 1920, but it, too, was vulnerable to the downturns of the export economy. As in Argentina and Brazil, the depression of the 1890s brought unrest, when an eight-month civil war brought down President José Manuel Balmaceda (1886–1891), who symbolized the corrupt, coercive system in power since independence. During Chile's Parliamentary Republic from 1891 to 1920, Chilean politics reached an impasse, because of the government's inability to meet the demands of the emerging classes. The working class increased in numbers as people moved into the mines and cities from the countryside. Inevitably, they sought ways to protest their brutal labor and living conditions through unions. In the 1890s, there were riots in the nitrate fields, where conditions were unimaginable. Conflict worsened in the first decades of the new century. Disturbances in Santiago in 1905 cost the lives of 60 people. Economic depressions in 1907–1908 and after World War I took their toll. The worsening economic crisis led to terrible strikes in 1919; one in Santiago involved 50,000 workers. Arturo Alessandri emerged in 1920, promising to accommodate the demands of the new classes, and won election to the presidency. The upper class continued their unwillingness to compromise, creating a political stalemate. Reformist military officers, impatient for change, overthrew Alessandri in 1924. Only then was the impasse broken, but only temporarily.

Thirty or 40 families, consisting of large landowners and businesspeople tied closely to the export sector, dominated Peruvian politics at the turn of the century. These upper class families often were more familiar with Paris than with the Peruvian countryside. Racist, as well, they viewed indigenous and castas as barbarians. Nonetheless, from the mid-1890s until 1919, Peru experienced an era of relative peace and stability, known as the "Aristocratic Republic." Like everywhere else, however, the inevitable downturns eventually brought discontent and unrest. *War of the Pacific*

The War of the Pacific (1879–1883) left the nation's economy and politics in ruins. Exports fell sharply. Andrés Avelino Cáceres, a hero of the War of the Pacific, brought some order to Peruvian politics and government finances from 1885 to 1895, first as president and then through puppet rulers. His successor Nicolás de Piérola (1879–1881, 1895–1899) presided over a considerable measure of development, by expanding exports of agricultural commodities and minerals. However, increased agricultural exports caused landowners to expand their territory at the expense of individual and communal landholdings, which created widespread unrest.

During World War I, Peru experienced rebellions in the countryside, uprisings of Chinese immigrant laborers, and protests by university students. Social unrest exploded in 1919 with huge strikes in Lima and Callao. The presidential election in 1919 returned to power former president Augusto B. Leguía (1908–1912, 1919–1930), who ruled for the next 11 years. His solution to the nation's economic problems was an extensive program of public works construction that he devised to provide employment.

In Mexico, General Porfirio Díaz ruled for 35 years (1876–1911), in conjunction with the landed upper class, the military, and a cadre of professional bureaucrats. Building his regime on a shrewd combination of consensus and coercion, Díaz wove an intricate web of alliances among once fragmented regional upper classes. He bound them together using the revenues generated by his export-based economic strategy. Don Porfirio, as people called him, was a masterful politician who people simultaneously admired and feared. He was a war hero, recognized as one of the commanders at Puebla, where Mexican troops won a great military victory against French invaders on May 5, 1862. (The *Cinco de Mayo*, or Fifth of May, is a national holiday in Mexico.) Díaz was often magnanimous in victory, when it was to his political advantage. He could be equally ruthless, however. When, early in his regime, a subordinate asked him what to do with captured rebels, Díaz told him to "kill them in cold blood." His rural police, the *Rurales*, kept order in the countryside. (One practice was to shoot prisoners, even those guilty of minor offenses, while allegedly trying to escape.)

During Díaz's rule, Mexico's economy grew spectacularly. Domestic peace and the end of foreign invasions combined with burgeoning markets for Mexican agricultural commodities and minerals and the inflow of international capital to cause unprecedented economic expansion. The Díaz government oversaw the investment of $1 billion in U.S. capital and a ninefold increase in trade from 1877 to 1911 and sponsored the construction of more than 10,000 miles of railroad.

Despite peace and prosperity, however, Mexico's economy and politics had a dark underside. As did other export economies, Mexico endured periodic booms and busts. Downturns struck during the mid1880s, the early 1890s, and from 1907 to 1909. The booms brought prosperity, but the busts produced widespread suffering among the urban and rural working class. Economic depressions caused political disruptions by undermining the conditions of the emerging working and middle classes and by unbalancing the delicate system of political arrangements between Díaz and regional upper classes. Díaz's web of political alliances depended on his ability to reward cooperation with jobs, tax exemptions, subsidies for businesses, and other benefits. The economic downturn in 1907 allowed him insufficient resources to pay for cooperation. Ungrateful upper class allies looked for opportunities to free themselves from the dictator.

While the economic crisis undermined his support among the upper classes, the countryside reached the point of rebellion. Improved transportation and widened markets for agricultural commodities, both in Mexico and abroad, sharply increased land values. Political officials and large landowners, particularly in the mid1880s and in the decade after 1900, undertook to expropriate the lands of small owners and the communally held lands of indigenous villages in order to expand both their landholdings and the pool of cheap, landless labor. As a result, there was an undercurrent of agrarian discontent throughout the dictatorship. This discontent evolved into crisis in 1907, when the economic downturn and the upper classes' land grabbing limited the alternative employment possibilities of landless people in rural areas. Previously, they had found jobs in the mines, the cities, and the United States, but the depression deprived them of these employment opportunities. The Díaz dictatorship also had eliminated elections to local offices by creating a system of appointed district leaders *(jefes políticos)*. Some of these district bosses proved extraordinarily intrusive, meddling even in private matters. Not surprisingly, country people protested this loss of local autonomy.

Coinciding crises helped bring down the dictatorship after 1900. The immediate furor was over Díaz's succession. Díaz was 74 when reelected as president in 1904. His vice president, Ramón Corral, got the post because he was one of the most unpopular officials in Mexico and was, therefore, no threat to Díaz. None of the obvious successors dared to show ambition, despite the fact that if Díaz won reelection in 1910 at 80, few expected he would live out his term. The second crisis was the depression of 1907, which erased many of the gains of Díaz's economic miracle and ruined the businesses of the emerging middle class. The middle class suffered discrimination in taxation, the courts, and the banking system under Díaz's regime, and the economic downturn laid bare this rampant unfairness. The last crisis was the squabbling among and eventual division of the upper classes. Enemies of the dictator, who bided their time and been content to be bought off, saw an opportunity to even old scores. These combined crises left the urban and rural working classes with little to lose, the embryonic middle class falling back toward poverty, and the upper classes uninterested in supporting the dictator, at best, or quietly working against him, at worst. The oil that greased the wheels of the dictator's political arrangements evaporated. It was time to fight, and Díaz's time ended.

The export boom the upper classes presided over disguised inherently unfair societies everywhere, because the prosperity accrued to only a small minority. The new middle classes were extremely vulnerable to economic downturns and saw their modest gains erode during the depression following the turn of the century and the inflation of World War I. The mines and new factories paid pitiful wages and offered miserable working conditions for new migrants from the countryside and immigrants from abroad. Workers protested for better compensation, improved working conditions, and against the regimentation that domestic and foreign employers tried to impose upon their daily lives. Meanwhile, rural people lost their lands and livelihoods to the forces of the export economy. Some migrated in search of better opportunities elsewhere, but others stayed where they were and revolted in an attempt to regain or retain their landholdings and their control over their daily lives. Resistance then was inevitable in the face of the intrusion of the world market and national authorities.

National leaders in a number of countries grappled with the question of how best to draw indigenous peoples into the new capitalist nation-state. Other upper class and urbanized middle classes regarded the indigenous population as a serious impediment to national progress. Positivists in Mexico shared this view, and the Díaz regime alternated between ignoring and trying to exterminate indigenous peoples. Apaches in the north of Mexico were at times subject to bounties on their scalps. Conversely, some of the victorious factions in the revolution that overthrew Díaz adopted a conscious policy of glorifying the nation's indigenous heritage. Archaeologists and historians rediscovered the great cultures that existed in Latin America before the arrival of the Europeans, while the brilliant muralists of the 1920s and 1930s illuminated the Indian past.

The place of indigenous peoples also provoked much discussion in Peru, where the humiliating defeat in the War of the Pacific caused a reevaluation of the nation's priorities and policies. Peruvian intellectuals concluded that Indians required "reform." Fired by the 1889 novel *Aves sin nido* by Clorinda Matto de Turner, which exposed the harsh exploitation endured by indigenous in a small Andean town, a new movement, *indigenismo*, resolved to rediscover Indian Peru. U.S. archaeologists rediscovered Machu Picchu, the long lost Incan city, further fueling interest in pre-European Peru. After World War I, the indigenismo movement shifted from willingness to study Indians to a more revolutionary stance. A few envisioned a new nationalism that glorified the indigenous past. A second strain of indigenismo arose from José Carlos Mariátegui, the noted Marxist intellectual, who tied indigenismo to socialism. He advocated radical land reform to end the centuries old oppression of indigenous by the hacienda system.

Not everyone accepted the notion that modernization and economic development were good, as is illustrated by the Latin Americans who threw stones at passing railroad cars. The first, and perhaps most crucial, source of opposition to modernization arose in the countryside. During the first half of the nineteenth century, political disruptions and inadequate transportation kept land values down. After midcentury, Liberals, following the models of England and the United States, attempted to create a class of small farmers they believed would form the basis for both capitalism and democracy. Their efforts to break up the landholdings of the Catholic Church and communal indigenous villages backfired, however, because politicians and large landowners inevitably ended up with much of this property. A number of nations, notably Argentina and Mexico, gave away vast tracts of public lands to the politically well connected, which concentrated landholding even further. Unlike the peaceful, political attempt to create social equity described above, country people sometimes violently resisted modernization. Two such movements erupted in Brazil. The first occurred in Canudos, an estate in the northern part of the state of Bahia, where Antonio Conselheiro and his followers set up a community in 1893. Located deep in the backlands, it grew into a considerable city of 20,000 to 30,000 people. The local upper class—and eventually the national government—viewed Canudos as a threat. Several military expeditions went to Canudos in an effort to oust the residents and break up the community, but the residents defeated the soldiers. Finally, in October of 1897, the federal army destroyed the city and slaughtered its last 5000 residents. Euclides da Cunha made these events notorious in his book *Rebellion in the Backlands*. Another movement, the *Contesdado*, took place in the border area between the states of Paraná and Santa Catarina in southern Brazil. The rebellion began in 1911, led by José Marfa, who his followers regarded as a saint. The processes of modernization in rural and urban areas alienated many of the people who joined the movement, including small farmers thrown off their lands as railroads spread across the country and railroad workers abandoned to unemployment when their contracts expired. Despite the deaths of their leaders, including José María, rebels continued to fight until late 1915. Meanwhile, widespread banditry swept Brazil during the period of the Canudos and Contesdado rebellions. Many of the poor dark skinned people who made up the majority of the rural population lost their lands or ended up on the wrong side of local political disputes, so they filled the bandits' ranks, having few other options. The people of Canudos and the Contesdado sought only to be left alone, to control their daily lives in peace. Unfortunately for them, they encountered a centralizing government.

Nowhere was the impact of the rapidly developing export economy dominated by foreign investors clearer than in Mexico, where a diverse coalition

(handwritten margin note: Canudos movement)

of profoundly discontented people waged a revolution of unprecedented duration and cost. In 1910, a multiclass alliance of dissidents from the upper class, middle class people who suffered financial ruin in the depression of 1907, country people whose lands the upper class expropriated, and unemployed workers rallied around Francisco I. Madero, a disaffected, wealthy landowner, who toppled Porfirio Díaz from power. The depression of 1907, the uncertainty of succession, and the deteriorating state of the army and police badly weakened the Díaz regime. In the spring of 1911, the coalition ousted Díaz, who prudently embarked on a comfortable retirement in Paris, never to return to Mexico. The consensus among Madero's followers soon crumbled as landowners and landless country people clashed over land reform and the middle and lower classes disagreed over the importance of property rights. Dormant regionalism, suppressed temporarily by Díaz, reawakened as well.

In 1913, supporters of Díaz took advantage of the disintegration of the revolutionary coalition and the resurgence of regionalism to reestablish briefly the old regime without Díaz. General Victoriano Huerta, Madero's most important military commander, took over the reins of the counterrevolutionary movement, betraying Madero and ordering his execution. Others then formed a loose partnership of revolutionary movements to defeat Huerta in 1914. Their leaders included Venustiano Carranza, another alienated northern landowner; Pancho Villa, a bandit-businessman from Chihuahua (also in the north); and Emiliano Zapata, a village leader from the state of Morelos (just south of Mexico City). This alliance quickly disintegrated. Carranza, representing the dissident landowners, clashed with the lower class *Zapatistas* (followers of Zapata) who advocated wide-ranging land reform and Villistas, whom Carranza considered criminals. Carranza and Villa intensely disliked each other. Villa and Zapata allied, for they had a common enemy. The three factions set upon each other in a brutal civil war that lasted until 1917.

By 1917, however, Carranza emerged triumphant with the stalwart assistance of his best general, Álvaro Obregón, another northerner. Carranza owed much of his victory to his ability to win over the working class and some rural people with promises (later unfulfilled) of reforms. Carranza also appealed to members of the middle class, because he defended private property rights and offered political patronage. The revolutionaries promulgated the Constitution of 1917, which provided for extensive land reform, workers' rights, and other wide-reaching reforms. Carranza then split with Obregón over the extent to which the government would implement the provisions of the constitution. Obregón, who favored reforms, overthrew Carranza in 1920. Meanwhile,

Zapata and Villa continued guerrilla warfare until 1919 and 1920, respectively. Mexico's bloody struggle lasted a decade and cost the lives of between 1 and 2 million people. The revolution devastated the nation's economy. It would be well into the 1930s, before most economic indicators recovered to 1910 levels.

Conclusion

In 1920, middle-aged and elderly Latin Americans could look back on the enormous changes that occurred in their lifetimes. Those who lived in the cities saw signs of "progress" all around them—streetcars, automobiles, modern office buildings, banks, and factories. In the more fashionable parts of towns, they marveled at the lavish homes and other symbols of the upper classes' conspicuous consumption. More people could read and write than ever before. Outside the cities, railroads crisscrossed the countryside, although they were concentrated along routes that served the new export economies. Large estates and modern farm machinery produced crops for sale in nearby cities and overseas markets (while small farmers, however, found it increasingly hard to produce the subsistence crops they needed to support themselves and their families). With the notable exception of Mexicans, this generation of Latin Americans experienced fewer wars than their parents or grandparents, but only the most naive among them would have predicted that this peace would last indefinitely. Workers, women, and country people would inevitably seek to benefit from modernization.

Timeline

1876   Porfirio Díaz takes power in Mexico
1888   Abolition of slavery in Brazil
       Empire overthrown in Brazil
1891   Chilean civil war; Balmaceda ousted; Parliamentary Republic begins
1910   Mexican Revolution begins
1912   Argentine Sáenz Pena Law
1916   Irigoyen elected President of Argentina
1917   Mexican Constitution
1918   Semana Trágica in Argentina

How Historians Understand

Why Do People Rebel?

The era from 1880 to 1920 was a tumultuous one for Latin America. Emergent working and middle classes jostled for a place in politics, economy, and society. Upper classes struggled to maintain their positions. Country people sought a return of the protection they had enjoyed under the Catholic monarchs of the Iberian empires. Technological innovations disrupted society at all levels. The international movement of ideas, people, and money reinvented the ways that men and women worked, lived, and interacted. Yet, despite all these upheavals and rapid changes, only in one country, Mexico, the people rose up in revolution. It is an enduring and important question in Latin American history as to why only the Mexican lower and middle classes allied to destroy the old regime.

Most people in Latin America lived with a degree of day-to-day oppression. The daily struggle to subsist consumed their days; they had little time or energy to plan, let alone carry out, a rebellion. At some points in history, however, individuals ignored survival in order to rise up against their oppressors (though such occurrences are rare). Historians have almost universally failed to discern what causes such rebels to risk everything.

In the case of the Mexican Revolution, as in any social revolt, historians and sociologists have numerous questions: Why some groups or individuals rebelled and others did not? Why did some country people, such as permanent residents on the haciendas, remain uninvolved, while northern small landowners led the overthrow of Porfirio Díaz? Why did some large landowning families join the revolution, while others fought it to the death?

Most difficult to answer, perhaps, is the question of why individuals participated in uprisings, because very few sources exist to give scholars insight into individuals' motivations. Historians researching the Mexican Revolution have compiled many oral interviews and discovered criminal court records, both of which reveal personal stories. Unfortunately, these sources are not available for all regions or eras.

Of all the groups that rose in rebellion against Díaz in 1910, the most elusive are country people. Everyone concedes that rural people were central to the Mexican Revolution, but there is disagreement as to why exactly they revolted. Did country people fight to restore their lost lands? Did they resist the encroachments of centralized government on their local prerogatives? Do people risk their lives for land or religion or local autonomy? It is extremely difficult for twenty-first century historians to penetrate the worldview of late nineteenth century rural dwellers.

(continued)

(continued)

Historians and social scientists have formulated various theories, based on such factors as rising expectations, class conflict, moral economy, and mob behavior, to try to understand why people rebel. The paucity of evidence, however, has made it impossible for scholars to validate or confirm any of these theories of motivation. Analysts have tried to circumvent the lack of direct evidence (also called *primary sources*, such as accounts of participants' actual words) by examining the possible grievances, the economic circumstances, and the political crises that might have alchemized discontent into revolution. Thus, historians build circumstantial cases without proof of causality.

Perhaps the most convincing and plausible attempts to understand the mental and emotional states of various revolutionaries have appeared in the works of fiction written during and after the Mexican Revolution. The works of such authors as Mariano Azuela (*The Underdogs*), Martín Luis Guzmán (*The Eagle and the Serpent*), and Carlos Fuentes *{The Death of Artemio Cruz)* give insights into the rebels' reality through the imagined conversations and thoughts of their characters. The novelists often portray the revolutionaries as petty, greedy, and murderous, with few heroes among them. (For instance, Azuela's Demetrio Macías was less than admirable.)

How, then, do historians obtain an accurate picture of the revolutionaries and their motivations? It is unlikely that we ever can. Pieces of the puzzle will always be missing.

Latin American Lives

Evaristo Madero (1829–1911), Patriarch of the North

In 1910 a 37-year-old rancher and industrialist from the northern state of Coahuila, Mexico, Francisco I. Madero, led a political movement against the long-term regime of Porfirio Díaz, setting off what was to become the Mexican Revolution. Defying enormous odds, he overthrew the dictator and became president. Not 2 years after his victory, he fell to assassins' bullets. The martyred Madero achieved perhaps the highest rank in the pantheon of Mexico's heroes.

Sometimes forgotten is the fact that Francisco I. Madero was the scion of one of the richest families in Mexico. The Madero, based in Parras, Coahuila, and Monterrey, Nuevo León, were at the fulcrum of the crucial network of northern entrepreneurs who were crucial to the Mexican economy from the mid nineteenth century through the Porfiriato, Revolution, and post-revolution. Evaristo Madero, its patriarch, built a great empire through shrewd entrepreneurship and familial and political connections. In 1910, the *El Paso Morning Times* referred to him as a "Mexican Croesus." He had a personal fortune estimated at US$20,000,000. The Madero were important cattle raisers, cotton growers, and guayule producers in the Laguna region of Coahuila, and were involved with many industrial and banking concerns, among which was the largest Mexican-owned mineral smelting operation in the nation. Family members reportedly owned 7 million acres of land, with holdings in Chihuahua, Coahuila, Durango, San Luis Potosí, and Zacatecas.

Despite their vast economic resources, the patriarch's difficult relations with Díaz and his representative in northeastern Mexico, General Bernardo Reyes limited their political influence. The family's ambiguous relations with Díaz at times thwarted its economic interests, as well. Subsequently, family members stood at the forefront of local and statewide opposition to the national regime during the 1890s and the first decade of the twentieth century. Eventually, this led to Francisco I. Madero's seemingly quixotic campaign for the presidency in 1910.

The patriarch of the family, Evaristo, was born in the late 1820s. He began his career as a freighter along the recently drawn border between Mexico and the United States after the war between the two nations. At first, he operated mule and wagon trains in Coahuila, soon moving on to trading contraband silver bullion, wool, and hides across the border in return for dry goods and manufactures. Evaristo Madero earned a fortune in border trade, in particular generating enormous profits from Confederate cotton during the U.S. Civil War during the l860s, when the Union Navy blockaded southern ports, leaving only outlets through Mexico to export to markets in Europe. In his illicit trade, Madero benefited from the protection of Santiago Vidaurri, then the political boss of Nuevo León and Coahuila. Evaristo used the income from his mercantile business to buy land and expand into industry and banking. His first investments were a huge ranch in Coahuila that included an old winery, a number of flourmills, and a textile mill. From the late 1860s to the 1880s, he bought large haciendas in the Laguna region.

(continued)

(continued)

The Madero relied heavily on their family connections. Evaristo Madero had 18 children, and between them his children, grandchildren, and great grandchildren numbered 124. Many married into prominent families. His first marriage in 1847 brought him as his brother-in-law and long-term business partner Antonio V. Hernández. Also important were his son Francisco's marriage to Mercedes González Trevino, a member of a family of important landowners and politicians in Nuevo León, and his daughters' marriages to Lorenzo González Trevino, Melchor Villarreal, and Viviano Villarreal. He also had marriage ties to prominent Monterrey families such as Zambrano and Sada Muguerza. With nine sons and numerous sons-in-law, he had a substantial pool of managers to succeed him.

Evaristo was governor of Coahuila from 1880 to 1884, when Porfirio Díaz, whose rebellion in 1876 he had opposed, allied with rivals to force him out. The Madero family retained local influence in Parras and continued to compete in state politics but was unable to reestablish itself at the top. Despite maintaining cordial relations with the científico faction within the national regime, the Madero found themselves badly disadvantaged by a series of decisions made by the old dictator during the first decade of the twentieth century. This quite likely led to considerable disgruntlement among family members toward Díaz and may very well have led to Evaristo's grandson's revolution. Evaristo died in 1911 before Francisco I. became president.

Slice of Life

A Chilean Mining Camp

LIFE IN THE MINING camps of Brazil, Chile, Mexico, and Peru was difficult, dangerous, and expensive. Spanish and Portuguese colonial enterprises had little success in attracting voluntary labor to the camps without substantial monetary inducements or coercion. The indigenous peoples steered clear of the mines as much as possible. The advent of a freer labor market and the introduction of modern technology during the nineteenth century did not improve the living and working conditions. As one observer noted, "Labor in the copper mines of the nineteenth century was harshly disciplined, intense, and brutal."

Chilean copper mines were small and totally lacking in modern technology. Mine owners had no capital, suffered poor transportation, and lacked a dependable labor supply: Who would want to work in a copper camp? The mines were usually isolated, accessible to the outside world only by several days of hard travel through rugged terrain. Most were located in the mountains, buffeted by inhospitable weather.

The miners suffered abominable treatment. The physical labor was arduous and included working with heavy hammers and chisels and carrying 200-pound sacks of ore up rickety ladders. Charles Darwin observed that the miners were "truly beasts of burden." Miners had little time for meals, working from dawn until dusk. Adding insult to injury, armed guards patrolled the camps, and if miners were caught stealing ore, they were subject to corporal punishment.

Conditions changed somewhat during and after World War I, when copper prices rose because of increased demand. After the war, large international corporations invested in the copper industry. They brought in new technology, such as the widespread use of dynamite. The big companies paid relatively high wages and provided better living conditions than the small Chilean operations. This was not saying much, however.

The skyrocketing cost of living in the camps offset better wages. Slightly improved working conditions did not change the fact that life in the mines was unendurable: The mine tunnels were hell-like, either unbearably hot from the venting of underground gases or cold and wet. Copper dust swirled in the air, making it nearly impossible to breathe and causing rampant respiratory disease. Cave-ins, falls, asphyxiation, and dynamite explosions were constant hazards, resulting in injury or death. Housing for single workers was makeshift; in the smaller camps, it usually consisted only of tents. Often, 20 men packed into one room. Families fared no better, residing without ventilation, electricity, or light in hovels made of wood and aluminum boards. There was no heat, and the cold was unbearable. Two families often shared two-room, dirt-floored apartments in the barracks.

(continued)

(continued)

The mines recruited workers from the southern agricultural regions, especially the Central Valley, where the concentration of landholding pushed landless people to seek work in the mines and cities. *Enganchadores* (less than honest recruiters) haunted the bars and plazas, buying drinks for hungry, desperate men, getting them drunk, and convincing them to sign work contracts. The following morning, these men woke up, hung over, only to find themselves on a train bound for the north, often having been advanced money from the enganchadores that had to be worked off. Because the mining companies needed workers who were at full strength to do the arduous work, they often rejected men supplied by these recruiters.

Agricultural labor went back and forth between the farming regions and the northern mines, and levels of turnover in the labor force were high. Many rural workers spent a year in the mines to earn the relatively high wages and then returned home to pay their debts or settle on a plot of land. Still others worked just long enough to amass some cash and then left without notice. The companies did not always pay departing workers what they owed them. In 1917, El Teniente employees averaged only 18 to 20 days' work. The high job turnover had numerous causes, including the harsh working conditions; exhaustion, injury, and illness; and racial discrimination, especially from foreign supervisors employed by the large companies.

Women moved in and out of the camps, working as domestic servants, preparing and selling food and alcohol, and working as prostitutes. Women came to the camps mostly independent of men, looking to earn and save money, perhaps to start again elsewhere. They ran their own households, raised children, and struggled mightily to make ends meet. Formal marriage was infrequent, because life at the mines was too transient.

Both men and women resisted the efforts of large foreign companies to institute labor discipline. Mobility and independence were highly valued by the workers and widely opposed by the companies. It took decades to instill the industrial work ethic into rural workers.

Workers and bosses frequently clashed over control of aspects of everyday life. This struggle was a microcosm of the relationship between the upper classes and lower classes throughout Latin America during the nineteenth century.

Nature's Way

Antigua, Guatemala: Rising from the Ruins

Guatemala is located on the "'Ring of Fire," a horseshoe of volcanoes and seismic fault lines" that run along the Pacific Coast. Near Antigua, the Acatenango volcano has two peaks, Pico Mayor (Highest Peak) and Yepocapa, which is also known as Tres Hermanas (Three Sisters). Acatenango joined with Volcán de Fuego and collectively we know the volcano complex as La Horqueta. Guatemala is the home of thirty-seven volcanoes. El Volcán de Fuego is the most active in the world. In total, three of the volcanoes are active and the others dormant. If that is not dangerous enough, Guatemala lies in a hurricane zone, as well.

The history of the old colonial capital, Antigua, which sits at the center of the region of destruction, is one of extraordinary resilience. Earthquakes razed the city three times. Since 1543, the region endured a dozen major disasters (earthquakes, volcanic eruptions, floods). After earthquakes destroyed the town in 1773, the colonial government moved to what is now Guatemala City. That year the earthquake killed 600 people and another 600 died from disease and starvation caused by the event. Royal officials ordered the remaining inhabitants to evacuate and relocate. Scavengers plundered the town of usable building materials. Some residents stubbornly refused to abandon the town. Antigua miraculously recovered during the nineteenth century, benefitting from the nation's coffee boom.

Guatemala experienced damaging earthquakes in 1816, 1902, and 1917. In the latter year, a series of earthquakes over two months caused massive landslides. Three years later, the Santa María volcano erupted. These disasters probably set the stage for the long dictatorship of Jorge Ubico (1930–1945). Another earthquake occurred in 1942. In 1944, just a year before the military overthrew him, President Ubico declared Antigua a national monument. Restoration began yet again.

All of this another major earthquake destroyed in 1976. In Guatemala an estimated 22,545 died, 74,000 hurt, and a million displaced. The earthquake destroyed the town of Chimaltenango, nine miles from Antigua, leaving only the health clinic and town hall standing and killing more than 9000 residents. The guerrilla war, then in its fifteenth year, intensified, because the destruction disproportionately affected poor indigenous. Chimaltenango became a center of the insurgency. Some historians look on the seismic events of 1976 as a turning point, when Guatemalans concluded that current institutions were unsatisfactory. Unfortunately, this meant another two decades of civil war.

The resilient Antigua recovered once more, stimulated by its achieving status as a United Nations World Heritage Site in 1979. It experienced an inflow of tourists. The establishment of a number of reputable Spanish language schools also helped a renaissance.

(continued)

(continued)

The civil war ended in 1996 with signed peace accords. Nonetheless, more disasters were to come. Terrible hurricanes slammed Guatemala in 1998 (Mitch) and 2005 (Stan). Two disasters occurred in 2010, mudslides from the Volcán de Agua and tropical storm Agatha. An earthquake struck in 2012. Volcán de Fuego erupted in 2018. Hurricane Stan killed 600 and destroyed 35,000 homes. Accompanying mudslides swept away entire towns. Tropical storm Agatha hit in May 2010 the day after the Pacaya volcano erupted. Mudslides left 20,000 homeless, the storm killed 300. The 2012 eruption left 50 dead and 5000 homeless.

The eruption of Volcán de Fuego (ten miles from Antigua) in 2018 laid bare once again the tensions and inequities in Guatemala. The event killed at least 165 people with another 260 missing and presumed dead. The infrastructure of the region was in shambles. Thousands were in temporary shelter. Despite the influx of outside aid, the government expended only a quarter of all funds designated for relief seven months after the disaster. In some instances, the government dispatched military to assist in indigenous villages. The Maya in particular refused their help. The deep distrust inculcated after the thirty-six year civil war and two decades of unsteady peace was evident.

Tourism, which accounts for 7.4 percent of Guatemalan GDP, remains the foundation of Antigua's survival. Natural disasters cause the numbers of visitors to ebb and flow.

6

Between Revolutions: The New Politics of Class and the Economies of Import Substitution

upper class allied with military (handwritten)

THE ERA FRAMED by the end of the Mexican Revolution (1910–1920) and the beginning of the Cuban Revolution (1959) continued, augmented, and refocused the conflicts and dilemmas of Latin America's politics and economy, which emerged from the transformations experienced in the preceding four decades. Battered by recurring crises—two world wars and a debilitating depression—and the exigencies of the superpower confrontation we know as the Cold War, Latin America struggled to answer the questions raised at independence and the decades afterwards: Who was to govern (and for whom) and how were they to govern? Latin American upper classes fiercely resisted the strident demands of the middle and urban working classes. Refurbished and reformed militaries established themselves as crucial actors in politics, mostly as conservatives, but on occasion as moderate and even radical proponents of social justice. For the most part, however, the upper classes allied with the military against labor organizations and popularly based political parties, the primary advocates of the lower classes. Armed forces anointed themselves as the ultimate arbiters of civil society, intervening periodically when differing versions of democracy faltered.

The profound changes brought about by urbanization and incipient industrialization altered relationships not only between classes but also between men and women. Women entered the public political and economic arenas, forcing readjustments to traditional patriarchy. Old notions of women's role, sexuality, and honor underwent important transformations. During this period, women fought for and eventually won suffrage.

The rise and fall of democracy and dictatorship reflected the constant battles between moderates and hardliners in the upper classes and militaries.

M. Wasserman, *Modern Latin America Since 1800*,
https://doi.org/10.1007/978-3-030-96185-5_6

Many members of the upper classes and allied military officers realized the necessity of altering the economic and political systems, at least to minimally satisfy the demands of the lower and middle classes for better living and working conditions and for electoral and economic fairness. Compromise was difficult because the ruling classes of most nations were no longer homogeneous, making consensus virtually unattainable, and intransigent elements of the upper class—military alliance were unwilling to make concessions. The most notable divisions arose because export economies created a brash new class of industrialists and entrepreneurs whose interests were not always in harmony with the landowning class. The militaries divided as well, usually between old-line upper class senior officers and up-and-coming middleclass junior officers.

The lower classes strove for their voice in politics and the economy by joining labor unions, though these mostly served skilled workers. With expanded male suffrage, workers were valuable allies for rival middle and upper class political parties. Left political groups, such as the Socialists and Communists, experienced only modest success. With the exception of the brief Socialist Republic proclaimed in Chile in 1932 and popular fronts (alliances of Left and center political parties) governments of the late 1930s and early 1940s in Chile and Cuba, none of the leftist parties ever shared national power. The working class more commonly attached itself to a rising political leader, such as Colonel Juan Perón (1946–1955, 1974–1976) in Argentina, who traded concessions, such as wage increases, for support. A number of other democratic leaders and dictators also relied on the support of the middle and lower classes. Populism, comprised of cross-class alliances brought together by a charismatic leader advocating social reform, dominated the politics of the era.

The struggle for control over their everyday lives continued to be at the center of lower class demands. Although the increasing migration of people to the cities muted somewhat the demands for local autonomy in the countryside, they remained at the core of Mexican politics into the 1940s (and perhaps longer). The strength of regionalism forced even dictators like Juan Perón in Argentina and Getúlio Vargas in Brazil to ally with provincial and state political bosses, who obtained the support of the people of the countryside by defending local customs and traditions.

At the same time, important sectors of the national ruling classes came to realize that they could not obtain their goals of modernization without national governments becoming more active in the economy. The prolonged economic crisis of the 1930s strengthened and expanded governments' role. Concerned with the industrial base of national security, the new industrialists and organized labor joined elements of the military to institute extensive tariff protection for domestic manufacturing. The resulting policies and strategies of import substitution industrialization dominated the resurgent drive for modernization.

Nonetheless, exports fueled the economies of Latin American nations throughout all the crises. The plight of the region depended on the booms and busts of the international markets for agricultural commodities and minerals. Political instability or stability and the choice between dictatorship and democracy often (though not always) derived from the status of the economies of the individual nations.

Three Crises   -export boom, world war, great depression

The export boom from the 1870s to the 1910s stimulated industrialization, mainly in the form of processing agricultural commodities. The boom ended after 1920, however, when three great crises—the two world wars and the Great Depression—disrupted international trade and capital markets for prolonged periods (1914–1919, 1929–1941, and 1939–1945). Latin American upper classes reassessed their nations' reliance on exporting commodities and importing consumer goods.

World War I revealed the extreme uncertainties and costs of the booms and busts associated with economic reliance on exports. The war should have stimulated exports and benefited the region, as European countries placed their economies on a wartime footing. Instead, the war exposed Latin America's vulnerability to temporary stoppages in the flow of goods and capital back and forth across the Atlantic Ocean. During the early part of the war, the demand for Latin American commodities plummeted. Government revenues dropped sharply, which led to government deficits. When the demand for strategic materials finally rose, other factors, such as the rising cost of imports, mitigated the benefits. Latin American exports earned high prices, but only for a short period.

This brief boom proved detrimental to Latin American agriculture in the long term, because many farmers responded to the temporary increase in demand by borrowing money to increase the amount of land under cultivation. When Europe recovered its agricultural capacity and the world access to European markets, these farmers faced ruin. The most startling case of this agricultural boom and bust was the Cuban "Dance of the Millions." In 2 years, sugar prices soared from 4 cents to more than 20 cents a pound, only to plunge to prices even lower than where they began. In anticipation of booming demand and prices, Cuban sugar growers greatly expanded landholdings and production, only to confront disaster when prices dropped.

With competition from abroad cut off by the war, domestic manufacturing seemingly had unprecedented opportunities. Unfortunately, machinery and capital were not available. The United States furnished an alternative market, but during the war, it could not supply Latin America with all the needed industrial equipment, materials, and capital.

Despite the lessons of the world war and the nasty, though brief, depression in 1920 and 1921, Latin American economies remained export oriented throughout the decade. Unfortunately, overall international trade grew far more slowly than it had in the previous decades. From 1913 to 1929, the volume of trade rose an average of only 1 percent per year. To make matters worse, Latin American nations confronted harsh postwar competition for this stagnant global market. It was nearly impossible to increase market shares of primary commodities because other, often cheaper, producers arose elsewhere. Latin American nations were already operating at high efficiency, so they could not significantly decrease costs.

Circumstances were right for the development of modern manufacturing. Urbanization brought together a relatively more affluent population that demanded consumer goods. The expanding middle and laboring classes furnished a growing market. Improved transportation and communications expanded the market to the countryside. Domestic manufacturing, however, could not compete successfully against its external rivals unless protected by government. Internal markets were simply too small to obtain economies of scale.

As the 1930s began, Latin American economies remained highly concentrated on a few export commodities sent to a handful of markets. For 10 countries (Bolivia, Brazil, Colombia, Cuba, the Dominican Republic, El Salvador, Honduras, Guatemala, Nicaragua, and Venezuela), one product in each accounted for at least 50 percent of the exports. Four nations, the United States, Great Britain, Germany, and France, provided 70 percent of the trade. This concentration put the region in serious jeopardy when the century's worst economic crisis hit.

The worldwide Great Depression wreaked havoc with Latin American economies. Between 1928 and 1932, export prices tumbled by more than half in 10 countries. Mineral producers in Bolivia, Chile, and Mexico experienced the worst, as both unit volume and prices declined. Argentina's exports fell by two-thirds from 1929 to 1932. The Cuban sugar industry was all but ruined.

Recovery from the depression began between 1931 and 1932. Real GDP in Colombia exceeded its pre-depression level in 1932. The same was true for Brazil in 1933, Mexico in 1934, and Argentina, El Salvador, and Guatemala in 1935, while Chile and Cuba, where the depression was most severe, recovered later in the decade. Honduras, solely dependent on bananas, did not regain its pre-crisis GDP until 1945. The recovery of external trade in the 1930s was at least partly the result of a shift away from markets in Great Britain and the United States to those in Germany, Italy, and Japan.

The depression acted much like World War I in that it impeded the flow of imports to Latin America. Low productivity, the result of shortages of cheap power, the lack of skilled labor, the lack of credit, obsolete machinery, and overprotection (tariffs that were too high), continued to hinder industrial development. The depression shut off the flow of capital into the region from Europe and the United States. The only way available for Latin American countries to modernize was through some form of government intervention. National governments established agencies such as CORFO (Chilean National Development Corporation) in Chile to foster industrialization that the private sector was unable or unwilling to undertake.

World War II hit Latin America harder than the depression and previous world war. The British market shrunk when it went on war footing, and the British blockade of Europe cut off recently expanding continental European markets. U.S. programs such as Lend-Lease and the Export-Import Bank never replaced the shortfall in either finance or commerce. Inter-Latin American trade made up some of the lost markets.

The drop in U.S. and European imports after 1939 should have provided impetus for further Latin American industrialization, but wartime inflation eroded real wages and purchasing power, limiting any expansion of domestic markets. Nonetheless, industrialization expanded in several nations. In a few cases, the United States fostered industry by supplying technical assistance. Governments established non-consumer industries, such as the Volta Redonda steel works in Brazil.

Dictators and Populists

Peacetime solved few of the region's problems. First, as in the aftermath of the World War I, Latin America suffered from the decline of U.S. purchases of primary products and the elimination of the cooperative mechanisms for funneling technical assistance and capital into the region. Second, to make matters worse, the inter-Latin American markets gained during the war diminished as cheaper European and U.S. products flooded the region. Latin American nations were further disadvantaged because their governments did not devalue their currencies, making their exports more expensive abroad. Third, the United States, confronted by the threat of Soviet communism, turned its attention to rebuilding Europe, so U.S. government resources were no longer available, and Latin America had to rely on insufficient private sector capital investment. Fourth, slow European recovery (until the advent of the Marshall Plan for European recovery in 1948) limited potential markets. The outbreak of the Korean War (1950–1954) sent prices up again, but only briefly. Fifth, Latin American nations faced a dilemma as to how to spend the large foreign exchange reserves they built up during the war before inflation eroded those reserves. Some, like Argentina, repaid external debt. Argentina also purchased its foreign-owned railroads. Mostly, however, Latin American governments spent the reserves, setting off a wave of inflation.

Facing dismal market opportunities and with only limited resources available from abroad, Latin America turned inward in the late 1940s. Most governments instituted tight restrictions on imports, both to end the spending spree and to protect domestic manufacturing. Postwar depression in Europe erased traditional markets with no prospects for quick recovery. Latin America shared only minimally in the vast postwar expansion of international trade. The growing consensus among government officials and intellectuals was that Latin America could no longer rely on the export model. Some nations sought to diversify their exports, others adopted the policies of import substitution industrialization (ISI), and another, smaller, group attempted both. These goals were illusive. The most advanced countries (Argentina, Brazil, Chile, Colombia, Mexico, and Uruguay), already took the easiest steps toward industrialization. The next stage was to be far more demanding in terms of capital and technology. Domestic enterprise was unable or unwilling to risk capital. This left the field open to either multinational corporations (which were eager to enter protected markets) or state-owned companies.

Unfortunately, the ISI strategy for development was critically flawed. Domestic manufacturers could not compete with multinational companies either in their home markets or abroad. The small size of domestic markets meant no economies of scale. Often, domestic manufacturers operated at less than full capacity. Industrialization was import intensive; it needed capital goods and technology available only from abroad, creating a further drain on scarce capital. With the exceptions of Brazil and Mexico, the 1950s were a time of economic stagnation in the region. Meanwhile, the developed nations were on the path to unprecedented prosperity, leaving Latin America behind.

The Social Question remained preeminent in Latin American politics throughout the years of world wars and economic crises. The constant conflict and negotiation among the upper, middle, and lower classes (at least the organized elements) and between genders defined political parameters. The region's nations alternated between limited democracy and dictatorship, for the most *women couldn't achieve goals*

from resistance

part, but not always, in correlation with the booms and busts of the world market. Good times allowed democracy to function; bad times increased conflict between classes and led to the imposition of coercive governments by the upper class allied with the military.

During the 1920s, a wave of popularly elected leaders prepared to make concessions to the new aspiring classes and the changing circumstances of women. Unfortunately, both Hipólito Yrigoyen, the head of the Radical Party in Argentina, and Arturo Alessandri in Chile eventually fell victim to military coups. Augusto B. Leguía in Peru and Gerardo Machado in Cuba turned from populism to dictatorship when economic depression eroded their support.

The 1920s and 1930s were troubling times for the traditional social order. The upper and, to some extent, the middle classes feared their societies were coming apart as challenges by the lower classes increased. Perhaps the greatest uncertainties evolved from the transformation of women's roles. Women worked in visible urban settings in factories and offices. They organized and staged strikes. The new "free" woman—sexually active, cigarette smoking—was not the reassuringly pliant, passive mother of old. As in the case of those who were agitating for the improvement of working and middleclass conditions, however, feminists found it difficult to obtain their goals in the face of resistance from the male hierarchies that composed the government, religious institutions, and financial establishments. Feminists did not achieve their major objective, to obtain equality in law, until the 1930s, and suffrage (the right to vote) took even longer.

Women's organizations received assistance from liberal and populist political parties. A handful of liberals viewed changing laws to reflect women's new roles to be part of the modernization process crucial to societal development. Women were active participants in the multifaceted campaigns for social reform all over the region. They sought not only the right to vote but also better working, sanitary, and health conditions for everyone. As Latin American governments haltingly involved themselves in public welfare, women made these activities their own.

In both Argentina and Peru, the upper classes, through populist leaders Yrigoyen and Leguía, shared power with the middle class. As long as the export economy stayed strong and the national government did not attempt far-reaching reforms, this tension filled alliance held. The Great Depression of the 1930s, however, put the upper and middle classes into competition for rapidly shrinking resources. Ultimately, the upper classes used coercion (by the police, thugs, or the military) to maintain their status. In Chile, politicians could not reach consensus about the Social Question. As a result, the

1926 enactment of the law of womens rights

younger elements of the military twice intervened to force reforms that would improve conditions for the middle and lower classes.

In Argentina, the Radical Party alliance between the middle class and elements of the landowning upper class dominated the country's politics during the 1920s. A major accomplishment was the 1926 enactment of the law of women's civil rights, which provided that women had all the rights of men, thereby removing gender limits to the exercise of all civil functions (but, crucially, not the vote). Heavily reliant on government patronage to bolster their support, the Radicals required prosperity to generate the revenues to pay for their strategy. The economic downturn that began in 1928, however, sharply curtailed the ability of the Radicals to provide patronage employment for their followers. In September 1930, the military, overthrew Yrigoyen, who won a second term in 1928.

Yrigoyen's case clearly illustrates that populist politics succeeded only when government revenues were sufficient to fund patronage and that the precarious alliance between the upper and middle classes disintegrated rapidly when the two groups competed for scarce resources or when their interests clashed. Their ties, forged from their mutual fear of the lower classes, proved unstable. When in conflict, the side with the strongest links to the armed services, most often the upper classes, won out.

Peruvian politicians, like Argentina's Radicals, sought to find answers to the Social Question by appealing to the middle class and by adopting a vast, program of patronage. Former president Augusto B. Leguía (1908–1912, 1919–1930) returned from exile in 1919 to topple the "Aristocratic Republic." With strong backing from middle and lower class voters, he proclaimed *La Patria Nueva* (the new fatherland). He proposed a stronger interventionist state, which would modernize and grow the economy, financed by foreign investment and increased exports. The center of his administration was a massive program of public works. He rebuilt Lima into a beautiful modern city and constructed nearly 10,000 miles of roads. Leguía's plan was successful until 1930, when the depression sharply limited the funds available.

Leguía focused on the middle class and country people as his bases of support. To appeal to the former, he vastly expanded the government bureaucracy and the educational system, quadrupling the number of public employees and doubling the number of students. Leguía took advantage of growing unrest in the countryside, where indigenous peoples and landowners were at bitter odds, to undermine landowners whom the president regarded as impediments to his drive to centralize power. The end of Leguía's efforts to forge an alliance with country people came when the army and local authorities killed 2000 small farmers and landless residents during two uprisings in 1923. Like

Yrigoyen and so many after him, Leguía learned that populism was only as successful as its economic program. Leguía could not survive the depression and fell from power in 1930.

The Chilean upper classes, unlike some of their counterparts in Argentina and Peru, steadfastly refused concessions to the middle and lower classes. As a result, Chile's Parliamentary Republic (1891–1920) simply did not work. Social unrest escalated as the government was unable to ameliorate the economic crisis and hardship brought on by World War I. Strikes tore apart the northern nitrate region. Out of the turmoil of the late 1910s rose veteran politician Arturo Alessandri Palma. Drawing support from the working class, promising sweeping reforms, and professing an interest in women's issues, he won the presidential election of 1920. For 4 years, however, he was unable to overcome congressional opposition to his program. Impatient junior officers, led by Major Carlos Ibánez del Campo and Major Marmaduke Grove Vallejo, seized the government in 1924. In 1925, their administration decreed a law that extended the property rights of married women; they also penned a new constitution that restored strong presidential rule (lost in the 1890 civil war). Ibánez took office as president in 1927, and his foreign loan-financed spending spree brought a measure of prosperity. The impact of the Great Depression, however, was especially harsh in Chile, because it heavily depended on mining exports. Massive street demonstrations forced Ibánez to resign in mid 1931.

In Cuba, populism also evolved into dictatorship in response to the depression. The terrible collapse of sugar prices in 1920, and a two-decade-old tradition of ineffective, corrupt government, exacerbated by the Platt Amendment to the Cuban Constitution of 1902, which installed the United States as the island's protector paved the way for Gerardo Machado to win election as president in 1925. Like other populists, he initiated a massive foreign loan-financed public works program. In 1929, sugar and tobacco prices crashed, and the ensuing crisis wore away Machado's popularity. His regime thereafter was increasingly brutal. He lasted until August 1933, when a coalition of students and military officers forced him out of office.

In Argentina, Peru, Chile, and Cuba, leaders with reform programs emerged, supported by the urban middle and working classes. Yrigoyen, Leguía, Ibánez, and Machado encountered difficulties when economic depression limited their ability to provide employment in government and build public works projects. All turned to coercion.

Each of these leaders lost the confidence of the middle and working classes and the military toppled them.

Mexico's situation differed from these other cases because its middle class, allied with workers and country people, won the revolution and controlled the national government. The new ruling group, comprised of middle class northerners (from the state of Sonora in particular), did not share power with the upper classes the civil war ruined. The main problems facing the revolutionary regime were rebuilding the economy, satisfying the demands of the victorious revolutionaries, and unifying an army fragmented by regional and personal loyalties.

From 1920 until the mid-1930s, Mexicans struggled to balance reconstructing their nation's economy after a decade of destructive civil war against satisfying the various revolutionary factions. Middleclass demands for equal and fair access to education, employment, and economic opportunities were, perhaps, the easiest to meet. The middle class sought, in particular, the expansion of government to provide them with jobs. The needs of country people and urban workers, however, encountered more government resistance because they threatened private property rights, of which their middleclass allies were the firmest advocates. Landless villagers fought in the revolution to regain the lands stolen from them and their ancestors by hacendados. The Constitution of 1917 guaranteed the return of these lands. Nonetheless, the revolutionary government redistributed land only when politically necessary, because government leaders feared that land reform might undermine private property rights and decrease agricultural production, and thereby impede economic recovery. A further impediment arose during the 1920s when a new landowning class, many of them ex-revolutionary military officers, emerged to oppose the implementation of land reforms. The revolutionary regime was willing to allow industrial labor to organize as long as the unions affiliated with the Regional Confederation of Mexican Workers (CROM). Presidents Alvaro Obregón (1920–1924) and Plutarco Elías Calles (1924–1928) balanced reconstruction and reform and survived a series of major rebellions. Obregón won reelection in 1928, but an assassin's bullet killed him before he took office. Calles ruled from behind the scenes, as three interim presidents filled out the 6-year term until 1934. He solved the problem of the fragmented army by founding (1929) and building a new political party, the National Party of the Revolution (PNR), which brought together the disparate factions and wayward generals.

Brazil's middle and lower classes were the politically weakest in Latin America in 1920. Nonetheless, the old order fell apart when it experienced the depression. The power-sharing arrangement among the upper classes of the largest states gradually broke down during the course of the succeeding decade. When the upper classes of Sao Paulo (the other participants were the states of Rio de Janeiro and Minas Gerais) refused to alternate out of the presidency in 1930, their action set off a rebellion. Plummeting coffee prices added to the crisis. A coalition of dissident regional upper class, disgruntled mid-rank army officers, and disparate members of the urban middle class revolted to overthrow the Old Republic. Out of the uprising, Getúlio Vargas, governor of Rio Grande do Sul, the defeated presidential candidate in 1930, emerged to rule Brazil for the next 15 years.

To meet the crisis of the Great Depression of the 1930s, most of Latin America turned from democracy to military dictatorship or to civilian dictatorship with strong military support. The major exception was Mexico, which, instead, constructed a one party regime. A number of important experiments took place during this period, such as the *Concordancia* in Argentina, the Socialist Republic in Chile, the *Estado Novo* in Brazil, and the revolutionary administration of Lázaro Cárdenas in Mexico. Almost all were short lived, and although each aimed to end conflict between classes, only Cárdenas's reforms succeeded.

Leftist ideologies, such as socialism and communism, often flourished as intellectual exercises, particularly among university students, but they were no match for upper class and military opposition. More eclectic, and at times relatively radical, leftist political parties, such as the American Popular Revolutionary Alliance (APRA) in Peru and the National Revolutionary Movement (MNR) in Bolivia, proved more enduring and influential. In the short term, local variations of rightist ideologies, most importantly corporatism and fascism, had greater impact, but quickly receded.

By 1932, the moderate military, led by General Agustín Justo (1932–1938), formed an alliance (known as the Concordancia) comprised of old-line conservatives, independent Socialists (primarily from Buenos Aires), and, most importantly, anti-Yrigoyen Radicals. The new conservative alliance confronted the depression by balancing the budget, paying the foreign debt, encouraging exports, and discouraging imports. The Justo administration introduced Argentina's first income tax, which substantially cut the government's reliance on trade taxes for revenues, and established a central bank, which gave the government unprecedented influence on the management of the economy. The depression did not hit Argentina as hard as it did other Latin American nations, and, as a result, the upper class regime was relatively benign. The moderate Concordancia continued to govern when Roberto M. Ortiz took over as president in 1938.

In Chile during the 1930s, the upper classes made concessions to urban workers and women but were unwilling to accommodate demands for land reform in the countryside. For a year and a half after the fall of Carlos Ibánez, Chileans stumbled from one government to another. One of these was the Socialist Republic, led by Marmaduke Grove, which lasted for 100 days in

1932. Former president Arturo Alessandri won a new term in 1932. By 1935, Chile had recovered from the economic crisis, which allowed Alessandri to make overtures to the lower classes. He permitted extensive labor union organization and instituted a very effective process of mediating employer-employee disputes. A law in 1934 expanded women's freedoms and property rights, though men still maintained legal authority in the family. Alessandri cracked down hard in the countryside. Pedro Aguirre Cerda, the candidate of a coalition of center and Left parties known as the Popular Front, captured the presidency in 1938.

Brazil's social ferment and economic crisis led it to dictatorship. Like the post-revolution Mexican government during the same period, Brazilian dictator Getúlio Vargas (1930–1945) obtained the support of white collar and industrial workers. He was unable to create a wide political consensus, however, instead ruling by decree. Vargas's appeal to the masses was more show than substance. Three years after winning election as president by vote of a constituent assembly (1934), Vargas engineered a coup against his own government to prevent new elections and established the *Estado Novo* (New State) in 1937. At this point, he no longer made even a pretense of popular support.

In Peru, various forms of populism failed because the military remained steadfastly opposed. Luis M. Sánchez Cerro (1930–1933) represented the same middle class that had formed the core of Leguía's following. His "Conservative Populism" promised to restore the old social and economic structure, but at the same time offered the lower classes land reform, social security, and equal rights for indigenous. After a bitter election campaign in 1931 against APRA's Victor Raúl Haya de la Torre, Sánchez Cerro survived 16 terrible months of civil war and economic crisis until assassinated. General Oscar Benavides (1933–1939), a former provisional president (1914–1915), took over. He engaged in a continuing struggle with Haya's followers in APRA. Peru recovered more quickly than other nations in the region from the depression, as exports surged beginning in 1933. Benavides cancelled the 1936 elections when it became apparent he was losing and ruled as dictator for the next 3 years. Modest conservatives inclined toward slightly expanding the role of government served as presidents from 1939 to 1948.

Mexico experienced the most far-reaching reforms and consequently the longest era without upheaval. By 1934, the Mexican Revolution seemingly reneged on its promises. Seventeen years after revolutionary victory, however, the country's new president, Lázaro Cárdenas, finally implemented long awaited reforms. His major accomplishment was to redistribute 49 million acres of land to 15 million Mexicans, one-third of the population. Rural Mexicans fought the revolution for land, and Cárdenas fulfilled Emiliano

Zapata's promises to return these lands to the lower classes. As a result, the president bestowed an aura of legitimacy on the post-revolution regime that lasted for half a century. The Cárdenas administration more than doubled the average wage of urban workers. In 1938, Cárdenas expropriated the foreign-owned petroleum companies operating in the country when they refused to obey a Supreme Court order to increase the wages of their employees. In addition, the president undertook major efforts in public health and education. He also reorganized the official party in 1938, transforming it from a loose alliance among revolutionary generals, regional bosses, and labor leaders into an organization responsive to four major sectors: labor unions, rural campesino organizations, the military, and government bureaucrats (middle class). Cárdenas did not fulfill his promise to amend the Constitution to ensure equal rights for women. Reform reached its acme in 1937. Cárdenas had gone as far as he could, for there was enormous opposition among the post-revolution upper class to any further radical policies, and the nation did not have sufficient resources to carry out further reform.

During the 1950s, the Revolution moved to the center, shifting to policies for economic growth that produced the second great Mexican economic miracle (the first occurred under Porfirio Díaz). Mexico flourished as the official party consolidated its support among the middle class by providing large numbers of jobs in the government bureaucracy and government operated businesses and free education at the fast expanding National University (UNAM).

In all of Latin America, only in Mexico was the ruling group substantively responsive to the demands of the middle and working classes. Country people and the urban middle class obtained the land and opportunities for which they had fought so long and hard. As a result, Mexico prospered until the 1960s and maintained unparalleled political stability.

Cubans rose up in popular rebellion against Gerardo Machado in 1933. The victorious revolutionaries, comprised of a coalition of university students, noncommissioned military officers (sergeants, corporals), and political opponents of Machado, encountered strong disapproval from the U.S. government. Sergeant-stenographer Fulgencio Batista emerged from the plotting and violence as the power behind the scenes. Batista used methods similar to those of other populist leaders of the era, appealing to the working class from which he had come. He won election as president in 1940 and led the island through World War II. He retired peacefully and moved to Florida in 1944. Cuba, like Mexico, had achieved a measure of stability through concessions by a government run by the middle class (with a few leaders from the lower classes as well) to the needs of the middle and working classes.

Argentina became the setting for the most notorious populist regime in the Americas during the twentieth century, when the charismatic Juan Domingo Perón and his wife Eva Duarte de Perón emerged from a series of wartime political crises. The two towered over postwar Argentine politics. Perón, though the military ousted him in 1955, was a major influence until his death in 1974. *Peronism* was the most important example in Latin America of an alliance between a charismatic populist and the lower classes. As a member of a military government in 1943 and 1944, Perón built a base of support among organized labor, known as the shirtless ones *(descamisados)*. Military hardliners pushed him out of the government in 1945, but a massive demonstration by workers in October 1945 rescued him, and he won the presidential election in 1946. Unlike Yrigoyen and Leguía, both of whom drew support from the middle sectors, Perón's populist politics depended on the urban working class with strategic allies among conservative bosses in the provinces. Perón repaid the working class for its support, greatly improving working conditions and benefits. The president opened the way for massive government involvement in business enterprise with the establishment of one state agency for marketing all of the nation's agricultural exports and of another that administered industries confiscated from German citizens during the war. His government also operated shipbuilding and steel firms. He nationalized the railroads and telephone service. Like the other populists, Perón found that when he was unable to pay for his programs in times of downturn, he lost support. In response, he shifted his strategy from popular appeal to repression, generating bitter opposition from the middle and upper classes. Nonetheless, he maintained his hold on the masses, overwhelmingly winning reelection in 1951. The economy stagnated, inflation rose, and his regime grew increasingly harsh, leading to a military coup in 1955.

A unique aspect of Perón's rule was the crucial role played by his wife Eva Duarte de Perón, a former actor. Popularly known as Evita, she exerted enormous influence through her Eva Perón Foundation, which funded medical services and provided food and clothes for the needy. Evita rose from the lower classes, and became Perón's connection to them. Evita died prematurely in 1952 and with her passing, her husband lost a crucial connection to his political base.

Extreme politics emerged with peace after 1945. The first major revolutionary movement to arise from the ashes of World War II occurred in Guatemala in 1945, when a group of young, reformist military officers overthrew the long-running dictatorship of Jorge Ubico (1930–1945). The second was in Bolivia in 1952, when a coalition of country people, miners, and the middle class, under the banner of the National Revolutionary Movement (MNR), toppled the conservative government backed by landowners, industrialists, and the military. The Bolivian Revolution implemented widespread land reform, destroying the traditional landowning class; nationalizing the tin mines, the producers of the nation's major export; enfranchising all males and females; and virtually eliminating the military.

More common, however, was a movement right, when the upper class military alliance, in the midst of the international Cold War between the communist Soviet Union and the capitalist United States, reacted against the threat of communism in Latin America. Anti-left dictators arose in Chile, Colombia, Cuba, and Venezuela in the early 1950s.

After a number of years under the rule of Left and Left-center coalitions, Chile turned to former dictator Carlos Ibáñez, who took advantage of widespread discontent to bring together an odd coalition of Socialists, feminists, the middle class, and deserters from various parties to win the election of 1952. Unable to build consensus, he repeated his earlier policies of repression. His major innovation was to vastly intensify and broaden government involvement in the economy, establishing a central bank and state enterprises in major industries such as sugar, steel, and petroleum. Colombians looked to Conservative General Gustavo Rojas Pinilla (1953-1957), who as dictator tried to bring peace to a nation wracked by civil war, but he could not survive an economic downturn. Fulgencio Batista returned to rule Cuba in 1952, overthrowing a corrupt, democratically elected regime, and presided over a measure of prosperity on the island until the late 1950s. Batista, like Ibáñez and Rojas Pinilla, used harsh repression to govern instead of his earlier appeal to the masses. A young lawyer, Fidel Castro, led a rebel band in the mountains of southeastern Cuba, which gradually attracted support and allies among the middle class and workers in the cities to defeat Batista's army in late 1958. Reformers alternated with dictators in Venezuela. A group of officers, calling themselves the Patriotic Military Union, overthrew the president of Venezuela in 1945, but the Democratic Action Party (AD), led by Rómulo Betancourt, outmaneuvered the officers and installed a civilian government. Three years later, Marcos Pérez Jiménez took the reins as dictator until 1958, when the military overthrew him and returned Venezuela to democracy. In Brazil, GetúlioVargas joined Batista and Ibáñez as former presidents, once discredited, who returned to power. He won election as president in 1950 mainly because of the support given him by the working class of the big cities. Economic stagnation and inflation, however, badly eroded real wages and drastically undermined his base among workers. Amid a scandal over his role in the attempted assassination of a political rival, Vargas killed himself on August 23, 1954. Ironically, his death at his own hands prevented a military coup and paved the way for the continuation of civilian rule under Juscelino Kubitschek (1955–1960).

In each of these cases, neither populism nor coercion succeeded in establishing social peace. Reform was possible only in times of economic boom. Populism disintegrated during economic downturns. Efforts to win the support of the middle and lower classes through public patronage and concessions to labor unions required booming economies to pay for them. Coercion was unsustainable without some concessions to the middle and lower classes. The upper classes and military were willing to make only superficial accommodations. The basic unfairness and unjustness of Latin American society remained.

Failures on the Left and Right

The major populist experiments all failed in the long term. Their success, as in the cases of Yrigoyen's Radical Party and Perón's movement (known as *peronismo* or *justicialismo*), were tied closely to the fortunes of their nations' export economies and the unbending opposition of the hardline elements of the military and upper classes.

Perhaps the most auspicious failure of populism in Latin America was that of the American Popular Revolutionary Alliance (APRA) in Peru. Victor Raúl Haya de la Torre founded APRA in 1924, with support among labor unions and the middle class. APRA's program consisted of opposition to U.S. imperialism, unification of Latin America, internationalization of the Panama Canal, nationalization of land and industry, and solidarity for oppressed peoples. Although its leadership was middle class, the party extolled the indigenous past and sought to adapt the majority of Peruvians, who were indigenous, into modern life. Haya believed that socialism was not possible in Peru, with its tiny industrial working class. He envisioned, instead, the middle class leading a cross-class alliance.

With the upper classes and military adamantly opposed to Haya, he was never to gain the presidency, though APRA was often an influential force in Peruvian politics. Haya moved APRA to the center during the 1940s, eliminating its antiimperialist rhetoric to the point of exhibiting a favorable attitude toward the United States. During much of the 1940s and 1950s, the government banned APRA. After losing the 1951 election, Haya led an unsuccessful revolt. He, like Perón, even in defeat was to remain a gray eminence in politics for decades.

The most successful and extensive social reforms in Latin America took place in Bolivia. The National Revolutionary Movement (MNR) sought to create a strong centralized state with middleclass leadership of a cross-class alliance. In 1943, the MNR helped Major Gualberto Villaroel overthrow a conservative military government. He, in turn, fell in 1946 without accomplishing much reform. Conservative governments followed until 1951, when the MNR, which adopted a much more radical program, won the presidential election with its candidate Victor Paz Estenssoro. After the military intervened to prevent Paz's victory, the MNR rose in rebellion in 1952 allied with organized labor. The MNR carried out extensive land reform; nationalized the tin mines, which produced the nation's most important export; and enacted universal suffrage without literacy requirements. For the first time in centuries, the indigenous population had access to land and politics. After these initial radical transformations, the MNR balanced the rival interests of small landowners, who had become conservative when they received land, and tin miners, who sought additional radical changes. The MNR maintained its power until overthrown by the military in 1964.

The APRA failed in Peru and the MNR succeeded in Bolivia because the APRA alienated the military, which remained unalterably opposed to it, while the MNR initially defeated the Bolivian military. Just as importantly, the MNR, unlike the APRA, enjoyed a cross-class alliance between the middle and urban and rural lower classes.

Industrialization and urbanization transformed the place of women in society. In the nineteenth century, women always worked, whether inside or outside the home, and were often single heads of households. At times, women were crucial participants in politics, as in the military aspect of the Mexican Revolution from 1910 to 1920. The white upper class men who controlled governments had to find satisfactory ways to recognize the realities of these transformations. This required a reassessment of such concepts as public and private space, honor, and gender.

Latin American feminists of the early to midcentury (the first wave of Latin American feminism) were comfortable with defining themselves as mothers and wives, emphasizing their childbearing and nurturing capacities. They did not seek to gain equality with men but rather to eliminate laws and conditions that impeded their traditional roles. They also used their status as mothers and teachers to further their argument for their participation in the public sphere. The early successes of feminists included revising civil codes to eliminate the legal inequality of married women and raising important social welfare issues. Because elections were meaningless in many Latin American nations, suffrage was not an important issue to feminists until the 1920s. Not all feminists

— did not want equality
— sucess

Table 6.1 Women's enfranchisement

Nation	Tear	Nation	Tear
Ecuador	1929	Argentina	1947
Brazil	1932	Chile	1949
Uruguay	1932	Bolivia	1952
Cuba	1934	Mexico	1952
El Salvador	1939	Honduras	1955
Dominican Republic	1942	Nicaragua	1955
Panama	1945	Peru	1955
Guatemala	1945	Colombia	1957
Costa Rica	1945	Paraguay	1961
Venezuela	1947		

some women did not want to be in politics

agreed on the value of women participating in the corrupt male world of politics. In fact, some doubters believed that the female vote would be overwhelmingly conservative and thus impede their progress. Thus, prior to World War II women obtained suffrage in only four Latin American nations (see Table 6.1).

Conclusion

Import substitution economics and populist politics dominated the era from 1920 to 1959. Latin American ruling classes sought to industrialize and modernize their nations, while maintaining the political status quo. The urban middle and working classes simultaneously looked to better their living and working conditions and to have a meaningful say in government. In the countryside, small property owners and landless workers wanted either to maintain what they had or to acquire lands previously stolen from their ancestors by the greedy upper class and to defend their control over their local traditions and values.

Import substitution, which protected Latin American manufacturing from foreign competition, did not succeed in stabilizing economic conditions, despite the opportunities for improvement afforded by two world wars and the depression. Most Latin American countries were too poor to constitute markets extensive enough to enable domestic industries to achieve economies of scale. The capital required for industrialization was available from only three sources: domestic private credit, domestic public funds, or foreign investment. Given the high risk involved with such enterprises, domestic private capital was unwilling to invest. Although Latin American banking had emerged by 1900, it had only a scattered impact on import substitution industrialization (ISI).

Because foreign investment was unavailable through much of the period because of the world wars and economic crises, Latin American upper classes had to turn to domestic public funds, expanding the role of government in economic enterprise. Both public and private capital, however, relied almost entirely on the export sector to generate revenues for investment. The export sectors were subject to booms and busts and therefore unreliable.

As for the Social Question during this era, the answer seemed at times to be populism, with its cross-class alliances. Charismatic leaders such as Yrigoyen and Perón, who were willing to distribute patronage and other economic benefits to their loyal followers, enabled years of social peace. The price was high: sham elections and loss of institutional independence for popular organizations. More important, populism, like ISI economic policies, built on sand. It relied on booming exports to pay for the public works, expanded bureaucracy, and higher wages and benefits. When export booms ended, populism often deteriorated into oppressive dictatorship.

The struggles of ordinary Latin Americans remained much the same as they had since independence. The upper classes, as always, sought to maintain their wealth and power and were reluctant to share either. Those at the bottom of the economic scale fought to preserve their control over their everyday lives: to feed, clothe, and shelter their families and to maintain their local values and traditions.

The inability of Latin American economic policies and politics to lead to development and to answer the Social Question intensified societal tensions. When combined with the threatening specter of the Cold War struggle between communism and capitalism, these tensions would produce the conditions that in turn created two decades of tyranny and civil wars.

- Timeline

1914–1918   World War
1919–1930   Leguía dictator of Peru
1924   Young military overthrow Alessandri in Chile
1933   Cuban Revolution overthrows dictator Machado
1937   Getúlio Vargas stages coup, established Estado Novo
1939–1945   World War II
1946   Perón elected President of Argentina
1952   Batista returns to power in Cuba

How Historians Understand

Reconstructing the Semana Trágica (The Tragic Week) in Argentine History

Class conflict was always just beneath the surface in Latin America. The political outcomes of these confrontations depended to a considerable extent on the middle class. When the demands of the lower classes threatened the middle class (which they nearly always did), its members sided with the upper class-military alliance against workers and country people.

One of the first instances of this was the *Semana Trágica*, which occurred during the "red scares" (Communist scares) after World War I. The middle class panicked, believing the government lost control over the lower classes. Class conflict was not the only factor in the horror, it also focused on the festering prejudices Argentines felt toward the vast wave of new European immigrants that poured into their country over the preceding half century. In particular, it exposed Argentine anti-Semitism, for much of the violence Argentines committed was against the Jewish community.

The events began in December 1918 with a strike in a metallurgical factory in Buenos Aires. As the month wore on, the single factory strike spread throughout the city. It continued into January of 1919. Fueling the tension, rumors flew about plots from abroad, and the badly frightened urban middle and upper classes believed the government "lost control" of the situation and allowed a communist conspiracy to run amok. This led to violent reprisals from the upper classes, carried out by vigilantes who formed militias to protect their neighborhoods from the workers. President Hipólito Yrigoyen sent police and the army to subdue the strikers.

The situation culminated horribly in the Semana Trágica, which lasted from January 10 through 14. Many upper class Argentines blamed Jews for the troubles. The upper classes identified Jews with the Left, because most Jewish immigrants in Buenos Aires had come from Russia, where a Communist revolution had recently (1917) taken place. Acting on their fears, groups of vigilantes took to the streets. Allied with the police, they attacked Jewish neighborhoods, arresting people and destroying property. The Argentine Navy played a crucial role in encouraging, arming, and leading these middle and upper class vigilante groups.In mid-January, the government finally brokered an agreement that ended the strike and the conflict. In light of the universality of the anti-Left riots of the post-World War I era (the Palmer Raids in the United States, for example), historians paid little attention to the anti-Jewish aspect of the event. Later, Argentina, like most of the world, closed its doors to Jews fleeing Nazi Germany during the 1930s. Again, because the situation was commonplace, historians found this unremarkable. Many commented, however, on the military rightist regime's affinity for Germany during World War II; Argentina had steadfastly refused to declare war against the Axis powers until the last day of the conflict.

(*continued*)

(continued)

Anti-Semitism reappeared publicly during the dire crisis of the 1960s and 1970s. The military governments (1966–1973 and 1976–1983) fired Jews from positions of prominence. In the early 1970s, rightist paramilitary groups killed Jews suspected of Left sympathies. When the army instigated the "Dirty War," Jews disproportionately bore the brunt of the violence. The harrowing story of newspaper publisher Jacobo Timerman's imprisonment and torture was, perhaps, the least daunting, for many Jewish young people filled the rolls of "the disappeared ones."

Looking back through the context of Argentina's growing anti-Semitism over the course of the twentieth century, historians are reevaluating the initial assessment of Semana Trágica, which too easily dismissed the tragedy.

Latin American Lives

Elvia and Felipe Carrillo Puerto

ELVIA CARRILLO PUERTO (1876–1967) and her brother Felipe Carrillo Puerto (1874–1924) were, respectively, among the foremost feminist and radical leaders of the post-revolutionary era in Mexico. Elvia once said, "I want… women to enjoy the same liberties as men … to detach themselves from all the material, sensual, and animal, to lift up their spirituality and thinking to the ideal … to have a more dignified and happier life in an environment of sexual liberty and fraternity." As the radical governor of the state of Yucatán (1922–1923), Felipe carried out the most extensive redistribution of land outside of Morelos. In their brief time in power, the siblings created the most progressive state government in post-revolutionary Mexico in terms of women's rights.

Elvia and Felipe Carrillo Puerto were 2 of 14 children born in the heart of the *henequen* region. (Henequen was used to make twine.) Their father was a small merchant. Both lived and worked during their formative years among the poor Maya of the region, learning their language, customs, and traditions.

Elvia Carrillo Puerto was a feminist, an activist, a politician, an administrator, and a teacher for the first two-thirds of the twentieth century. She was a controversial figure in Yucatán as the governor's sister, and her activities defined Yucatecan feminism during the 1920s. Married at 13 and widowed at 21, she scandalized Yucatán's traditional society by living with men to whom she was not married, as well as marrying three times. When her brother was killed during a rebellion in 1924, she fled the state and returned only once during the next 40 years.

Elvia worked as a rural schoolteacher to support herself and her son after her first husband died. She saw firsthand the horrors of poverty and malnutrition in the countryside. She was well read (Marx, Lenin, and others), especially for a woman of her status and time. She joined the movement against the dictator Porfirio Díaz in 1909 and continued her work as a teacher and organizer through 1915. In 1912, she organized the state's first feminist league. In the late 1910s, she moved to Mexico City, for a short time sharing a house (1921–1922) with her brother, who was then a deputy in the federal congress. She married again, divorcing in the early 1920s, and remarrying in 1923. In 1921, Elvia was the first woman elected to a seat in the state congress of Yucatán. After her exile from Yucatán, Elvia held a series of administrative posts in the capital. She continued to organize feminists, founding a succession of important feminist groups.

Felipe, as the governor of Yucatán, led one of the failed "Laboratories of the Revolution" during the 1920s, only to be killed in a brief rebellion that failed nationally but succeeded in Yucatán. As a youth, Felipe was a small landholder, mule driver, trader, and railroad conductor. During the 1910s, he spent time with Emiliano Zapata's agrarian movement in Morelos before attaching himself to General Salvador Alvarado, the socialist governor of Yucatán. Felipe took over the Socialist Party of the Southwest, the governing political party of the state,

(continued)

(continued)

when Alvarado left in 1918. Felipe encouraged the people to become involved in politics, and he advocated Mayan culture and history. Felipe, however, was too radical for the Sonoran Dynasty made up of presidents Alvaro Obregón and Plutarco Elías Calles. They readily abandoned him during the revolt by army officers, led by Adolfo de la Huerta, in 1923.

The Carrillo Puerto siblings symbolized the unfulfilled promise of the Mexican Revolution at its turning point during the 1920s. A series of local and state radical initiatives all fell victim to the harsh practicalities of rebuilding a war-ravaged nation and the hard-eyed greed of the victorious generals. Elvia, however, who lived into the late 1960s, never gave up her dreams of women's equality.

Slice of Life

Colombian Coffee Farm in 1925

COFFEE IS PRODUCED in two distinct ways: on plantations (fazenda in Brazil, *finca* or hacienda elsewhere) and on small, family operated farms. The latter predominate famously in two nations, Costa Rica and Colombia. Smallholdings required, as one historian observed, a "lifetime struggle in which ingenuity, hard work, and a good measure of luck ..." were crucial elements.

The small operators did not always own their own property. On the huge plantations in the older coffee regions, permanent workers (*arrendatarios*) obtained the right to farm a small parcel on which they grew corn, yucca, plantains, and sugarcane and raised fowl or livestock. In return for the use of the land, the worker undertook an obligation to labor ranging from a few days to nearly a whole month on the plantation, depending on the size and quality of his plot. The coffee estates also employed temporary workers, small farmers from other areas, contracted for harvest and paid according to the amount of coffee beans they picked. Temporary labor weeded the groves as well. A third type of worker, the *colono*, contracted to open up new lands for coffee production, clearing the land, planting new trees, and caring for them for 4 years. The colono then sold the trees to the plantation owner and renounced all rights to the land. The colono also cultivated food crops between the trees for family subsistence.

In the newer coffee regions, small and medium-sized family farms predominated, the latter operated by sharecroppers or renters. The sharecroppers received half the harvest in return for caring for the trees and processing the beans. They received only one-third, however, if they did not dry and de-pulp the beans. Although some medium-sized farms operated with the help of sharecroppers, they mostly relied on family labor.

Small farmers had to adapt to the environment and the family's limited resources. The topography of Costa Rica and Colombia made it impossible to use mechanized machinery, so farmers used axes and fire to clear the land and hoes to weed it. Colombian farmers planted their crops in vertical rows on the severely steep slopes so they could weed standing upright. (Weeding bent over is excruciating work.) The farmers planted using a *barretón*, a heavy wedge-shaped implement with an iron tip and a long, straight wood handle that the farmer poked into the soil. The farmer then placed corn or a coffee seedling into the resulting hole in the ground. He cleared with a *peinilla* or *machete*. Farmers planted food crops between the rows of coffee trees not only to provide sustenance for themselves but also to help prevent erosion. They planted shade trees, such as plantain, to inhibit erosion and provide leaves that fertilized the coffee trees. Shade also slowed the growth and ripening of the coffee beans, so that they matured at the proper pace. Pigs and fowl wandered in the fields, eliminating insects and supplying fertilizer. Family farms grew many crops, but the smallest farms concentrated on subsistence staples such as plantains, bananas, manioc, corn, and beans. They grew corn on the least fertile land.

(continued)

(continued)

The work of growing coffee was hard and long. Men usually did the heavy work of clearing, planting, and weeding. Women and children helped with the harvest, including de-pulping, washing, fermenting, drying, and selecting. Once this process was complete, women and children were responsible for putting the coffee beans into burlap sacks and transporting the sacks by mule or horse, on difficult trails, to coffee towns, where the farmers sold the coffee to merchants and traders.

Farm families lived simply. Corn, eaten in soups and bread, was the staple of their diet. It also was feed for the fowl and pigs, which, in turn, the family ate on special occasions. The usual meal was soup and then some kind of starch with small bits of salted beef or pork purchased in town. The farmers also bought most of their vegetables. Many farmers grew citrus and mango trees and, in the warmer zones, sugarcane. From this sugarcane, they produced brown sugar cakes called *panelas* and the molasses that was later fermented and distilled to yield *aguardiente* or rum. These provided sweets and alcoholic beverages.

To survive, the families had to be frugal and self-sufficient. They usually produced most of what they needed, except for some of the men's clothing (pants, shoes, and boots). Poor children wore little or no clothing. The women made baskets, mattresses, and candles.

Small farm coffee growers lived in houses consisting of bamboo walls, thatch roofs, and dirt floors. The women did their wash in local rivers and streams. Human waste went in the fields; this unsanitary practice fouled water supplies and resulted in the transmission of intestinal diseases, including intestinal parasites, which were common.

Nature's Way

El Nino/La Nina: The Southern Oscillation (ENSO)

El Nino refers to an exceptionally strong and prolonged period of warm sea surface water in the eastern Pacific Ocean associated with air pressure deviations in the east and west Pacific, the Southern Oscillation. The two components of ENSO are the opposites: El Nino, which consists of warming water, and La Nina, which consists of cooling water. ENSO affects the atmosphere and ocean systems as well as natural ecosystems. When the east to west winds in the Pacific weaken, it causes the ocean water off the west coast of South America to warm. This means that the movement of cold water from deep in the sea lessens. As a result, the nutrient rich cold water does not come to the surface, reducing plankton production and the available food for fish and birds. La Nina has the opposite effect. The cold water from the deep sea rises and increases plankton production. At the same time, the phenomenon causes climate change. The impact of ENSO is varied. In Central America, El Nino causes heavy rains on the Caribbean coast, while the Pacific coasts stay dry. Large amounts of rain fall on the coast of Ecuador, northern Peru and southern Chile. In Ecuador, Peru, and Bolivia El Nino leads to drought in the Andes. It reduces precipitation in Venezuela and Guyana and drought in the Brazilian northeast. Rainfall increases in Argentina, Paraguay, and Uruguay. Temperatures rise in southern Brazil. In the Caribbean, it can engender conditions favorable for hurricanes. The events occur every three to seven years between December and January. They last between nine and twelve months.

The Lima Geographical Society first reported El Nino in 1891. It is likely, however, that eleven other events occurred before then. Investigators found instances of heavy rains that began in December in 1790, 1804, 1814, 1828, 1845, 1864, 1871, 1877, 1878, 1884, and 1891. The twentieth century experienced thirteen more.

The phenomenon has the most detrimental effect on Peru in the form of heavy rains, which cause flooding and mudslides. The northern coast of Peru is in normal times arid, which magnifies the impact. The most damaging occurrence took place in 1983 when heavy rains instigated a landslide that killed 596 people and property destruction in the range of $US 2.4 billion. Similarly, El Nino of 1997–1998 hit Peru particularly hard with intense rains in the northern and Amazon areas causing major flooding and mudslides. The rains badly damaged roads. Two hundred and three people died. The precipitation was equally as intense and destructive in Bolivia, Ecuador, and Paraguay, where the death toll together reached nearly 300 and flooding badly damaged roads, bridges, homes, schools, and hospitals. The changes it caused in precipitation patterns also affected Argentina, Brazil, Chile, Colombia, Mexico, Panama, and Venezuela. In 2010, El Nino induced floods in Peru that took 158 lives. The latest catastrophe occurred in 2017, when 80 people lost their lives. The rains washed away 1360 miles of main roads, 577 miles of secondary roads, 194 bridges, 417 miles of irrigation canals, estimated at $US 1.4 billion in damages.

Of particular danger is the higher levels of water in rivers brought on by the rain. Studies also associate increases in the occurrence of mosquito-borne diseases, such as malaria, dengue, and viral encephalitis, with ENSO. Scientists argue about the impact on agriculture. Heavy rain is detrimental to cereal crops, but benefits crops like maize. El Nino decimates the fishing industry off the coast of Peru. Because of the lack of plankton food, anchovies, which are the basis of the fish meal industry, disappear.

7

People and Progress, 1910–1959

- altering gender roles
- transition from rural to agriculture
- city living conditions got worse bc of people.

The first half of the twentieth century was a time of vast transition from rural, agriculture-based traditions to urban middle and working class "modern" life. Change manifested not only in the politics of popular organizations and upheaval, but also in all aspects of everyday life, such as employment, housing, food, entertainment, and art. The prolonged processes of altering gender roles, begun in the nineteenth century, continued. The struggle by common people for control over their everyday lives went on, as well.

People resisted transformations of their long-held values and practices, not only rural dwellers, but also many members of the upper classes, the nominal promoters of change. The latter looked on popular culture as vulgar—the products of the slums—and regarded with suspicion the repercussions of migrations and industrialization. The wealthy and powerful who sought to modernize their nations and the lower classes worried about whether they could control these changes.

The transition from countryside to city and from rural agricultural to urban industrial worker or middle class did not transform the attitude of the upper classes toward the lower, who the rich and powerful continued to fear. The wealthy grappled with the Social Question in politics and economics. Ultimately, they allied with the armed services and the middle class to control the masses. The Brazilian saying: "The social question is a question for the police," reflects their attitude. It was not enough, however, for the upper classes merely to maintain their control over the lower classes through government coercion. The wealthy tried mightily to force all aspects of social life and culture to conform to their need to rein in the urban lower classes. They sought to transform immigrants and migrants into a quiescent proletariat

© The Author(s), under exclusive license to Springer Nature Switzerland AG 2022

M. Wasserman, *Modern Latin America Since 1800*,
https://doi.org/10.1007/978-3-030-96185-5_7

loyal to the nation (sometimes known as the *patria,* or fatherland). They attempted to exert similar influence over the transformation of gender roles, particularly the place of women, in the rapidly changing urban society. Through the state, Latin American upper classes sought to shape the families, relationships, homes, leisure time, and tastes of workers to maintain their (male) hegemony (patriarchy). This meant potentially massive intrusions into local and personal prerogatives. moving to cities

The movement of people from the countryside to the cities was and continues to be the most crucial process in Latin America. In 1950, 61 percent of the population was still rural. From 1950 to 1960 alone, nearly 25 percent of rural Argentines abandoned the countryside for the cities; 29 percent of Chilean country people and 19 percent of Brazilian rural folk did the same. They left their homes because neither land nor jobs were available to them. Increasing concentration of land ownership severely limited their opportunities to obtain their own plots. "Land reform" projects distributed only marginally productive properties and did so without the opportunity to obtain credit to purchase equipment and make improvements. Burgeoning populations added to the pressures on the accessible land. Making matters worse, large landowners required fewer year round laborers because of technological innovations and changes in crops. Many export commodities needed only seasonal workers, at planting and harvest. In contrast to the deterioration of conditions in rural areas, cities offered more employment, better opportunities for education—and therefore upward mobility—and improved health care. However miserable the living conditions in the slums of the cities, they were infinitely better than in the countryside, and however limited the possibilities in the metropolises, they were shining rays of hope compared to the darkness obscuring economic opportunities for the poor on large estates and in villages.

Even in the cities, of course, everyday life remained a constant struggle, as in the nineteenth century. Most Latin Americans continued to be poor and uneducated. The literacy rate for those older than 15 years of age was 50 percent. Only 7 percent of the people possessed a secondary education. As for work, if anything, it became harder. Large companies rather than small, family operated workshops now employed most industrial workers. Impersonal bureaucracies replaced personal relations. City streets, noisy and smelly, polluted and unsanitary in the previous century, deteriorated further. The vast influx of people from the countryside and from abroad increased the pressures on existing facilities and public works beyond the breaking point. Like the Europeans and North Americans before them, Latin Americans who advocated modernization cared little that their relentless drive for economic development decimated their forests and pastures and polluted their water and air.

The contrasts between rich and poor, and the ironies they generated, were striking. Latin American upper classes during the first half of the twentieth century rebuilt the cores of the largest cities to emulate London or Paris. Governments built the Teatro Nacional (now the Palacio Nacional de Bellas Artes) in Mexico City and the Teatro Colón in Buenos Aires and constructed the elegant avenues of Rio de Janeiro and the Avenida de Mayo in Buenos Aires. While resplendent buildings and gleaming boulevards appeared in the cities' centers, however, more and more people crammed into the decaying tenements in the vast tracts of the city untouched by renovations.

Proletarianization and Patriarchy

Conditions in rural areas deteriorated steadily for the lower classes since independence, and life for farm tenants and other workers was as precarious as in the preceding century. Work on the farms and ranches, if available at all, remained as hard and as badly paid as ever. Employment was erratic or seasonal. It was difficult to eke out the barest living. Most rural workers faced lifelong indebtedness. At a ranch in the northwestern part of the state of Sao Paulo, in Brazil, in 1929, for example, 50 laborers rose at 4 A.M. to eat a breakfast of bread and coffee, after which they cleared fields to plant pasture for cattle. The men ate lunch at 8 a.m. and consumed their third meal consisting of beans, rice, and pasta at 2 P.M. Their toils did not end until dusk. Although the food was plentiful, they received no more after the early dinner. Famished at the end of their long day, workers purchased additional food—perhaps cheese and bread or candy—from the ranch store, buying it on credit charged to their salaries. On Chilean estates, tenants obtained a house and a small parcel of land in return for their labor. Their status was precarious, because the landowner could change the arrangements at a moment's notice and evict or move the tenants. Protest was futile, for the police and military were at the service of the landowner. In short, conditions for rural workers had not changed since the nineteenth century.

Living in any one of thousands of small villages in Peru or Mexico was little better. The villages were often isolated, reachable only over muddy or dusty potholed roads hours from any city. There was no electricity. Many of the inhabitants of the indigenous and mestizo villages, especially women, spoke only their Indian language, such as Quechua and Aymara in the Andean nations or Nahuatl in Mexico.

It was nearly impossible to feed a family on the produce of small, individually owned plots, despite the families' modest meals—Andeans, for example, ate simple stews of potatoes, other vegetables, and, in good times, shreds of chicken, beef, or pork, accompanied by wheat or barley bread. As a result, country people sought work on neighboring estates and farms, in mines, and in cities. The movement of people from place to place was continual from the mid nineteenth century on. Country people in Chile, for instance, often left their farms for short periods to work in the mines, drawn by high wages and the possibility of saving enough to buy their own land. After a few months, when the farmer-miner had accumulated enough money, he returned to his own parcel of land or to the estate, where his family members were tenants. Manuel Abaitúa Acevedo, who first traveled to Chile's El Teniente copper mine in 1924 from his home village, was typical of the early migrants, who traveled back and forth between farm and mine. Initially, Abaitúa Acevedo worked 9 months in the mine before going home. The next year, he mined for 4 months, and in the following 2 years, 1 month each. In 1928, he worked in the mine for 5 months. His dream, like that of others in his situation, was to save enough money to buy his own land. *new machines for*

Rural working conditions improved somewhat early in the twentieth century, in large part due to the arrival of two machines. First, in Mexico, the *molino de nixtamal,* which ground soaked maize kernels into damp flour to make tortilla dough, revolutionized the everyday lives of women, allowing them to escape the centuries-long practice of grinding corn by hand, which required hours and hours of work. Second, the sewing machine, many of which operated through foot power rather than electricity, facilitated home piecework production, permitting women to work and tend to their families, and forming the basis of the clothing cottage industry. Sewing machines also eased the transition from wholly traditional to more western-style, modern clothing. Access to electricity and the radio would have enormous effect on rural life, as well, but they were not universally accessible until the 1950s. Only 40 percent of the residents of Huaylas, a village in Peru, for example, had electricity in 1963.

Despite these improvements, however, rural life in the first half of the twentieth century was so difficult that vast numbers of country dwellers left their homes and migrated to the mines and cities in hopes of finding better work. These women and men bravely left their villages and estates in order to improve their situation by entering the unfamiliar culture of mining camps and urban landscapes and acquiring new skills. When necessary, they moved from job to job.

The history of María Elisa Álvarez illustrates this situation. She arrived in Medellín, Colombia, at age 16 after toiling on a coffee plantation for 5 years. She also sold cured tobacco, sweets, and produce on the streets of her hometown. In the city, Álvarez worked in domestic service for a year and then went to the textile mills. She worked there for a few months and then labored at a small dyeing shop and a local hospital. Having learned enough as a nurse's assistant to care for a patient, she gained employment caring for the invalid son of a wealthy family. After quitting because the son was unpleasant, she obtained employment in the factory she worked in years before and then found a position in another mill, where she stayed until retirement.

Migrants from the countryside, such as Álvarez, arrived in the cities or mining camps only to face a long process of socialization and accommodation. The very sights, sounds, and smells were different, and as if this was not disorienting enough, the newly migrated workers became immersed in struggles over their customs, traditions, and demeanor with their employers.

The conflicts between laborer and company are evident in the histories of two important industries, textile manufacturing in Medellín, Colombia, and copper mining in Chile. In both cases, companies required a reliable body of workers, but this proved difficult. Medellín textile workers were notorious for being uncooperative and mobile.

Companies sought to transform rambunctious and itinerant country bumpkins into passive, stable, productive workers. Workers resisted mightily. With the new century came critical changes in labor relations and market conditions, technology, and gender relations. In response to these changes, large companies attempted to control workers' lives to an extraordinary extent. *Strikes*

First, labor strikes during the mid-1930s in Medellín led company owners to formulate new strategies to instill stronger discipline into their unruly workers. Second, firms had grown larger and more bureaucratic, so owner families no longer supervised their operations from the factory floor, which, in turn, meant that they no longer fostered personal relations with their employees. Third, textile mills commonly used large looms capable of weaving much more cloth at one time. These new machines increased productivity, but—together with the attempt to keep women "in their places"—caused a drastic shift in the gender makeup of the workforce. Bosses replaced women loom operators with men. Medellín's textile and clothing factories, like most in Latin America, heavily employed women through the 1930s, but by the end of the 1950s, men were the majority.

These transformations left employers struggling to reacquire control over the workplace during the 1940s by devising a new, two-pronged strategy: on

replaced women with men.

one hand, providing desirable benefits for their employees, and on the other hand, seeking to influence all aspects of their employees' lives.

The first part of this strategy included improving working conditions and keeping salaries relatively high. The corporations that owned the mills and mines hoped that good pay would ensure a steady supply of able laborers, but it soon became clear that high pay would not persuade workers to abandon their freedom of movement or reform their behavior. Employers tried repressive tactics, but they proved to be equally ineffective at creating a body of compliant, respectable workers.

This led industries to the second part of the strategy: to influence every aspect of their employees' lives. Thus, corporations adopted paternalistic (fatherly) practices, making workers' lives more comfortable—and the job more attractive—by providing bonuses for attendance, establishing social and cultural organizations, setting up schools, and offering inducements to form traditional nuclear families.

As a result, Colombian mills paid workers well and provided them with such amenities as cafeterias surrounded by landscaped patios that served subsidized meals. The companies subsidized housing and grocery stores and paid for medical care, chapels, and schools.

Similarly, in Chile, the foreign-owned mining companies sought to ensure a stable, resident, skilled labor force by offering workers schooling, movies, libraries, organized sports, and clubs—the last of which were to substitute for labor unions—in hopes of simultaneously attracting and altering them.

The Chilean state became involved in the socialization of workers during the 1930s in order to incorporate the middle and lower classes into the new conception of the nation. The government sought to build a citizenry of disciplined and responsible people. This, of course, coincided exactly with the goals of the foreign copper companies. Both the government and the corporations committed to successfully implementing new responsibilities for the lower classes, who were to be "disciplined, educated, and responsible [in order to] fulfill the demands of citizenship for the national community."

Workers, nonetheless, wanted to rule their own lives. Miners resented attempts to control them by both the companies and the unions, and they continued to get drunk, play cards, and fornicate. At the El Teniente mine in 1922, an exasperated foreman fired close to 100 employees for "disobedience, laziness, fighting, insolence … leaving the job, carelessness, sleeping on the job, gambling, thieving, and incompetence."

The efforts made by the Chilean government and mining companies, as well as by the Colombian textile industry, to reform workers quickly became the aggressive reassertion of traditional, patriarchal definitions of gender roles.

With the encouragement of the Chilean state, the mining companies, for instance, created a masculinized culture of work. The workers were to overcome the difficulty and danger of the labor with their sense of dignity. Pride was to overwhelm the dehumanization that accompanied modern mining.

Masculinizing work was one-half of the process; the other half was reemphasizing women's traditional roles. Latin American culture at the time—like most cultures— viewed female workers as a threat to the "proper" relationship between men and women, because when women earned wages, they redefined narrow definitions of gender. Further, owners believed that they could not maintain patriarchal and paternalistic authority in the factory if it no longer functioned in the family setting—that is, if employment in mills or mines provided women with the means to be independent of the authority of fathers, husbands, brothers, and sons. Only single women could work

Crucial to patriarchal beliefs and authority is the notion of female "virtue," specifically virginity. If women worked only when they were (theoretically) virgins, and the comforting assumption was that all unmarried women were, the factory maintained its patriarchal standing as "father" figure. So mills and mines stopped hiring married women and single mothers. This way, women could work only while awaiting marriage, rather than working as independent females who would provide for themselves and potentially remain unincorporated into the family system.

In the midst of modernization, the mines and mills altered women's status to conform to centuries-old beliefs, but practicalities stood in their way. Women played a large part in helping the mining camps function. Women worked as domestics, as petty traders, and in the bars and brothels (which they sometimes owned) that sprouted like mushrooms around every camp. Like the men, many of these women hoped to save some money and move on. They usually came to the camps alone and often entered into sexual and domestic arrangements with men after their arrival.

Foreign companies that owned the mines believed that this transient and unruly population of women, especially prostitutes, in the camps added to the instability and lack of discipline among the miners by adding to and exacerbating the problems caused by rampant alcohol use and gambling. The companies sought to regulate the sex lives of the workers and the women in the camps. The mine managers even went so far as to force men and women found alone together either to marry or to leave their jobs. During the 1930s, some companies offered a monthly bonus and an extra allowance to workers who had families and were willing to formalize their relationships. This induced many couples to enter into civil unions and legitimize their children.

In addition, the companies sought to "civilize" the women in the camps, as well as the men. Company-sponsored programs, for instance, taught house-keeping skills to wives. Especially important in these lessons were the pointers in managing money and making ends meet, because the companies feared that poverty would tear apart the nuclear families they were trying so hard to create. As for single women who became pregnant or had abortions, the companies' solution was simple—they fired the women.

All of these policies, programs, and attempts to reinforce traditional gender roles succeeded in creating a stable mining workforce during the 1930s and 1940s. They could not eliminate the difficult working conditions in the mines. What neither the companies nor the state anticipated was that their efforts to masculinize the work culture would generate not only an increased sense of pride on the part of male workers, but an equal increase in their disdain for authority.

Neither the miners nor the women of the camps ever became entirely passive. Union activity continued, as did women's economic activities. Women sold food and beverages from their homes, took in laundry, and brought in boarders. Some even operated as female bootleggers (smugglers of illegal alcohol). Some married women managed to obtain a degree of economic independence through their involvement in the informal market sector.

The story below illustrates the ways in which the companies' tactics failed. Ana (Nena) Palacios de Montoya worked as a domestic in Medellín when she met Jairo, who became her husband. He was a driver for the local textile factory and used his contacts to obtain a position for her in the factory. Palacios de Montoya loved working in the mill. With funds cobbled together from yearly bonuses, mill loans, and the help of friends, she and her husband bought land and built a house. She gradually constructed her dream home, adding to the original structure as the family saved enough money for more materials. Amazingly, she managed to marry and have a child without her bosses discovering and firing her from her job. The bosses obtained two good workers, and their employees earned a good life—but, precisely contrary to the companies' efforts, Nena and Jairo clearly maintained their independence.

Work at the copper mines paid better than any other occupation in Chile. By the mid1940s, miners earned 50 percent higher wages than any other employment. Despite this, mines frequently experienced labor shortages until the relative stabilization of the workforce during the 1930s. When demand for labor grew, the companies sent to rural areas recruiters (*enganchadores*), *who* got farmers drunk and told them about all the money they could earn in the mines. The desperate, drunken men "agreed" to become miners, signed contracts (which they could not read) and then loaded onto trains headed to the mines. The farmers woke up, hung over, only to find themselves at a mine miles away from their villages, contractually bound to their new employers, and in debt to the recruiters, who often advanced them funds on their wages—which, of course, had to be repaid by working in the mines. If the farmers protested or tried to leave, the threat of police intervention persuaded them to cooperate. Despite these recruiting practices, turnover was a continual problem.

Regardless of how they had arrived at a mine, however, most miners' lives were similar to the description of the daily work at El Teniente, described below.

At four or five o'clock in the morning, a Chilean copper miner rose and ate breakfast at a cantina or the house of a family. By six, he was on his way to the train, completely enclosed and dark, that took him up to the mine. When he arrived, the miner reported to the foreign supervisor, who recorded his time of entry. A giant elevator then transported the miner and some 600 of his fellow workers to the different levels of the mine, where they joined their teams, which consisted of 15 people, and began work in the tunnels.

The lead miners entered the designated tunnel first, laying pipes and tubes that brought in compressed air and water for the drills. As the miners drilled, the machines sprayed water on the work site to prevent dust from filling the cavern. (Despite this precaution, the tunnels filled with so much dust that the miners could see only 5 or 6 feet ahead.) Miners inserted dynamite into the drilled holes—a delicate, highly skilled process—and blew up the walls, creating access to the veins of ore. Other team members then lay rails in the tunnels for cars that hauled in timbers to support the shaft's walls and ceiling, and then hauled out the ore. Once they accessed a vein, miners began the grueling work of chopping the ore out of the rock walls. They loaded ore into the railcars, which they pushed to and emptied into chutes that carried it to the concentrating plants.

Mining was brutal work in terrible conditions. Foremen, under relentless pressure from the companies to increase productivity, pushed the workers hard. Miners learned these varied skills—all of which were dangerous and required enormous strength—on the job. When they exhibited proficiency, they moved on to better positions, though some refused to take the most dangerous assignments. A few became foremen. Work in the concentrating mills also required a great deal of skill and was even more dangerous than work in the tunnels, because the refining process released toxic fumes. Protective equipment was never sufficient, so the miners who labored in the plants inevitably acquired silicosis, a respiratory disease. Concentrating plant workers were lucky to survive a dozen years.

Living conditions in the El Teniente mining camp were generally abhorrent. Lodgings for families had no electricity, light, or ventilation. "… [T]he barracks for single workers [were] so awful as to be irrational." Miners with their families lived in two room apartments in barracks buildings. Often, two families shared one apartment. A member of a family consisting of nine children and parents wrote: " … [W]e women had the bedroom because there were six girls and three boys, so in the big bedroom there were only women, in the other were my father with the boys, and in the other the kitchen." The company did not allow electric heaters or irons, so families used small wood and kerosene burning stoves, but both were expensive. There were common taps for water and toilets.

The worst disadvantage of living in the camps, perhaps, was the extraordinarily high cost of living, which badly eroded the real value of the nation's highest wages. Food was especially expensive, which meant that workers' and their families' nutrition suffered. Monopoly prices were at the heart of the problem.

Miners often resisted the difficult conditions. New miners often skipped work after a few days to recover from their aches and pains. Ultimately, because miners were in perpetually short supply, they had the advantage of being able to find another job if the work environment was unacceptable.

Urbanization and Social Change

The transformations sweeping through Latin American society during the first half of the twentieth century were nowhere more apparent than in the growing cities of the region. They were particularly evident in the conditions of the middle class and attitudes toward women.

Latin American cities were overcrowded, unsanitary, overrun by epidemic diseases, and teeming with uneducated migrants from the countryside and abroad. At the beginning of the century, the upper classes in Rio de Janeiro, Buenos Aires, and other cities determined to alter dramatically their metropolises' physical and social space while simultaneously inculcating moral values in the masses. Urban redevelopment, electrified public transportation, and massive population growth transformed the cities economically, spatially, and culturally.

The divide between the wealthy and the lower classes widened and grew more obvious. Rio de Janeiro, whose population was half Afro-Brazilian and where immigrants flooded in by the thousands, was really two cities, one of the poor, on whom the authorities cast suspicious eyes, and another of the "decent" upper and middleclass folk, who made up less than 20 percent. The upper classes imposed their will on the lower classes through cleaning up downtown spaces, instituting new health and housing codes, regulating recreation, and strictly enforcing laws against public nuisances such as prostitution.

Massive urban renewal took place in Rio de Janeiro from 1902 to 1910, clearing working class neighborhoods and moving their inhabitants to the city's outskirts. As migrants continued to flow into the city, urban services remained woefully inadequate. Terrible epidemics tormented the city. By 1920, disease ravaged downtown streets and abandoned girls, beggars, and prostitutes were everywhere.

The most startling example of super-urbanization during this era was Mexico City. Country people thronged into the city in increasing numbers from 1940 to the present. Much of the nation's new industry established in Mexico City—one-fourth of the country's factories were located there by 1970. Between 1940 and 1970, millions of people left the countryside to seek their fortunes in the metropolis, increasing the capital's population from 1.5 million to 8.5 million. The number of automobiles jamming city streets also grew exponentially during that time, choking the city with carbon monoxide fumes. The government erected architectural splendors such as the National Autonomous University and the Museum of Anthropology. Skyscrapers sprouted in the core of the city and along the beautiful, tree-lined, statue-ornamented Paseo de la Reforma, while migrants overflowed burgeoning barrios, such as Netzahualcóyotl.

Generally, life was better in the city than in rural areas and offered more opportunity to improve one's conditions. In 1960, *capitalino* (resident of Mexico City) family income was 185 percent more than a rural family's income.

The middle class expanded because government bureaucracies grew larger, the foreign businesses multiplied opportunities in growing economies, and education became available to more than just the wealthy. What mattered to the members of the middle class, as it had to the gente decente in the nineteenth century, was maintaining their respectability and their distance from the lower classes. Because their economic situation was chronically precarious, middle class people—who were only marginally more financially well off than the working class—concerned themselves primarily with keeping up the appearance of their status.

White-collar workers lived perpetually on the edge; their paychecks barely covered basic living expenses (see Table 7.1). Pawnshops were the only source of ready credit. White-collar workers found it nearly impossible to buy a

Table 7.1 A Typical Middle Class Budget in Mid-Twentieth Century Peruvian Soles

Rent	100
Food	240
Soap, toothpaste	20
Transportation	36
Water, electricity, garbage	14
One servant	50
Kerosene	12
Movies, once a week	20
School fees for oldest child	80
Total	572 on income of 600 (a meager sum at the time)

Source: Tat No. 16 (July, 1949), pp. 1819, cited in D. S. Parker, *The Idea of the Middle Class: White Collar Workers and Peruvian Society, 19001950* (University Park, PA: Penn State University Press, 1998), p. 212.

home. It was difficult to save money for a down payment or a financial cushion in case of emergency. No banks existed to keep saving or to provide mortgages.

Middle class health was barely better than that of the working class. Lima's white-collar workers were less likely to die of epidemic diseases such as typhoid, cholera, bubonic plague, or yellow fever than poor Peruvians, but they succumbed to tuberculosis, which accounted for one-third of all white-collar mortality in the city, a result of working in badly ventilated spaces and residing in damp, overcrowded apartments. It is likely they were malnourished as well.

Despite these obstacles to financial security, white-collar workers tried to emulate the rich, concerned mostly with appearance. Middle class women followed European fashions, while men who worked in commerce in Lima, during the 1920s joined shooting clubs, played billiards or wore English cashmere.

Because living spaces were so small and unpleasant, many people frequented cafes. Walking the streets of Lima was a way to show off respectability---of seeing and being seen. Crucial to the middle-class psyche was the notion that they were demonstrably different from the working class. Middle class workers were willing to commute for hours so they could reside in respectable areas of the city. The middle class sought forms of entertainment beyond films, radio, and sports—all favored by the working classes—and began to travel.

Women made up only 1 percent of the white-collar workforce in 1908 in Peru and did not enter this sector in numbers until the 1910s, when they filled positions in post offices, telegraph offices, and telephone companies. In the 1920s, they moved into retail, then banking, insurance, and commerce.

Five percent of working women were white collar by 1931. The typical images of white-collar workers, however, remained those of a young bachelor or of a family man whose wife did not work. Respectability demanded wives stay at home, even if the result of living on one salary meant that the family lived more modestly than it otherwise might have. Despite this tacit cultural injunction, however, it is probable that married middleclass women worked outside the home.

In Peru and elsewhere in Latin America, the number of white-collar workers expanded from 1930 to 1950, as businesses grew larger and more complex and public bureaucracies swelled. As in Chile's mines, traditional paternalism gave way to hierarchies and impersonal relations. Many more women entered the white-collar ranks during this period, although usually at the lowest paid levels. After the 1930s in Lima, mestizos comprised the largest number of white collars. White-collar workers' children eventually gained access to university educations.

Urbanization and industrial work, with its accompanying financial freedom, instilled a new attitude in women, many of whom became what the era called "the modern woman." (They were in Mexico and elsewhere *las chicas modernas,* or modern girls.) Although at the beginning of the twentieth century women office and factory workers— that is, women holding nontraditional jobs—were only a small minority of the female workforce, they caused much public discussion. At that time, most working women toiled as domestics, as they had in the previous century. The 1920s brought with them the notorious flapper—self-confident women who were racy, flirtatious, and assertive. This unprecedented image of the independent, sensuous female shook male culture, because female "virtue" was the very center of patriarchy—and such virtue certainly did not include self-reliance, self-determination, or a sense of self-worth inherent rather than bestowed by a father or husband. In Latin America, as elsewhere in the Western world at that time, modernity indicated economic progress and healthy, rational sexual and family relations when applied to men, but it meant a dissolute lifestyle and loose morals when applied to women.

In Brazil, as in other Latin American countries, the upper classes, government officials, and conservative Catholics worried about the low rate of marriage among the poor, the high rate of infant mortality, and the increasing numbers of women and children in the industrial workforce.

The irony, of course, was that middleclass women in Brazil (and other nations) were entering the white-collar workforce because it was harder and harder for families to make ends meet on one salary. Given this reality and despite governmental policies designed to keep women in their place, more and more middleclass women took advantage of educational opportunities and went into the professions. By the 1920s, women's employment did not elicit the disapproval among the middle class that it had in the past.

Women's fashions of the 1920s disconcerted the upper class males who dominated Brazil (and probably disconcerted a significant percentage of middle and working class males and some females). Compared to the clothing of the previous century and the turn of the century, during the early part of the decade, women wore lighter, shorter, and more comfortable dresses. Later in the decade, hems came up all the way to the knee, worn with silk stockings and high heels. Less cumbersome bras and panties replaced corsets. Short haircuts and the use of makeup were the style. Women exposed arms and legs on the beach. Women were revealing themselves physically as never before.

Fashion was not the only aspect of women's lives changing drastically. Women now smoked cigarettes in public. Films and magazines celebrated a glamorous, decadent life and encouraged women to aspire to it. Dances and music became scandalous: The tango, foxtrot, Charleston, and shimmy were all the rage.

To upper class males, women's virtue was under attack, and the Brazilian state, like the Chilean state, sought to defend patriarchy from these challenges. The regime of Getúlio Vargas (1930-1945) adopted policies intended to adjust the traditional role of women to meet the new economic and cultural conditions of the twentieth century, while maintaining the patriarchal structure of society. Its targets, of course, were women and the poor, the groups believed to pose the greatest threat to upper class men's—and the state's— status. The goal was to strengthen traditional marriage. Women were, after all, crucial to society not only because they reproduced but also because they educated their children. Therefore, it was necessary to "reeducate" women and reemphasize traditional values, so that women would inculcate their offspring with the "proper" values and attitudes. To accomplish this, the government adopted protective legislation limiting women's access to the workplace, in the hope this would limit women's ability to support themselves, essentially forcing them to find husbands simply to survive. The government also instituted social service agencies to monitor the urban poor. In addition to these governmental policies, industrialists even set up model villages to control the domestic lives of their workers.

The Brazilian ruling class and government were, however, willing to make minimal concessions to women. Early in the century, Brazilian legislation altered the wife's status to "companion, partner, and assistant in familial responsibilities." (Nonetheless, this legislation firmly maintained the husband as head of household, and women still did not have the power to control their own property.) In 1940, the government's penal code eliminated the distinctions between male and female adultery. There was also an attempt to end the legal tolerance of crimes of passion. (Law permitted a husband to kill his wife, if he caught her in adultery.) Women, like the middle class, struggled enormously to better their conditions, and succeeded somewhat, but their situation remained precarious. As the middle class had not achieved equal status with the wealthy and powerful, neither had women obtained legal, economic, or cultural equality with men.

The Arts

The vast movement of people from the countryside to the cities and from the rest of the world to Latin America during the first half of the twentieth century deeply affected the region's popular culture (folk songs, dance, and crafts) and its high culture (orchestral music, theatrical dance, painting, sculpture, literature, etc.). Improved communications and transportation not only brought more people together domestically, but facilitated travel among countries and the introduction of foreign influences. The art tied closely to the construction of national identities, and Latin Americans struggled to find their way in the space between their own artistic traditions and those of Europe and North America, which the upper classes much admired. The changes wrought by industrialization, migration, and urbanization on Latin American dance, music, and painting, in particular, were extensive.

Connected with rural music and songs that protested the miserable conditions in the teeming tenements and the industrialization of urban work, the tango, born in the slums of Buenos Aires, Argentina, during the late nineteenth century, was a fitting symbol for these profound transitions. Before World War I, dancers performed the tango primarily in the outskirts of Buenos Aires, where rural tradition was still stronger than in the heart of the city. The tango melded various aspects of Argentine society, combining the music of the rural *milonga*, the Spanish *contradanza,* and influences of African Buenos Aires. Its form was a protest against conventional mores: Danced by couples whose bodies closely entwined, the tango was modern, urban, and explicitly sensual, it eschewed more innocent traditional (folk) dances performed in groups. Radio and film made the tango part of popular culture, and the upper and middle classes, who disdained the dance for the first several decades of its life as being symbolic of the poor, later embraced it as a symbol of Argentina.

The Brazilian samba, too, was an object of upper class scorn during the nineteenth century. In fact, the Brazilian government outlawed it for a time. Nonetheless, the samba became the symbol of Brazil's mixed heritage of African and European culture. Arising from the poor Afro-Brazilian neighborhoods of Rio, during the 1920s samba clubs took over Carnival (the festival before Lent). The clubs' leaders shed the bad reputations of their predecessor organizations and convinced parents in the poor neighborhoods to allow their daughters to participate. Not only did samba—the dance of the poorest Brazilians—become the symbol of the nation, but it also illustrated how women, who were now active and public participants in Carnival, were no longer restricted to private spaces.

In painting and literature, the conflicts inherent in the processes of urbanization, modernization, and finding national identities emerged at the turn of the twentieth century in movements such as *modernismo* and *indigenismo* (nativism). Nicaraguan poet Rubén Dario founded modernismo, a literary movement that sought to express the Latin American experience. The visual arts followed, also seeking a uniquely Latin American presentation of the region's culture. Latin American artists, most of whom trained in Europe, set aside the perspective of the continent and looked at their homeland up close. Mexican artist Saturnino Herrán (1887-1918), for example, depicted indigenous and mestizos living and working in their local environs in such paintings as *El Trabajo (Work)* (1908) and *La Ofrenda (The Offering)* (1913). Herrán, who never studied in Europe, was one of the first twentieth century Mexican artists to look to the country's pre-Columbian past for subject matter. Similarly, Ecuadorian painter Camilo Egas (1899-1962) depicted the life of Indians over the centuries since the conquest in huge horizontal panels, such as the *Fiesta Indígena (Indian Festival)* (1922).

At the heart of the Mexican search for national identity and art's place within it was Geraldo Murillo, widely known as Dr. Atl (1875-1964). He was a crucial link among European movements (such as impressionism), Mexican popular culture, the famous Mexican muralists, and the revolutionary government. Dr. Atl was an important sponsor of the muralist movement in the 1920s. He brought *arte popular* into the forefront in 1921 when he organized an exhibition of popular art and wrote its accompanying text, *Las artes populares en México*. A talented painter in his own right, Dr. Atl's works, such as *El Volcán Paricutín en erupción* (1943), for instance, showed his eclectic approach to art. Uruguayan Pedro Figari (1861-1938), son of an Italian immigrant, depicted life on the vast plains of the Pampas, as well as creole and black dance. He, like Herrán and Egas, painted the lower classes in the countryside, as one critic observed, "never before represented with such boldness and candor. ..."

Perhaps the most well-known and the most important artistic movement that grappled with the intertwined dilemmas of modernization and national identity—most crucially the place of indigenous peoples within the revolution—were the Mexican muralists. The most famous of these were Diego Rivera (1887–1957), David Alfaro Siqueiros (1896-1974), and José Clemente Orozco (1883-1949), but the group also included Alva de la Canal, Chariot, Fernando Leal, Xavier Guerrero, Roberto Montenegro, and Dr. Atl. According to one art historian, Jacqueline Barnitz, "The artists faced two major challenges: that of introducing a new public monumental art requiring special technical skills, and that of creating an effective visual language for propaganda purposes." José Vasconcelos, the minister of education during the administration of President Álvaro Obregón. (1920-1924), set out quite pointedly to incorporate and indoctrinate the masses through public art. Vasconcelos sought to educate the mostly illiterate Mexican population about their country's culture and identity—in short, to make them Mexicans,

Siqueiros's manifesto of 1923 set out the muralists' goals: "the creators of beauty ..." must ensure that "their work presents a clear aspect of ideological propaganda." The muralists introduced workers and country people into their art on a grand scale and rewrote Mexican history in their enormous paintings on walls. The stairwell murals in the National Palace in the Zócalo (central plaza) of Mexico City depict Mexico's history from the conquest through the Cárdenas (1934-1940) era. Art, to the muralists, was inherently political. In a nation in flux during the 1920s, art seemed a way to help construct a sense of nationhood in a country blown apart during the previous decade's revolution.

During the 1930s, artists' concern for the lower classes intensified. In Mexico and Peru, indigenismo art took center stage as these nations struggled, as they had for centuries, over the place of the indigenous population in their societies. The Mexican muralists were the primary purveyors of the new indigenous image, which romanticized pre-Columbian civilizations and denigrated Spanish colonial culture. Indigenismo, both in art and literature and as a political problem, was a complex phenomenon. On one hand, intellectuals sought to extol the great heritages of the indigenous civilizations. On the other hand, modernizing upper classes saw Indians as backward rustics. At best, the more thoughtful members of the upper class sought to place the Indians in industrializing society. Pride in the accomplishments of native peoples dovetailed nicely with intensifying nationalism, which was a crucial aspect of populism, the political answer to the Social Question during the

1930s and 1940s. Nonetheless, to the upper and middle classes, modem indigenous people were impediments to progress.

Brazil had to confront its national and cultural identity not only in terms of indigenous, but of African peoples, as well. Traveling the path of the Mexican muralists, Tarsila do Amaral (1886-1973) returned from her European training in the early 1920s to paint the everyday existence of poor Brazilians, who comprised the nation's largest population. Another Brazilian painter, Candido Portinari (1903-1962), according to Barnitz, also depicted the "poor and the dispossessed, haggard and weak, with the staring eyes and distended stomachs of the malnourished."

During the 1920s, with a movement centered in Sao Paulo, modernist Brazilian artists ended the nation's denial of its past and set about incorporating it into a national culture. They rejected regionalism and sought to make Brazil Brazilian. Novelist Mario de Andrade became a leader of the search for what constituted "Brazilianness."

Similarly, sociologist Gilberto Freyre sought Brazilianness in the country's various traditions and regions. Brazil could be whole, he argued, only by allowing regional differences to flourish within the nation. Both men rejected foreign models, none of which had stood up to Brazilian requirements.

Conclusion

At the core of Latin American struggles during the first half of the twentieth century were economic and physical survival. Most people were poor and struggling day by day to survive. Although education and health care made great gains—more people were literate and they lived longer—Latin Americans' standards of living lagged far behind those of people living in Western Europe and the United States.

Latin Americans also grappled with the widespread effects of industrialization and urbanization. Everyday people, particularly in the countryside, fought to retain their cherished traditions and control over their daily lives. The onslaught of the factories, railroads, highways, telephone, radio, electricity, and centralized government, however, was too strong. Nonetheless, the urban and rural working classes and small landowners were remarkably independent and resilient. They selectively adopted new ways and adapted to new conditions. Their resistance to the dictates of the upper classes and military, however, caused the latter to seek drastic solutions to the decades-old Social Question. Two decades of violence and trauma ensued.

How Historians Understand

The Voice of the Lower Classes

The most difficult task historians confront is the construction of the past of the rural and urban lower classes. Mostly illiterate, they did not often record their own histories. The upper classes, whose fear of the masses we have discussed extensively in these pages, were in charge of governments, universities, and media and excluded the stories of those who were not of their own status in national histories. The less wellborn, among them the poor, country people, urban workers, and non-elite women, appeared in official history books only as no-account, lazy subjects of justifiable oppression, exotic objects of sympathy, criminals, or irrational protestors. As in the cases of the well-known Mexican historian Lucas Alamán and the liberal historians of nineteenth century Argentina and Chile, upper class fear and disdain of the lower classes was clearly evident.

Foreign visitors, the most famous of whom was Fanny Calderón de la Barca, the wife of the Minister of Spain to Mexico, who recorded her observations of nineteenth century Mexico, provided perhaps the best glimpses into the lives of everyday people. They tended, however, to see Latin Americans through the narrow focus of wealthy, white Europeans or North Americans, with their racism and condescension undisguised. Their bestselling books pictured half-naked gauchos and tropical villagers, noble at their best, savage at their worst.

Pressured by the events of periodic, violent upheavals during revolutions in Mexico (1910), Bolivia (1952), Cuba (1959), and Nicaragua (1979) and the challenges of Marxism, populism, and feminism, twentieth century historians of Latin America delved into the histories of lower class people. The first efforts used traditional methods, exploring national institutions, such as labor unions, which had records to consult.

Traditional sources seemed to furnish neither description nor insight. Newspapers of the day, unless in opposition to the government—and these were rare—hardly paid attention to the poor. Few treated the lower classes with any degree of fairness. Strikes, for example, newspapers reported as the result of the manipulations of outside agitators. Not many journalists explored the lives of the people driven to these radical actions.

In the 1960s, dismayed by the massacre of hundreds of civilian protestors in Mexico City by government secret police forces, and in the 1970s, horrified by the emergence of vicious, repressive military regimes in Argentina, Chile, and Brazil, historians pushed harder to write the stories of everyday people. Local records provided the sources for this history.

The best sources for the history of common people lie in judicial, police, notary, and municipal archives, located in villages, towns, and cities. In addition, most recently, historians have discovered illuminating materials in the records of large companies and from modern large estates. Foreign mining companies in Brazil and Chile, in particular, proved rich depositories. Most of the archives contain "official" documents, of course, which reflect biased views of events.

(continued)

(continued)

Historians, despite the difficult conditions in local archives, such as poor lighting and ventilation, the threat of dangerous parasites from dust, and uncooperative bureaucrats, discovered invaluable materials. Judicial archives, for example, contain the records of suits concerning marriage, criminal trials, tax protests, litigation between heirs, and land disputes. Notarial records reveal family economic holdings, wills, business transactions, and contracts. Police documents tell us crimes committed and by whom. Municipal records detail taxes, rules, and regulations, the activities and tactics of local officials, and the reactions of the citizenry to official actions.

Although police and court records are not always representative samples of the general population, by using them historians can uncover the extent of such activities as drunkenness, wife beating, prostitution, and banditry. They can also estimate the extent of government interference in everyday life in its efforts to discipline the lower classes.

The picture produced by these records is, of course, never complete, but they have created history where none had existed previously.

Latin American Lives

Frida Kahlo

Frida Kahlo (1907-1954) was a tortured artist famous for her striking self-portraits and her stormy marriage to muralist Diego Rivera. Long after her death at 47, she achieved celebrity for her incorporation of distinctively female concerns, such as reproduction, children, and family, into her paintings. Critics consider her avowedly feminist in her treatment of her own body. She, like Elvia Carrillo Puerto, was a prominent example of Mexico's "new" woman who defied convention. Kahlo reached cult status among feminists for her merging of personal emotions and politics.

Four factors determined her life: a terrible automobile accident that left her with a fractured spine and pelvis and constant pain throughout most of her life, her tumultuous marriage to Rivera, her inability to bear children, and her prodigious talent (though unrecognized, for the most part, while she was alive).

When she was 15, a bus she was riding collided with a trolley. The crash inflicted terrible injuries, which resulted in 35 hospitalizations and operations. The remainder of her life she spent in constant physical torment. Kahlo and Rivera married in 1929. They divorced in 1939 and remarried in 1940. They were international stars, consorting with world famous artists and leftist politicians and thinkers. Rivera's notorious philandering marred their dreamlike lives, though Frida, herself, had affairs as well.

Personally and professionally, Kahlo was in the forefront of the movement to incorporate popular culture into art. She was flamboyant in her dress, wearing the traditional garb of the women of Tehuantepec, the isthmus in southern Mexico, and styling her hair in indigenous coiffures with bows, combs, and flowers. She bedecked herself in jewelry. She was an avid collector of popular, folk, and pre-Columbian art. Her artistic work rooted in pre-Columbian and colonial sources. Some commentators regard her as the Mexican artist who best combined popular art with the "modernist avantgarde." The merger of her concerns as a woman and her feeling for country people manifest themselves in her painting *My Nurse* (1937), in which she suckles on the breasts of a dark skinned indigenous woman. In her most famous paintings, we can observe her obsessions with her pain, her love, and her barrenness. In her work *Raices (Roots,* 1943), she portrays herself with vines growing out of her chest as she lies in barren land. Despite her inability to bear children, she insists on herself as part of and a contributor to the "natural environment." In *El abrazo de amor del universo, la tierra* [Mexico], *Diego, yo y el senor Xolotl (The Love Embrace of the Universe, the Earth [Mexico], Diego, Me and Senor Xolotl)* (1949), she holds a baby with Diego's face in her arms, combining both her obsession with motherhood and her love of her husband. *Las Dos Fridas (The Two Fridas,* 1939) resulted from her divorce from Rivera. The two women depict her traditional and urbane sides, only the former loved by Diego.

In the male dominated art world, Frida Kahlo was unappreciated until the 1980s, when her striking depictions of motherhood and her body fit into the new feminist art history. Some historians, however, have criticized the treatment of her as a victim, obsessed with her physical and emotional pain. Overlooked, they maintain, is "her active role in the formulation of the language of art, which questioned neocolonial values." Interpreted as '"the other,' the feminine and the unconscious," critics marginalized her in a similar way in which Latin America finds itself made exotic. Kahlo, however, does not interpret Mexican women (or herself) as victims, but rather as "an assertive presence with the power of life and death."

Slice of Life

Village Life in Peru

Historian Florencia Mallon extensive research in the villages of the neighboring Yanamarca and Mantaro Valleys, in the central highlands of Peru, illuminates the lives of rural people. The land is fertile and well-watered by the Yanamarca and Mantaro rivers. The area lies on the major transportation routes to both important mining regions and the tropics, which meant that the mines furnished a market for the area's livestock and produce.

Small to medium-size farms, proprietors of which enlisted the help of family labor to grow alfalfa, wheat, and vegetables, predominated in the region at the beginning of the twentieth century. In the higher altitudes around the valley, where the holdings were much larger, people raised livestock and grew potatoes and quinoa, drawing labor from local villages.

Some proprietors owned plots in three zones: the humid lowlands located in the center of the valley, the valley slopes, and the flat lands on the other side of the mountains. This practice replicated the ancient Incas' approach to farming and commerce. To illustrate how the country people diversified, Mallon tells us the story of Jacoba Arias, an Indian who spoke only Quechua, from Acolla in the Yanamarca Valley. She owned 14 hectares (2.47 acres = 1 hectare) divided into small parcels scattered in different growing regions. She had 40 sheep, 3 teams of oxen, 6 bulls, and a cow. These animals provided the family with milk, cheese, meat, and lard, as well as wool for her family's clothes. She also owned 3 mules, which allowed her to engage in small-scale commerce.

Farming the valley's slopes was no easy task. The environment often changed radically even within a single plot, resulting in variations in soil and climate. Farmers had to understand their land and to adapt their methods and crops according to the soil composition, the temperature, and the amount of sunlight and rain. Families also adjusted to the needs of the farm and the capabilities of their members. Young children and the elderly tended the livestock because these duties required less arduous work. No one wasted time. The shepherds, for instance, spun wool thread while they watched the flock.

Family farmers diversified their economic activities to make ends meet. Agricultural work was seasonal with everyone participating in planting and harvest. Spinning thread, weaving, and household chores were major year round tasks. Some men, usually those who were young and single, worked in the mines or as muleteers, transporting goods, during the offseason. Others made handicrafts, such as shawls, hats, ponchos, blankets, or woodcarvings. In good years of an agricultural surplus, farmers purchased extras, perhaps coca and alcohol. In bad years, the family sold handicrafts or even some livestock.

Agriculture was a risky enterprise under the best of circumstances. An early frost, hail, or too little or too much rain could bring disaster. Because family size was not planned, inheritance eventually divided the land into such small plots that no single family could subsist on them. Some families augmented their property's produce by working the farms of other owners in return for splitting the harvest between them. Some families tended other livestock owners' animals in return for half the newborn sheep or cattle. Another arrangement

(continued)

(continued)

included cooperation between a farming household and a livestock-raising household: The latter's sheep fertilized the fields of the former, and the two families tended to and shared the crops.

God-parenthood enhanced cooperation among local families. On the occasions of a baby's first haircut, baptism, marriage, and roofing of a new house, children obtained six godparents, who, tied with the bonds of affection and respect, looked out for them in difficult times. Usually, one of the families was better off, but the arrangement worked to the benefit of both families because the wealthier had access to labor (and perhaps political support), while the less affluent could expect assistance in case of poor harvests or conflicts.

Governance in each village in the region consisted of two or more administrative units with their own officials. These entities oversaw community projects such as cleaning the irrigation ditches or planting community fields. There were also *cofradias*, religious lay brotherhoods that sponsored the local saint's celebrations. Each of these organizations had a mayordomo to administer the celebration. He had to pay for the expenses not covered by the income from cofradia lands. The people of the community came together in these shared tasks. There was, of course, always conflict, ranging from petty arguments to serious disputes over landownership.

Natures's Way

Mexico City Earthquake, 1985

The Mexico City earthquake of 1985, like the Nicaraguan quake in 1972, was a classic example of government failure that ultimately led to the end of a long-term regime. While unlike Nicaragua, it did not stimulate an armed revolution, the event spawned a wide range of popular movements.

Mexico City experienced two earthquakes, one and a half days apart on September 19 and 20, the first of which rated 8.1 on the Richter scale and the second 7.3. The quake hit hardest in the central zones of the city, which built over water-saturated subsoil that once was a lakebed. The oldest, poorest sections of the capital suffered the greatest damage, but the ruin was everywhere. The official count of the dead was 7,000. It was more likely that 12,000 to 15,000 was the minimum number and some estimate as many as 20,000 perished. More than 100,000 buildings collapsed. Ruins lined the streets of the Avenida Juárez and the Paseo de la Reforma, the great avenues of the city. Mangled widow frames and glass hung precariously from skyscrapers. One of the casualties was the Hotel Del Prado across from the Almeida Park, where the stunning mural by Diego Rivera *Dream of Sunday Afternoon in the Almeida Central* had a prominent place on the wall of the lobby. Fortunately, the government rescued the mural. The Hotel Regis, another landmark, was a heap of rubble.

In response to the devastation, the one party state, run by the Institutionalized Revolutionary Party (PRI) sputtered and stumbled. Despite the clear distress of the people, the powerful President of Mexico Miguel de la Madrid disappeared for two days. When he finally showed his face, he downplayed the disaster and refused international assistance. The government failed. Whatever aid it distributed went only to loyal PRI supporters. One observer wrote: the earthquake...switched on the light to see the fragility and corruption of the system...."

The victims, known as damnificados, in spite of the government's seeming indifference organized, first to rescue people from the rubble and then to rebuild. In the first month forty local groups formed and joined in the Unified Coordinator of the Damnificados (CUD) in order to exert pressure on the one-party state to provide desperately needed assistance. The PRI responded at least to the immediate requirement of the residents of the central areas of the city, expropriating properties in the badly damaged sections to prevent landlords from evicting tenants. The CUD succeeded in pushing the government to build 45,000 new housing units.

The most striking project in the reconstruction took place in El Centro, where in 2002 the government partnered with billionaire Carlos Slim to renovate old properties, construct pedestrian malls, and install a new telecommunications system. The government also accomplished considerable improvements in creating monitoring and emergency response systems.

(continued)

(continued)

The criticisms of the government response are considerable. First, the renovation of the downtown had the perhaps unanticipated consequence of driving up rents and causing an outflow of the poorer residents. The government attempted to attract people to the core city through the "Bando Dos" program, but this, too, pushed up prices. Some owners sold their properties profitably and moved to the cheaper outskirts. Second, the vast preponderance of the reconstruction took place in the central districts; the government ignored the peripheral barrios. The government did nothing to regulate or formalize the informal settlements on the periphery. They remain as dangerous as ever. Cinderblock housing does not stand up well in an earthquake.

Some observers claim that 1985, similarly to the 1968 slaughter at Tlatelolco, was a step in the democratization of Mexico. It led directly to the formation of the Party of the Democratic Revolution (PDR) in 1988 in opposition to the PRI. Three decades later, however, nothing remains of the grassroots movements the earthquake engendered.

8

The Search for a Better Way, 1959 to the Present

The post-World War II promise of equitable politics and societies and prosperous economies remained unfulfilled in Latin America until the advent of a new millennium. The hopes of the years after 2000 though were short-lived, less than two decades of unprecedented achievements seemed dissipated by 2020. The questions remained constant. Who was to rule, how, and for whom? Would the wealthy and powerful willingly share with those who had neither riches nor influence? Were Latin American nations in control of their fates or were the trends of world markets and political and economic rivalries too great to overcome? For much of this period, no answers appeared, only failed formulas, tired politicians, angry, impatient military officers, and an endless series of lying, ultimately corrupt populists. Among politicians, saints were a rare breed and sinners were legion. However, despite these disillusionments, the political landscape changed substantially. The electorate expanded enormously. Women won full suffrage at long last. Governments eliminated literacy qualifications for political participation. How these transformations were to affect Latin America remains unresolved.

In the 1950s, grappling with the pressures of the nascent cold war and the disappointment of slow economic growth, Latin Americans turned to a cohort of old, former dictators, such as Carlos Ibáñez in Chile and Getúlio Vargas in Brazil, whose policies and practices failed earlier, or looked to new strongmen, as in Colombia and Venezuela. All of them failed. The victory of the 26th of July Movement in Cuba in 1959, its subsequent adoption of communism, and its close alliance with the Soviet Union, struck fear into the military-upper class alliance in the region. The combination of the threat of upheaval from below (echoes of the nineteenth century) and the uncertainties of

© The Author(s), under exclusive license to Springer Nature Switzerland AG 2022
M. Wasserman, *Modern Latin America Since 1800*,
https://doi.org/10.1007/978-3-030-96185-5_8

economic development strategies pushed the region into an era of darkness. During the twenty years that followed the Cuban Revolution, the Latin American Left experienced unprecedented success. Chileans elected Socialist Dr. Salvador Allende as president (1970–1973) and the Sandinista Revolution in Nicaragua (1979–1990) held power for a full decade. Major leftist insurgencies arose in Colombia, El Salvador, Guatemala, and Peru. The Salvadoran and Peruvian rebellions came within a hairbreadth of victory. Politics then polarized into brutal violence. Leftist guerrillas staged robberies and kidnappings, attacked police, and bombed buildings, and, in response, Latin American militaries embarked on a vicious reign of terror. The nightmare of terror and civil wars ended only in the mid-1990s. Vestiges remained in Central America into the 2010s. 2000's people went left.

The armed forces and their right wing allies (in some countries including the clergy and hierarchy of the Catholic Church) proved as incapable and corrupt as the politicians they disdained. Humiliated by battlefield defeat or scandal, often frustrated by their inability to foster economic growth, the military withdrew from direct governmental control in the 1980s, pushed out by the citizens of the nations they had ruled so badly. In the late 1990s and early 2000s, after an interim of wobbly democracy, still troubled by seemingly insurmountable poverty and severely inequitable income distribution, much of Latin America turned leftward once again. Many Latin American nations elected left-of-center leaders in what we know as the "Pink Tide." ("Pink" indicated left, but not so far left as to be communists or "reds.") After what appeared to be a series of striking successes in ameliorating poverty and installing responsible governments, by 2020 economic setbacks ended the leftward trend.

In the years after 1959, most Latin American regimes pursued policies of Import Substitution Industrialization (ISI). This required governments to protect nascent industries and often to invest heavily in sectors where private capital was unwilling to finance. ISI vastly increased the level of government intervention in the economy. Ironically, the right-wing take-over accelerated rather than curtailed government involvement. Gradually, though, it became evident that ISI failed. Starting with the Pinochet military government in Chile in 1973, Latin America embraced free market economics. With the collapse of communism in the Soviet Union and Eastern Europe in the late 1980s, no viable left alternative to capitalism was evident. By the end of the century, it was all too clear that the solutions of both left and right were unmitigated disasters for the middle and working class. ISI, state intervention, free market or neo-liberal models failed. What emerged next was a compromise, pioneered in part by Brazil in the 1990s, that followed the prevalent neo-liberal strategies, opening up the economies and shrinking government involvement, while simultaneously adopting programs to alleviate poverty and enhance health care and education. These policies were successful for several years until global economic downturns struck in 2008 and 2020.

The Revolutions: Cuba, Central America, Peru, and Colombia

[handwritten: Batista ruled after revolution and came back when politics failed after world war.]

Cuba

Some considerable controversy exists about the effect of the Cuban Revolution on Latin America. On one hand, some argue that it shattered the fragile political equilibrium of the region, because it introduced a new set of factors into Latin American political equations. According to this view, the (so-called) loss of Cuba to communism mobilized the United States' efforts in the area. Fidel Castro's call to revolution intensified the fears of the upper class-military alliance. Not coincidently, insurgencies rose all over Latin America in the 1960s and 1970s. On the other hand, some maintain that strictly domestic considerations instigated the events of these times. Certainly, "Che" Guevara and Castro became icons of the left, but they did not cause the various insurgencies. These were times of upheaval all over the world. Young people rose up everywhere against inequities and unfairness. Cuba and the other rebel movements in Latin America were parts of a wider phenomenon. More important, the elites of Latin America (and the middle classes, as well) distrusted, even feared, the popular classes dating from the independence era. The difference in the twentieth century was that elites no longer needed popular class support. They had a professional military to back them. If they operated dictatorships, they no longer needed popular electoral support either.

In the 1950s, Cuba seemed an unlikely location for a revolution. Only ninety miles from Florida, tied tightly economically to the United States, for American tourists and investment flooded the island and the United States was the largest market for Cuba's sugar, its people were among the best educated, healthiest, and wealthiest in Latin America. The island also had a seemingly invincible dictator in Fulgencio Batista. Batista dominated Cuban politics for a decade after the revolution of 1933. Then, after a number of years in comfortable, voluntary exile in Florida, he returned to the island in 1952, as one of the cohort of Latin American leaders who returned to power in the wake of the political failures after the end of the world war. As Vargas *how Castro invaded Cuba↓*

and Ibánez found to their chagrin, the second time was not easy. He hoped to regenerate Cuba, but his squelching of democracy and the rampant corruption of his regime alienated many.

Fidel Castro was one of Batista's earliest opponents. A veteran of the rough and tumble politics of the time, he proved a persistent enemy. On 26 July 1953, Castro led a small band in a disastrous attack on the army barracks at Moncada on the southern part of the island. The authorities captured him and he barely escaped execution. After two years in prison, during which he wrote his famous tract, "History Will Absolve Me," Castro received amnesty and then moved to Mexico, where he plotted and raised money for an invasion of Cuba. He returned in late 1956. He hid in the mountains in southwestern Cuba, establishing a small guerrilla band. The seemingly impossible happened, when the regime crumbled, as the movement grew stronger. The rebellion culminated, when Castro and his rebel army rolled into Havana January 1, 1959.

Castro was nothing, if not a student of Cuban history. He observed how during previous rebellions—the war for independence in 1898 and the uprisings of 1933—the United States suborned the movements, and politicians gave in to opportunities to enrich themselves rather than improve the lives of the people. He proclaimed, "This time the revolution is for real." Barely thirty-two, the oldest of the rebel leadership, Castro confronted multiple challenges. First, the 26th of July Movement had to consolidate its position. Other rebel groups and leaders sought a share of the victory. Second, the revolutionaries' youthful enthusiasm, dedication, and forbearance stood them in good stead as guerrillas in the sierras, but they had no experience in governance. They had no plan. Castro desperately needed reliable allies. Third, and perhaps most important over the long term, Castro had to find a way to neutralize the inevitable opposition of the United States. Castro resolved these difficulties in the early 1960s. Rival leaders almost magically disappeared. Most crucially, he proclaimed a socialist revolution, took on the Communist Party as a partner, broke relations with the United States, and allied with the Soviet Union.

These actions brought the Revolution almost immediately into two confrontations with the United States, which ultimately solidified his hold on Cuba. In April 1961, his army defeated an informal force of U.S.-trained and supported Cuban exiles, who invaded the island at the Bay of Pigs, making him a greater hero than previously. Then, in October 1962, the United States and the Soviet Union came close to war, when the Soviets installed offensive intercontinental ballistic missiles in Cuba. The United States Navy blockaded Cuba to prevent the arrival of additional missiles. A tense thirteen days of negotiations ensued before the superpowers reached accommodation with the Soviets removing the missiles in return for an American pledge not to invade the island. The United States, however, maintained an embargo on trade with Cuba for the next half century.

The Cuban Revolution, a regime in power to this day, met with mixed success. The twin pillars of its economic program over the first two decades were marked failures. One of the main goals was to decrease dependency on one export crop, sugar. Another was to create a "New Socialist" Cuban who would labor for the general good not individual gain. Sugar production plummeted during the first decade, but then the government reemphasized sugar production to supply the communist nations of Eastern Europe. The New Socialist proved unachievable as individual productivity dropped precipitously because of this policy. Castro then created a Soviet-style bureaucracy notable for its inefficiency and inflexibility. None of this fit well with his personal style, which led him to a series of erratic experiments with free markets and private enterprise. What saved Cuba economically was the Soviet subsidy of perhaps a billion dollars a year, mainly through the purchase of the sugar harvest. The loss of this support when communism collapsed created an enormous crisis in Cuba. Since then periodic shortages of staples and rationing were common. Nickel exports and tourism, most from Europe, have augmented the economy in recent times. In the years since 2000, the Cuban economy experienced one period of sustained growth from 2004 to 2009, but only unimpressive increases from 2010 on. Although private enterprise expanded, the government remains the major factor in the economy. Despite the almost constant hardships, Cubans are the best-educated and healthiest people in Latin America and they have the most equitable distribution of wealth in the Hemisphere.

Fidel Castro ruled Cuba until 2007, when he passed the leadership on to his brother Raúl. Fidel died in 2016. Raúl Castro was head of state until 2018, when he stepped down in favor of Miguel Díaz Canel. Cuba and the United States resumed diplomatic relations in 2014. Efforts to improve relations with the United States halted with the Trump administration (2017–2021).

↑ cuban revolution: 1) not rely on exports
Central America 2) create new socialist cuba

The prolonged guerrilla insurgencies that persisted in Central America from the 1970s through the 1990s resulted in the deaths of hundreds of thousands and the displacement and immigration of millions more. Although by 2000 the region experienced relative peace, the impact of the wars continued in the economic depression and the departure of millions more in search of better lives. The violence in El Salvador, Honduras, and Guatemala persisted to the terror of the population. In two of the three nations that experienced prolonged civil war, Nicaragua and El Salvador, former rebel groups eventually came to govern through elections. Neither obtained particular success, as economies either stagnated or grew at a slow pace, outward migration continued, and extreme poverty reached the highest levels in Latin America. Violence persisted to an extent unparalleled almost anywhere else in the world.

The left guerrillas won on the battlefield only in Nicaragua. In 1979, the Sandinista National Liberation Front (FSLN) overthrew Anastasio Somoza Debayle, whose brother and father before him ruled the country for a total of over four decades. The Sandinistas, then, became the only leftist revolution to lose control over the government in fair elections in 1989. In yet another first, they returned to power through elections in 2007.

The origins of the Nicaraguan revolution lay in the catastrophic earthquake that leveled Managua, the capital, in 1972. The Somozas misappropriated the relief funds that poured in from abroad, adding to their already enormous wealth, derived from the various criminal enterprises they operated with the National Guard (*Guardia Nacional*). The FSLN, comprised of rural people, students and disillusioned children of the middle and upper classes, organized in opposition appalled at the greed and impunity. Six years later, Somoza went too far even for the upper classes, which supported his family for decades, when he ordered the assassination of longtime rival Pedro Joaquín Chamorro. The FSLN raided and occupied the national palace that same year, indicating to all that the regime lost its iron grip on the country. Nonetheless, Somoza's hold was such that it took another seven years to oust him. He fled in July 1979, but not until he sacrificed 50,000 lives in a brief, bloody effort to retain his power.

The Sandinistas ruled for the next decade, but theirs was a troubled regime. For the first five years, the FSLN governed without an election. In 1984, Daniel Ortega, the leader of the FSLN, won the presidency. Tragically for Nicaragua, the United States, under the administration of Ronald Reagan, was implacably opposed to the FSLN and funded, secretly and illegally, the opposition, known as the *Contras*. The American-backed civil war cost another 40,000 Nicaraguan lives and severely damaged the country's economy. In 1989, the two warring groups reached a peace agreement.

Much like the Cuban revolutionaries twenty years before, the Sandinistas blundered badly in their administrative and economic policies. To make matters worse, the ongoing civil war badly disrupted business and cost billions of dollars in damages. The military draft instituted in order to fight the Contra war proved extremely unpopular. Nicaraguan mothers loudly objected to their children going to war. Perhaps, the most critical mistake of the Sandinista male leadership was the failure to incorporate fully women. The FSLN could not have won without the efforts of its women leaders. Much of their guerrilla leadership was female, and they endured the horrors of combat, rape, torture, and wounds. Nonetheless, many of these heroes felt dismissed and disdained after 1979. The massive loss of women's support played a large role in the defeat in the 1989 election.

Opposition candidate Violeta Barrios de Chamorro, the widow of the martyred Pedro Joaquín Chamorro, whose death had contributed to the victory of the revolution, won the presidency in 1989. Nicaraguan voters, exhausted by ten years of war, sought an alternative to the ineffective Sandinistas. The Sandinistas nonetheless remained the predominant political party, although Nicaraguans chose successive conservative presidents in 1996 and 2002, marking in the former instance the first time the office changed hands peacefully in Nicaraguan history. In the midst of the Pink Tide in 2006, Daniel Ortega staged a stunning comeback and then won reelection in 2011 and 2016. Unfortunately, the second act of the Sandinistas repeated the corruption and oppression of the Somozas. The Sandinista regime grew more and more repressive through 2021 with many political opponents jailed or forced into exile.

In El Salvador the nation's troubles originated in the brutal dictatorship of General Maximiliano Hernández Martínez (1930–1944), who rose to power in the aftermath of the infamous Matanza massacre of 300,000 Salvadorans in 1930. An alliance of wealthy coffee planters and the military succeeded him, maintaining their control through electoral fraud and repression. Guerrillas appeared in the 1960s. El Salvador held its first truly open election in 1972, but when it became clear that opposition candidate, moderate José Napoleón Duarte, won, the government nullified the results. Twelve years later, a new, legitimate election took place and Duarte won again. However, the military-upper class alliance continued to dominate the country. Between 1979 and 1989, the Agustín Farabundo Martí Front for National Liberation (FMLN) with an estimated 8000 combatants fought a civil war that came close to overthrowing the government. Only the massive assistance the United States provided the Salvadoran army prevented its defeat. Exhausted by a quarter century of fighting, Salvadorans elected as President Alfredo Cristiani of the National Republican Alliance (ARENA), a coalition of right wing groups. Much as Nicaraguans, Salvadorans turned to the Right to bring peace. Cristiani reached a ceasefire agreement with the FMLN in 1991. Three ARENA presidents succeeded one another in 1994, 1999, and 2004. In 2009, Salvadorans elected Maurisio Funas, a member of the FMLN as president. Another FMLN president succeeded him in 2014. In 2019, Salvadorans rejected candidates from both major parties and instead chose Nayib Bukele of the Grand Alliance for National Unity (GANA), who received fifty-three percent of the votes. The failures of both the right and left to lift the country from extreme levels of poverty and violence were all too obvious.

The guerrilla war and right counter-reaction was the most violent and most prolonged in Guatemala, where nearly four decades of fighting caused 200,000 deaths and perhaps millions more dislocations. Like El Salvador, Guatemala's nightmares began with the fall of a long-time dictator. A reformist group of young military officers overthrew Jorge Ubico (1930–1944) in 1944. They embarked on a program of widespread reforms that included the expropriation of uncultivated lands owned by the U.S.-based United Fruit Company. As a result, the U.S. Central Intelligence Agency fomented a successful revolt, led by a somewhat dimwitted Colonel Carlos Castillo Armas. He and his successors reversed all of the reforms of the previous decade. In 1960, probably heartened, as were the FSLN and the FMLN, by the Cuban revolution, a guerrilla movement that called themselves the Rebel Armed Forces took up arms. The military ruled behind the scenes for a decade and then for another decade generals governed as presidents, waging a campaign of murder and terror in an effort to eradicate the rebels. Death squads roamed the countryside committing what amounted to genocide among indigenous communities. Through a series of presidents, the war continued until 1996, when the government reached an accord with the guerrillas. A succession of elected presidents followed. Most notable was retired general Otto Pérez Molina (2012–2015), who resigned in an enormous scandal that engendered huge street protests. Entertainer Jimmy Morales succeeded him. As in in the other countries of Central America, repressive violence, poverty, and corruption accompanied erratic, mostly modest economic growth.

Economic and social conditions steadily worsened in Guatemala, El Salvador, and Honduras, the so-called Northern Triangle, during the 2010s with escalating violence and high unemployment. Desperate people from this area migrated in unprecedented numbers first to Mexico and then north hoping to find a better life in the United States. The mass of emigrants caused enormous disruptions in Mexico and became a highly controversial political issue in the United States.

Peru

From the late 1960s through the 1990s, Peru endured three distinct revolutionary movements. The first in 1968 consisted of reformist military officers who implemented far-reaching reforms. Second, during the 1980s and 1990s, a violent guerrilla organization terrorized the country, nearly toppling the government. The third upheaval occurred, when the president who had defeated the guerrillas ruled as an elected dictator in order to rebuild the economy. The first and last were more coups than revolutions, neither accompanied by prolonged violence. All three centered on a single leader and dissipated after his demise.

Each of the revolutions resulted from a long-term, frustrating impasse in Peruvian politics that pitted the military-upper class alliance against APRA and its leader Victor Raúl Haya de la Torre. The precipitating event for this series of upheavals was the election of 1962, which caused the military to stage a coup to prevent Haya de la Torre from becoming president. In a new election Fernando Belaunde Terry (1963–1968) won, but then governed ineffectively, paving the way for another coup, led by General Juan Velasco Alvarado, who set out to establish a "third way," neither communism nor capitalism. Velasco presided over one of the few leftist, military regimes in Latin American history. From 1968 to 1975, he redistributed more land than either the Mexican or Bolivian Revolutions, giving over half the nation's land to 375,000 families, one quarter of all rural dwellers. Velasco vastly expanded the government role in the economy, financing his program through massive borrowing abroad. The reform era ended, however, when Velasco became sick and stepped down. His successor Francisco Morales Bermúdez reversed some of the reforms and adopted austerity policies in order to repay the nation's debt. Belaunde won a new election and returned to the presidency in 1980, but had little to show for his term (1980–1985). Most important, however, was that during these years the *Sendero Luminoso* (Shining Path) guerrillas emerged.

The guerrilla movement revolved around a former university professor, Abimael Guzmán, the self-proclaimed "Fourth Sword of Marxism." (Marx, Lenin, and Mao were the first three.) The Sendero began in 1970 as a splinter group from the already fragmented Peruvian Communist Party. The name derived from a quote of José Carlos Mariátegui, the country's leading communist intellectual, who stated "Marxism-Leninism will open a shining path to revolution." Guzmán dismissed other Latin American leftists as traitors. He called the Cuban Revolution, for example, "a petty bourgeois, militaristic deviation." He advocated extreme violence. The Sendero as a purposeful strategy murdered thousands of political officials, small landowners, and so-called do-gooders. The brutality intimidated many Peruvians, but at the same time earned the undying enmity of many others.

The Senderos's organization was extremely disciplined and cohesive, in part because it offered opportunities their adherents did not have otherwise.

Sendero drew its strength from young people with poverty-stricken backgrounds in the countryside and the shantytowns of Lima. Many of these youths achieved a university education only to find that neither the government nor the private sector could provide them with satisfactory employment. The Sendero paid its soldiers well, making them an appealing alternative. The guerrillas were relatively egalitarian, as women comprised half its leadership. At its strongest, Sendero had perhaps 10,000 under arms and another 100,000 sympathizers.

By 1992, Sendero Luminoso demoralized Peru and brought it to the brink of collapse. The war cost 30,000 deaths, the military seemed to disintegrate, and panic gripped the nation. Then, on September 12, 1992, the tide turned, when the army unexpectedly captured Guzmán and much of the Sendero leadership. Without its highest echelons, the movement fell apart. Guzmán remains in prison.

The third of the Peruvian revolutions occurred in 1990, when Peruvians, desperate for a savior as the Sendero devastated the country, elected a little known figure, Alberto Fujimori, president (1990–2000). He brought an end the threat from the Sendero and supervised a period of substantial economic growth. However, in 2000 he was involved in corruption scandals, fled to Japan, and resigned from his office. Fujimori eventually returned to Peru, after which the courts convicted him, and he currently is incarcerated. The next year Peru elected its first indigenous president Alejandro Toledo (2001–2006). He and his successors Alan García (2006–2011), and Ollanta Humala (2011–2016) presided over centrist governments that worked within neoliberalism, which produced sustained high economic growth, reduced poverty, and low inflation. Unfortunately, scandal caused the next president Pedro Pablo Kucynski to resign in 2019. From 2019 to 2021 Peru had four presidents.

Colombia

The longest guerrilla war in Latin America endured in Colombia from 1964 until 2017. The Colombian government during this time often was near collapse, but it never went over the brink. Colombians appeared inured to some extent to cruel political warfare, for prolonged, bitter civil conflicts marred their history. The precursor to the guerrilla war, *La Violencia*, devastated the country from 1948 to 1958, when Liberals fought against Conservatives, resulting in the deaths of 300,000. The two parties ended the conflict in 1958, forming the National Front and agreeing to alternate presidential terms. One of the guerrilla remnants of the struggle evolved into the Revolutionary Armed Forces of Colombia (FARC). Other guerrilla groups formed in the later 1960s.

The guerrilla struggle and the underlying instability of Colombian politics resulted from two factors, the inequitable distribution of land in the countryside that worsened because of the policies instituted during the 1970s, and the closed political system that did not allow peaceful protest. The guerrilla groups expanded their numbers in the 1970s in response, organizing in remote regions, often newly colonized by peasants who cultivated coca. After a period of relative peace during the early 1980s, warfare resumed resulting in 300,000 more deaths and two million people displaced through 2002. (Some estimates calculate half as many deaths, but twice as many displacements.) Right-wing paramilitary, some allegedly financed by *narcotraficante* Pablo Escobar, contested the guerrillas. Assassinations and kidnappings were rampant.

Colombians elected Álvaro Uribe president in 2002 and 2006 and he and his successor Juan Manuel Santos (2010–2018) followed a dual policy of battling the FARC, while engaging in peace negotiations. The warring parties signed a ceasefire in 2016. Santos won the Nobel Peace Prize. A plebiscite rejected the first formal peace agreement, but subsequently, the government and FARC renegotiated. The war ended, though violence among criminal groups and right wing militias continues. Ivan Duque succeeded to the presidency in 2018.

Colombia confronted a new crisis, when more than a million refugees from Venezuela poured over the border to escape the latter's crumbling economy.

The Tyrannies: Brazil, Argentina, and Chile

right— military

In response to the successive failures of populism, during the 1930s and 1940s, the reprise of old dictators in the 1950s, and the renewed democracies in the 1950s and 1960s, combined with the threat of revolution from below, exemplified by Cuba in the 1960s, the nations of the Southern Cone and Brazil fell victims to the prolonged rule of rightist, military governments that seized power illegally and maintained control through the employment of terror and murder. Latin America, to be sure, endured military regimes in the past, but those that arose in the 1960s and 1970s were different, for they determined to remain in charge indefinitely and to remake their societies, employing all means necessary to restore traditional, patriarchal values with women subordinate to men, dedicated exclusively to caring for children and home. The military regimes ruthlessly eliminated leftist organizations, including political parties and labor unions, and targeted especially university students and faculty. Tens of thousands of people" disappeared." Even a larger number suffered imprisonment and torture. The military, police, and paramilitary "death squads" spared no one, rich or poor, men, women, and children, bureaucrats, priests, and nuns. Most citizens of these countries looked the other way in the face of the terror, some undoubtedly afraid for their own safety, others perhaps more in dread of a leftist takeover than the loss of their freedom.

As in the past, the armed forces and the upper and middle classes were the pillars of the rightist regimes. These groups were not always in accord, but united in the common fear of the left. To these we add two other supports. First, the United States government looked to the Latin American militaries as the last bastion against communism in the midst of a resurgent Cold War. Second, a new class developed of well-educated technocrats, who operated the expanding government bureaucracies and multiplying state-owned enterprises. The technocrats and military together created a political structure known as "bureaucratic authoritarianism."

The rightist regimes pursued an economic strategy that sought to encourage foreign investment, attracting it by keeping wages low. Their policies protected and enhanced the fortunes of the domestic upper classes, often to the detriment of the middle classes. Two ironies emerged. First, the supposedly conservative regimes expanded government ownership of various industries. Second, despite the advent of the technocrats, these government enterprises were inefficient and shockingly corrupt.

All of the military dictatorships were brutal. Brazil and Chile experienced a degree of temporary economic success. The others were abject failures. Brazil lasted the longest, twenty-one years, while Argentina seventeen, Chile sixteen, and Uruguay eleven. All crushed the purposefully overestimated guerrilla insurgencies that opposed them and virtually eliminated left of center political organizations. Each bequeathed a difficult, though ultimately successful, transition to democracy. In no case has the military returned to power.

Brazil

Brazil was the first country to fall to the right in 1964. Three tumultuous years preceded, during which an eccentric independent Janio Quadros won election as president (1961), only to resign a few months later, succeeded by the vice-president Joao Goulart, once a close ally of former dictator Getulio Vargas. Goulart was on shaky ground. He came to office only after agreeing to accept a conversion to a parliamentary system that limited his authority. A plebiscite restored his powers in 1963. He then proposed reform legislation that Congress rejected. Massive demonstrations took over the streets in Rio de Janeiro. Some sectors of the military primed to take over. The armed forces previously staged several failed coup attempts from the early 1950s. With Goulart obviously weakened, they struck in April 1964.

The military governments led by General Humberto de Alcantar Castello Branco (1964–1967) and General Artur de Costa e Silva (1967–1969) issued a series of Institutional Acts that severely limited civil rights. They also adopted wage-suppression-foreign investment economic development policies. President Emílio Garrastazú Médici (1969–1974) presided over the so-called Brazilian "Economic Miracle." He also intensified the war on left guerrillas who rose in opposition to the harsh regime. After nearly two decades, the elimination of the left complete, the military government proved as inept and corrupt as its civilian predecessors. Growing unpopularity led to a gradual transition to democracy known as the "*abertura.*" The Brazilian military, despite its long tenure was not as murderous as either the Chileans or Argentines.

The eight years of transition were difficult. The first elected president in two decades, Tancredo Neves (1985), died after two weeks in office. His successor José Sarney (1985–1990) served out his term despite economic hardship, which included cataclysmic inflation. The next president, Fernando de Collor (1990–1992), resigned amidst scandal. Democracy went back on track at long-last with the election of Fernando Henrique Cardoso (1995–2002), an internationally known sociologist, who previously served as Foreign Minister and Finance Minister. The Brazilian military remained out of politics since the mid-1980s.

Argentina

[handwritten: right]

[handwritten: Peronist, radicals, military]

The worst of the terror occurred in Argentina. The armed forces seemed more insular and more disdainful of civilian politicians than even their counterparts in the Southern Cone. The antagonisms between the major political parties, the Peronists (followers of Juan Perón, formally the Justicialista Party) and the Radicals (which split into two in the 1960s) and the military were an insurmountable obstacle to sustained democratic politics for more than three decades. The military overthrew Juan Perón in 1955. Even though he was one of them, the high command of the armed forces, especially the navy, alienated from him both because his popularity derived from his pro-labor policies and because they disapproved of his personal life. During two decades in exile in

Spain, the threat of his return was their nightmare. The Radicals equally disapproved of the Peronists and the military had no love for the Radicals. With the ban of the Peronists from 1955 to 1974 and the division of the Radicals, it was not possible for any candidate for president to win a majority vote. General Juan Carlos Onganía overthrew minority president Arturo Illia (1963–1966) in 1966. He set about to renovate society by outlawing political parties and expelling leftist students and faculty from the universities. In response, under the leadership of a coalition of auto workers and students in the interior city Córdoba, widespread protests erupted in May 1969. A guerrilla movement known as the *Montoneros* then staged a series of spectacular kidnappings. Even though the Montoneros proved ineffective and it turned out that one of their leaders was a government informant, their actions provoked an unprecedented, vicious response from rightwing death squads, sponsored by right-wing military and upper class. Successive military led governments presided over a disintegrating nation descending into murder and chaos. In desperation in 1974 the nation turned to Juan Perón, then seventy-eight years old and ailing. He won the presidential election, but lived for only a few months. His third wife María Estela Martínez de Perón ("Isabelita"), at his insistence the Vice-President, succeeded him. Neither Perón rescued Argentina.

The worst was yet to come. The military overthrew Isabelita in 1976. Argentina experienced the darkest chapter in its history from 1976 to 1983. The brutal rule of General Jorge Videla (1976–1981) replaced the due process of law with torture and murder. By 1978 the armed forces eradicated the guerrillas and most of the labor union leadership as far down as shop stewards. An estimated 30,000 people "disappeared," victims of the death squads, military, and police. The regime persecuted university faculty, disbanding whole departments it believed disruptive (psychology, for example) or Marxism-oriented. Horror stories of pregnant women thrown from helicopters into the South Atlantic abounded.

As in Brazil, however, the military proved incompetent and corrupt. As the economy deteriorated and their popularity plunged, the desperate generals went to war against Great Britain. In April 1982 Argentine forces occupied the Malvinas Islands in the South Atlantic, a territory which the British seized 150 years previously and which was in dispute ever since. President Leopoldo Galtieri (1981–1982) apparently misjudged the British response and the intentions of the United States. He evidently thought that Prime Minister Margaret Thatcher, since she was a woman, would not fight, and that President Ronald Reagan approved the action. The Argentine military suffered humiliating defeat and thoroughly discredited relinquished power. Argentine officers literally abandoned their troops on the battlefield.

Raúl Alfonsín (1983–1989), who long opposed the dictatorship, won the presidency in 1983. His was a difficult term, an enormous foreign debt and runaway inflation handicapped the economy and sectors of the military refused to accept the return to civilian rule, staging several failed revolts. Amnesty for the perpetrators of the terror remained a contentious issue. The Peronists, too, declined to cooperate. Nonetheless, Alfonsín began the healing. Although he left office six months early, he oversaw the first peaceful transition from one elected president to another since 1928. Peronist Carlos Menem succeeded him as president and served two terms. It is quite certain that as the hardest hit nation during the terror, Argentina took the longest to recover. Although the military did not regain power, it is not clear that it abandoned its pretensions as the nation's guardian.

Chile

While not as many "disappeared" in Chile as in Argentina, an estimated 3000 (Argentina had somewhat more than twice as many people, but murdered ten times the number as in Chile), the terror was equally as great and lasted longer. The dictatorship forever shattered Chile's reputation as the model Latin American democracy.

Like several other nations in South America, Chile turned to familiar names to solve its political and economic malaise in the 1950s, first former president Carlos Ibáñez (1952–1958), then the son of a former president Jorge Alessandri (1958–1964) with unsatisfactory results. With the left in the country growing stronger with each previous election, in 1964 the moderate and conservative parties joined to back Christian Democrat Eduardo Frei (1964–1970) against Socialist Dr. Salvador Allende. Despite considerable assistance from the U.S. Alliance for Progress, Frei failed to carry out a substantial reform program or pull the nation from the economic doldrums. In 1970 the center and conservative parties could not agree on a candidate, allowing for Allende to win the election with less than forty percent of the vote. The Chilean Congress approved his election, because the constitution required that if no candidate received a majority of the votes, Congress was to elect the president.

Allende was the first socialist head of state elected in Latin America. With only a plurality of support, a substantial number of Chileans suspicious of his policies, and a sector of the military bitterly opposed, the new president was

Allende failed
women opposed

on shaky ground from the beginning. Although he got off to a promising start, benefitting from high copper prices, winning local elections, and instituting a number of overdue reforms, he ultimately failed tragically. Allende was unable to win over the middle class on one hand or satisfy his radical supporters on the other. With middle class women protesting by banging pots and pans from their windows, peasants occupying lands in the countryside, workers taking over factories, and the upper classes and large corporations working in fierce opposition, Allende in retrospect was doomed. The military abandoned its long-proclaimed commitment to civilian constitutional rule and overthrew him on September 11, 1973. Allende died in the fighting.

The commander of the army General Augusto Pinochet led the coup and the dictatorship that went on for sixteen years. Pinochet, like his Argentine neighbors, set out to renovate society. The first step was to eliminate the Left. The military allies among the right instituted a reign of terror, imprisoning, torturing, and murdering thousands. Pinochet closed Congress, outlawed political parties, and eliminated labor unions. He also adopted neo-liberal economics, deregulating the economy and privatizing formerly government owned enterprises. His policies, like in the Brazilian case, resulted in boom times.

Chileans did not forget their democratic traditions. In a 1988 plebiscite they voted to end the Pinochet dictatorship. Patricio Alwyn won the presidential election in 1990 and Eduardo Frei Ruiz-Tagle succeeded him in 1994. The spectacular economic growth of the 1990s, averaging over seven percent a year, was a crucial factor in solidifying the transition from military rule.

Mexico: The End of the One-Party State

Unlike in the other major nations of Latin America, the military played a subordinate role in Mexico during the 1960s through the 1980s. The Mexican state, however, fought its own secret "dirty war" against the Left. It slaughtered protesters, assassinated rebel leaders, and intimidated any and all who contested the official party, the Party of the Institutionalized Revolution (PRI). Under the veneer of the Mexican "economic miracle" and regular elections, the one party regime bought off or repressed opposition and presided over widespread corruption. The formula of selective violence and patronage was quite successful. The regime's policies redistributed wealth downward from the upper income strata and upward from the lowest strata, bringing the middle class and skilled working class (represented by organized labor) a measure of prosperity.

The challenges to the PRI arose from two sectors, rural areas where access to land remained contested and independent labor unions unwilling to settle for what the PRI allowed in terms of wages and working conditions. The government often was willing to make concessions, though continued demands likely led to repression. A prime example was the case of Rubén Jaramillo, a peasant leader in Morelos, who rebelled on a number of occasions in a career that spanned four decades after the Revolution. During his last protest in 1962, federal soldiers assassinated him and his family.

By the early 1960s, after thirty years in power, the PRI lost touch with common folk and after withstanding a major strike of railroad workers and important demonstrations over water rights along the northwest border just a few years before, it apparently panicked when confronted with student protests in 1968. On October 2, 1968, unidentified police or military slaughtered an estimated five hundred unarmed demonstrators in the Plaza of Three Cultures in Tlatelolco, Mexico City. The regime stood exposed for what it really was. Nonetheless, it took thirty-two more years for Mexicans to vote out the PRI.

The discovery of vast oil reserves in the southeast, mostly along the Gulf coast, in the 1970s at first seemed an opportunity to renew Mexican economic growth, as the "miracle" faltered, and to maintain the PRI in power. The government, however, squandered the substantial revenue generated from petroleum production in an orgy of mismanaged spending and unprecedented corruption. It borrowed heavily abroad, based on future oil revenues. When oil prices fell and income plunged, Mexico confronted an enormous debt which it could not repay.

Mexico took the first halting steps to democratization in the early 1980s, when President Miguel de la Madrid (1982–1988) adopted reforms to eliminate fraudulent elections. Three events then occurred over the next dozen years that undermined the grip of the PRI. First, the massive earthquake that struck Mexico City in 1985 exposed the incompetence of the government. The response was an explosion of popular organizing to promote reconstruction. Second, the shocking, extensive fraud used to defeat the opposition candidate Cuahtemoc Cárdenas in the 1988 presidential election won by Carlos Salinas de Gortari (1988–1994) demonstrated the vulnerability of the PRI. Not only did Cárdenas garner a huge vote, but opposition parties took nearly half of the seats in Congress. Mexico, at long last, had a multiparty system. Third, in January 1994, the Ejército Zapatista de Liberación Nacional (EZLN) or Zapatistas rose up in the state of Chiapas. The movement crystallized the frustration with the inequities of Mexican economic development and the nation's semi-authoritarian political system. Simultaneously, Salinas signed the North American Free Trade Agreement, and his designated successor fell to an assassin's bullets. Under the new PRI president Ernesto Zedillo (1994–2000), the party acceded to further electoral reforms that resulted in the victory of the Partido de Acción Nacional (PAN) in 2000 and 2006. The PRI held power for seventy-one years, the longest tenure of any one-party state anywhere in the twentieth century.

The fragmentation of Mexican politics mitigated the impact of the end of the PRI's domination of the presidency. The winner of the presidential election received only a plurality of the votes in 2000, 2006, and 2012, a bare 36% in 2006. The PAN was a disappointment. Vicente Fox (2000–2006) elicited high hopes, but he produced little in the way of reforms, handicapped by a lack of a majority in Chamber of Deputies and, as critics maintain, an unwillingness to look to the daily administrative and political aspects of the position. Felipe Calderón (2006–2012), his successor, squeaked out a victory by half a percentage point. His opponent Andrés Manuel López Obrador protested and contested the result in court to no avail. Calderón took on the war on drugs, which set off an unprecedented wave of violence. Mexicans were obviously not pleased with the two PAN presidents,, because they returned to the PRI in 2012 when they elected Enrique Pena Nieto (2012–2018), under whose term the country fell into an even worse abyss of violence.

The Flow and Ebb of the Pink Tide

Latin Americans freed themselves from right-wing tyrannies and the terrors of the "dirty war" beginning with the fall of the Argentine military in the wake of the humiliating defeat in the Malvinas War in 1983, the Brazilian Abertura in the mid-1980s, and the end of the Pinochet dictatorship in 1990. With the exception of Colombia, the terrible, internal wars that devastated the region ended by the mid-1990s. New democracies replaced the dictatorships, but confronted seemingly unsolvable problems. Poverty was epidemic, in some countries surpassing half the population. The mal-distribution of wealth was insurmountable. Latin American economies, at this point nearly all implementing neo-liberal policies, featuring open trade, foreign investment, and deregulation, were incapable of creating sufficient employment for growing populations or providing the basic elements of social welfare, such as education and health care. The exuberant restoration of democracy did not immediately ameliorate the harsh conditions that existed all over the region.

everyone went left because of so many new problems

Consequently, many nations sought solutions in a turn leftward. The trend became known as the Pink Tide.

The Pink Tide in its heyday included Venezuela, Argentina, Brazil, Chile, Uruguay, Paraguay, Ecuador, Nicaragua, El Salvador and Bolivia, some 350 million people. Extraordinarily, a number of the new leaders fought as guerrillas against the military regimes. Political scientists divided these nations into two groups, radical and social democratic. The radicals included elected heads of state Hugo Chávez in Venezuela, Evo Morales in Bolivia, and Rafael Correa in Ecuador. These governments proclaimed their opposition to the neo-liberal strategy for economic development and the imperialism of the United States. They took Cuba as their model. These leaders turned back the clock, nationalizing large segments of their nation's economies, involving the state in redistributing wealth, and forming inter-American alliances to stand up against the United States. The social democrats sought to ameliorate the policies of neo-liberalism with a commitment to the welfare state. They looked more to European democratic socialism.

Venezuela and Uruguay illustrate the two opposite approaches of the Pink Tide. Hugo Chávez, a former military officer, who unsuccessfully attempted a coup in 1992, won election as president of Venezuela in 1999. Supported by the nation's considerable production of petroleum (it is a member of OPEC, the oil cartel) and the rise in oil prices after the September 11, 2001 terrorist attack on New York City, Chávez set out to raise the standard of living. His policies lowered the poverty and extreme poverty rates, lowered infant mortality, raised the number of children in higher education, and underwrote a number of left governments in the region. He accomplished this mainly by direct transfers of funds to poor people. His government also undertook the nationalization of critical economic sectors, including the oil industry, banks, electric power, telecommunications, mining, steel, and cement. In the meantime, with widespread popular backing and among the most open elections in the region, he eroded democratic institutions by ruling by decree and packing the courts.

However, the main weakness of Chávez's so-called Bolivarian revolution was the reliance of his domestic and international strategies on the continuation of high petroleum prices. Second, because direct transfers were the primary strategy for raising living standards, this in turn stimulated consumer demands and inflation, which was as high as thirty percent. Plummeting oil prices eventually precluded the success of this method. Third, the long-term viability of his nationalizing crucial industries was questionable in light of the dismal previous record of state-run industries in Latin America.

In foreign relations, Chávez was an outspoken critic of the United States and a close ally of Cuban head of state Fidel Castro. Venezuela in effect subsidized the Cuban economy by hiring Cubans by the thousands to work in Venezuela. He also cooperated closely with Lula in Brazil.

The drop in oil prices and the death of Chávez from cancer in 2013 jeopardized the Bolivarian revolution. Plummeting oil prices closed off access to food and medicine for the poorest Venezuelans. Dependence on extractive exports rendered the Venezuelan strategy unsustainable. To make matters worse, successor Nicolás Maduro had none of Chávez's charisma, and in the face of growing rightwing opposition, he intensified his authoritarian tendency. By 2021 the Venezuelan economy was in dire crisis. More than a million Venezuelans fled to Colombia and elsewhere.

Bolivia's experience was similar to that of Venezuela. Evo Morales, the nation's first indigenous president and former head of the organization of coca growers, nationalized natural gas production and cut off relations with the International Monetary Fund and World Bank. High prices for hydrocarbons financed his programs. The results were commendable. Poverty fell from sixty percent in 2006 to thirty-five percent in 2017. Extreme poverty lessened from thirty-eight to fifteen percent. Unemployment halved and minimum wages increased. Social transfer payments, much like in Brazil and Mexico, kept children in school and the elderly from hunger.

Like Chávez, however, Morales, came to think of himself as indispensable. He extended his term, ignoring the provisions of the constitution he created. When he proposed to run for a fourth term in 2019 and a plebiscite rejected the proposition, he ran anyway because the constitutional court overturned the plebiscite. He won a disputed election in October, but popular demonstrations caused him to resign the next month. Unlike Chávez, some of Morales policies over time were more conservative. He seemed to ally with agribusiness large landowners.

Uruguay was the most successful social democratic example. Tabaré Vázquez through non-consecutive presidencies (2004–2009 and 2015–2020) and José Mujica (2010–2015) of the Frente Amplio or Broad Front, a coalition of left parties, led the country into a set of rather remarkable achievements. They reduced poverty from forty to twelve percent. Unlike the other Pink Tide nations, Uruguay avoided corruption and tawdry scandals. According to one study, it ranked as the least corrupt country in Latin America and among the world's twenty-five least corrupt. It also obtained an almost perfect score on another study of political freedoms. (It is ahead of the United States.) It legalized abortion, same-sex marriage, and recreational marijuana.

Uruguay is one of only two Latin American nations in the "high income" category. Chile, another of the Pink Tide nations, is the other.

The left governments' achievements in both politics and economics, especially in the years from 2002 to 2012, were remarkable. Latin America became more inclusive, more democratic, and more equitable. Women took their place in leadership, holding in 2014 the presidencies of Argentina, Brazil, and Chile. They opened their societies to gay rights, legalized abortions, and even took on the military in an effort to uncover past crimes. The economic achievements under the left governments were even more impressive. They reduced the number of Latin Americans who lived in poverty from forty-five to twenty-five percent. The percentage of Latin Americans in the middle class increased to thirty-five percent. Ten million people obtained middle class status every year from 2002 to 2012. They undertook programs specifically targeted at redistributing income. The administration of Luiz Inácio "Lula" da Silva in Brazil organized the *Bolsa Familia* (family purse) which made cash payments to poor families as long as they kept their children in school and took them to regular health checkups. This reduced the Brazilian poverty rate by half, reaching fifty million people.

Pros of Pink tide under left

The Pink Tide began to ebb toward the end of the 2010s. Perhaps, the left governed too long. Hugo Chávez served fourteen years (1999–2013) until his death and his disciple Nicolás Maduro through 2020. Lula (2003–2011) and his successor Dilma Rousseff (2011–2016) governed for fourteen years in Brazil. Néstor Kirchner (2003–2007) and his spouse Cristina Fernández de Kirchner (2007–2015) led Argentina for a dozen years. Michelle Bachelet presided over Chile for two non-consecutive terms (2006–2010 and 2014–2018). Evo Morales (2006–2019) served as president of Bolivia for almost fourteen years before the people refused to accept his fourth reelection. Rafael Correa (2007–2017) was president of Ecuador for a decade. Some of them did not finish well. The economic expansion which fueled the unparalleled successes of the left government sputtered after 2012. The commodities export boom, which was at the heart of the prosperity, slowed markedly when the growth of the Chinese market for these products declined.

Perhaps, the most discouraging aspects of the ebb of the Pink Tide was the too often evolution into cults of personality and accompanying corruption. Hugo Chávez was a larger than life figure, particularly flamboyant on the international stage. Loyalty to his regime seemed to revolve around him, though his successor hung on for seven years and counting. Evo Morales as well appeared convinced of his indispensability; clearly, he pushed too far. The Kirchner/Fernández were personally controversial, probably even more so than their policies. Lula was another notorious figure, one who was a continuous presence on the political stage for decades. Daniel Ortega counts as one of the cultists also. Perhaps, it is not surprising that the larger-than-life leaders, so convinced of their own correct path, almost all tended toward authoritarianism as their rule endured. The less colorful leaders, such as Tavares and Bachelet left stronger legacies.

Despite their calls for reform and clean government, the left fell to temptation as had the military and politicians all over Latin America. One of the Pink Tide went to jail, albeit briefly, others found themselves indicted, and several confronted serious accusations. Neither of the two most radical, Chávez and Morales, faced accusations of personal corruption. Lula was briefly in jail after conviction. Rousseff was under investigation. So too were Fernández and Bachelet.

These partial successes and ignominious endings inevitably caused a backlash in some countries. In Argentina Maurico Macri, a conservative from one of the country's wealthiest families, became the first to defeat a Pink Tide candidate. Macri, though, lost his re election to Alberto Fernández, a Peronist in 2019. In Brazil the Congress impeached Rousseff for violating budgetary laws. Brazilians elected a former military officer, conservative Jair Bolsonaro as president to take office in 2019. Even the very successful Chile elected a right-wing billionaire Sebastián Pinera Echenique in 2010 and 2018, alternating with Bachelet.

The Global Economy

In the years after the end of World War II, the countries of Latin America pursued three general strategies to achieve economic development. The first was to promote and diversify exports, either by finding new primary products or by using the advantage of inexpensive labor costs to manufacture goods for European or U.S. markets. The second was Import Substitution Industrialization. Two versions of ISI appeared, one set forth by military dictatorships and the other by democratic governments. Both export enhancement and ISI required extensive government involvement, costly importation of capital goods, heavy borrowing abroad, and massive foreign investment. Widespread poverty severely limited domestic markets which in turn constrained the possibilities of development based on ISI. The third strategy, neoliberalism, embraced after the failure of ISI, threw open Latin American markets and removed governments from direct participation in the economy. By the early 2000s, the successful Pink Tide economies applied a variant of neo-liberalism heavily reliant on the export of agricultural commodities and extracted resources, such as oil, gas, and minerals.

All three models were subject to alternating booms and busts, because they relied on demand for their production on international markets, the availability and cost of global capital, and imported technology. Recession in the United States or Europe quickly damaged Latin America. Imprudent spending, reckless borrowing, and inefficient (at times foolhardy) monetary policies caused prolonged periods of debilitating hyper-inflation. Repayment of staggering foreign debt at exorbitant interest rates took most of government revenues, leaving little or no funds for social welfare.

The world petroleum catastrophe of the 1970s and early 1980s was an example of Latin America's vulnerability to the global economy. The rise in oil prices caused inflation, as the cost of fuels increased. To make matters worse, it exacerbated the region's perennial debt crisis. This era predated the discovery of Mexico's substantial oil reserves and the expansion of production in Brazil, Argentina, and Colombia. High oil revenues filled the coffers of the OPEC nations (Organization of Oil Producing Countries), most importantly Saudi Arabia and the Emirates, which in turn deposited their profits in Western financial institutions. The banks faced the dilemma of where to invest. At the same time, Latin American nations required enormous amounts for economic development. Most nations in Latin American imported oil, so borrowed funds likely went to pay for these imports. All was well and good as long as the economies of the debtors prospered, they could pay the interest on the loans. But when a new crisis hit in the early 1980s they could not repay. Mexico's debt increased five hundred percent. It came close to defaulting in 1982.

Some of the dependence on external markets lessened in recent times, because Brazil became the leading oil producer in the region, overtaking Venezuela, and Mexico, Colombia, and Argentina are notable oil producers, as well. Venezuela, Brazil, Peru, Argentina, Bolivia, Colombia, and Chile produce significant amounts of natural gas. Nonetheless, Venezuela, under the leadership of Chávez and Maduro, fell into the trap of borrowing heavily against future income from oil the prices for which were very high for a time, but when the market for a barrel of petroleum dropped from one hundred dollars to ten, the regime could no longer repay its debts or finance its programs. Mexico during its oil booms fell into a similar trap, borrowing in time of high prices and then unable to repay when prices dropped. The concept of putting funds aside for the down periods was, in fairness, not an attractive policy when the needs for social welfare and infrastructure were dire.

Domestic petroleum production was one major change Latin America's position in the global economy. Four others were worthy of note, as well. First, the enormous international transmigration of people, most importantly to the United States created a new source of funds in the form of moneys remitted by immigrants to their lands of origin. Second, the global trade in narcotics, cocaine in Bolivia, Peru, and Colombia, and marijuana in Mexico, profoundly affected the economies of these countries. Third and least studied, the illegal mining of gold in a few countries surpassed the revenues generated by narcotics. Fourth, China became a major purchaser of Latin American commodities and resources and a major investor in the region also.

The funds sent back to their home country by migrants, mostly from the United States grew in importance in the first years of the new millennium. In 2018 the total remitted to Latin American nations reached ninety billion dollars. This amount exceeds the Gross Domestic Products of thirty countries in the Western Hemisphere. Mexico led the way, receiving approximately thirty billion dollars. Remittances were the third largest revenue producer for Mexico behind only petroleum and tourism. Colombia, the Dominican Republic, and El Salvador were each recipients of between five and six billion dollars. With the exception of Colombia over eighty percent of the funds came from migrants in the United States. The majority of Colombia's came from Spain. Although analysts debate the pros and cons of these remittances, they generally agree that they contribute positively, though to what extent is difficult to measure.

The illicit business of narcotics is the most analyzed and debated topic in current Latin American Studies, perhaps other than the possible strategies for economic development and eliminating severe income inequities. Governments expended astounding amounts of money to destroy this trade, with frustratingly little success. Three major markets—the United States, the European Union, and Latin America (most especially Brazil) are involved. Only three countries in Latin America produce cocaine: Colombia (45%), Peru (35–40%) and Bolivia (15–20%). The estimates of the amount of revenue the illegal enterprise generates vary widely. One puts the total at $18–20 billion, another at less than $5 billion. Yet another estimates the sum at over $100 billion. The producers obtain a very small percentage of the money. Most goes to the retailers. But it is difficult to calculate the respective shares of the growers or cartels or retailers. Some analysts believe the cocaine economy equals that of the legal economy in Colombia and perhaps Bolivia. What is clear is that the narcotics trade creates enormous amounts of money. We know of its corrupting effect and its connection to violence, but it is not easy to delineate the actual economic impact.

The second, relatively unknown illicit business, by some estimates exceeding the narcotics trade in importance, is gold mining. Smugglers earned approximately $2 billion in Colombia and $2.6 billion a year in Peru in 2015. The gold yielding regions are remote and hard-to-access, so they are difficult to monitor. In Latin America, unlike the rest of the world where large, transnational corporations dominate gold mining, small-scale operators are prevalent. In 2014, 17,000 mines, employing 50,000 people, operated illegally. In Brazil 75,000 miners operated illegally. In many areas criminal organizations have taken over. In the case of Colombia, the FARC acquired twenty percent of its funding from gold mining. Although the mines provide in some instances above average wages, the overall effect is detrimental. Because government authority is scarce, workers are often subject to forced labor and debt bondage. Trafficking in young females is all too common. The miners destroyed the environment, laying waste to vast tracts of irreplaceable forest and jungle.

Illegal mining brought in money

Trade with China expanded rapidly in the new millennium. In 2018, it grew at 18.9 percent. While trade with the United States still dwarfs the Chinese $740 to 308 billion, the new market accounts for much of the export boom in extractive and agricultural commodities. Chinese demand for such products as soybeans shaped a significant part of the Brazilian economy, for example. China is Brazil's major trading partner. China also invested heavily in Latin America, primarily in Venezuela, Brazil, Ecuador, and Argentina. Its lending institutions invested $141 billion since 2005. The investment aimed at oil in Ecuador and Venezuela and soy in Argentina. Chinese investment and trade significantly helped the Pink Tide governments in Ecuador and Venezuela. China contracted for ninety percent of Ecuador's crude oil through 2024.

As the progress accomplished during the first two decades of the twenty-first century slowed, the question arises as to whether the region reached a plateau in development. Some of the challenges are obvious. The level of poverty and extreme poverty remain too high. The middle sector, while growing, consists of very vulnerable occupations, with the constant threat of falling back into the ranks of the poor. Without a substantial, secure middle class, the domestic market will not expand to provide the basis of permanent development. The inequitable distribution of wealth and income exacerbates this problem. Unequal access to education maintains a labor force unable to contribute in a technology—dominated world. In some areas, persistent violence creates an obstacle to development.

Analysts at the United Nations ECLA point to four additional new obstacles, which they claim resulted from longstanding weaknesses worsened over time: (1) stagnant or declining productivity; (2) the vulnerability of large segments of the population with unequal access to public services; (3) the growing dissatisfaction with public institutions; and (4) the impact of climate change. In economies based on exporting extractive and agricultural commodities, the tendency is not to invest in technology in the non-export sectors. The resultant low productivity undermines their ability to compete. Given that the Chinese market for extractive products flattened or declined, the affected nations need to create alternative engines for their economies. This is a twenty-first century version of the dilemmas presented by monocrop or mono-mineral enclave economies of the nineteenth century. The second "trap" is a consequence of the positive reduction of the number of the poor and the expansion of the middle class. The newly middle class, forty percent of the population, is precariously situated. Their jobs are usually low skilled, often part of the informal economy, and highly vulnerable to the ups-and-downs of global markets. The same analysts point out a third trap, the vast distrust of public institutions, which universally failed to provide the most basic investments in human capital. Lastly, the extractive economies that form the foundation of their (temporary?) prosperity are by their very nature environmentally unsustainable over the long term. How do Latin American nations solve these problems? The usual answers are (1) investment in education, in order to create more formal (obviously better and more secure) employment; (2) end corruption to restore (?) faith in public institutions; (3) improve the transportation and communication infrastructure, and (4) adopt a more environmentally sound economic model. In 2020 none of these seemed feasible, at least in the short and intermediate term.

Conclusion

Since 1945 Latin America seemed periodically on the brink of disaster. Most nations sustained economic development and political stability for no more than a decade, perhaps two. Economic progress has not necessarily accompanied political stability, neither right-wing dictatorship nor democracy, left or right. Political stability has not necessarily accompanied relative prosperity. Enormous natural resources made no apparent difference. No one found the formula for success. Import Substitution Industrialization, government intervention, neo-liberalism, and the Pink Tide all failed. The latter came the closest to obtaining social justice and economic equity, but reminiscent of the populism of a past era, it too often deteriorated into cults of personality or authoritarianism.

What then is the heart of the problem? What is the solution? Is there a solution? Analysts made much in the past of an international system that was inherently disadvantageous to producers of agricultural commodities and extracted resources. This argument mentioned in the "How Historians Understand" in this chapter posits industrialized countries—the United States and Western Europe—as the "villains," draining resources at cheap prices and selling manufactures and technology at high prices. The road to progress supposedly went through industrialization. The high levels of poverty rendered this an all but impossible task, for domestic markets were too small to maintain manufacturing. Local producers could not compete with external suppliers. But since the dependency paradigm appeared, globalization transformed markets. For example, once counted as less developed nations China, India, South Korea, and Taiwan emerged as industrial powers. They provided a new model, export industrialization. Since the collapse of the U.S.S.R., communism (the state version) was no longer a reasonable possibility. No other viable alternative to capitalism came forth. What remains is to look inward. For the rich and powerful to determine it is in theirs and their nations' best interest to mitigate the harsh effects of globalization. From 2000 many governments undertook such strategies with considerable success and in doing so secured the peace necessary to bring about a more prosperous and just society.

Timeline

1959   Cuban Revolution
1964   Brazilian military overthrow Joao Goulart
1968   Peruvian military led revolution
1970   Dr. Salvador Allende elected in Chile
1973   Chilean military overthrows Allende
1974   Juan Perón returns to Argentina
1976   Argentine military begins Dirty War
1979   Sandinista Revolution in Nicaragua
1982   Malvinas War. Argentina v. United Kingdom
1983   Military rule ends in Argentina
1988   Chilean plebiscite votes out Pinochet
1989   Sandinistas lose election
1990   Alberto Fujimori elected President of Peru
1999   Hugo Chávez elected President of Venezuela, beginning the Pink Tide
2000   National Action Party (PAN) ends seven decades of one party rule in Mexico
2006   Evo Morales becomes the first indigenous President of Latin American nation, Bolivia
2006   Michelle Bachelet becomes the first woman elected president of a Latin American nation, Chile
2018   FARC ends five decades of guerrilla war in Colombia

How Historians Understand

Theories of Economic Development and History

Theories of economic development greatly influenced not only the policies of Latin American governments, the behavior of businesspeople, and the plight of hundreds of millions of people, but also the interpretation of historical events and trends.

During the nineteenth century, ideas advocating free trade and comparative advantage dominated economic thinking. They fit nicely into widely accepted notions of Social Darwinism (the survival of the fittest) and the corollary belief in the superiority of white Europeans. Accordingly, Latin American nations were to supply agricultural and mineral commodities for export and open their markets for imports of manufactured goods. Argentina was the model. Its exports of beef and grain made it one of the richest countries in the world in 1914. The Great Depression of the 1930s challenged these perspectives. Economists no longer adhered to the belief that the export of primary products was a sustainable means to develop. In the late 1940s, the United Nations Economic Commission for Latin America (CEPAL), led by Raúl Prebisch, an Argentine, put forward the center-periphery paradigm, also known as structuralism. This view dominated Latin American economic thinking through the 1970s. The structuralists argued that export economies tended in the long run to suffer from a decline in the terms of trade. In other words, the prices received for primary goods decreased because the demand for them would not rise as fast as income, while at the same time the prices of industrial products rose over time. The structuralists believed that the only way Latin America could develop was to substitute domestic for imported manufactures. Import Substitution Industrialization thus became the most widely adopted development policy in Latin America after World II.

By the 1960s, ISI clearly failed. Dependency analysis emerged to explain Latin America's lack of development. Two schools of *dependencia* arose—the neo-Marxist and the reformist. Dependency advocates believed that peripheral (underdeveloped) countries, like those in Latin America, and center nations (Western Europe, the United States, and Japan) were involved in an unequal exchange that would always exploit the former and benefit the latter. Two ways were available to change the system: overthrow it, which the Marxists favored, or reform it. The translation of dependency into policy resulted in further government involvement in the economies of Latin American nations to reduce the influence of the developed center. Ironically, in order to finance their interventions in the economy, governments borrowed huge sums from the industrialized countries.

In opposition to the dependency school, the diffusionist model maintained that technology, capital, trade, political institutions, and culture spread out from the advanced to the backward nations. Dual societies grew within the underdeveloped nations in which coexisted an advanced urban sector and a backward rural sector. The diffusionist claimed that ideas and capital spread from urban to rural. They proposed that the advanced nations cooperate with the middle class of underdeveloped nations to modernize the latter. Contrary to the diffusionists, the dependistas concluded that the diffusion of capital and ideas made the less developed countries reliant on the giving country, widening the gaps between advanced and less advanced nations. The pattern repeated in the dual domestic society.

(*continued*)

(continued)

The failure of the ISI and intense government involvement in the economy disillusioned Latin Americans. The collapse of the communist states (with the exception of Cuba) in the late 1980s and 1990s meant that no alternative sources for capital were available other than in Western Europe and the United States. The institutions providing capital, such as the International Monetary Fund (IMF) and the World Bank exerted tremendous pressure to readopt the nineteenth century liberal paradigm, now rebranded as neo-liberalism. The notion that market forces will eventually create equity reestablished itself.

In the decades since 1959, the changing approaches to development affected the way historians viewed the past. All of the theories emphasized outside factors as causes of Latin America's economic woes. Logically, then analyses lessened the importance of domestic circumstances. They reduced the lower classes to virtually meaningless nonparticipants. Emphasis on international factors underplayed the consideration of regional and local conditions, so important since pre-Columbian times, leaving out the most meaningful aspects of culture and society, and focusing attention on economics. For historians, dependency's inability to incorporate change over time was another crucial weakness.

More recently, historians turned to studies of everyday life, traditions, and culture, focusing more on the popular classes. They have shifted their concerns from the international to the local.

Latin American Lives

An Argentine Military Officer

The years from 1976 to 1983 were Argentina's nightmare. The military, police, and right-wing vigilantes seized, tortured, and killed thousands of its citizens. Military officers threw naked, drugged civilians from airplanes over the South Atlantic Ocean. Squads of white Ford Falcons arrived at homes in the middle of the night and took away their occupants, whom no one ever saw again. Soldiers raped female prisoners. Terrorist gangs kidnapped pregnant women, taking their babies, and murdering the mothers. Few military officers ever showed remorse for the deeds of this era. Who were the soldiers who committed such acts? What was it about the institution of the military that led members to turn viciously on its own people?

In 1995, retired Naval Captain Adolfo Scilingo and half-dozen ex-officers publicly confessed to murder. While stationed at the Navy Mechanics School as a junior officer in 1977, Scilingo flew on two flights during which he personally threw more than thirty living people into the ocean. He reported that his superiors told him that these were extraordinary times requiring drastic actions.

The Argentine military at almost every point before 1976 divided into two main groups: those who would maintain the constitutional order, even if they opposed the policies of the civilian government, and those who would overthrow any civilian government. Splits also arose between the generals and lesser ranking officers. They argued about personalities and management styles. Lastly, the branches of the armed forces, the army, navy, and air force, were often at odds. The military previously ousted governments in 1930, 1943, 1955, 1962, and 1966. Between 1976 and 1983 they papered over their discord in what they believed a holy mission to save the fatherland. The generals vowed to stay in control indefinitely.

Latin American military officers lived in a world apart. They trained at their nation's military academy, where in their first year they chose their branch (for the army, the cavalry, infantry, or artillery). The rigorous training emphasized character and tradition. Men who graduated from these institutions acquired a worldview that was "very subjective and very romantic...." Officers experienced rigid discipline under the complete authority of their commanding officers, who often exercised control of the junior officers' social life, including approval to marry. They earned promotions periodically: sub-lieutenant in four years, to captain in eight. Officers attended new schools at regular intervals. Selection to the status of general staff officers through examinations assured higher ranks. Those who earned the rank of colonel after twenty years received a year of advanced military studies. Many traveled abroad, often to the United States. In earlier times, German practice heavily influenced the Argentine military.

The military experience was not all positive. Salaries eroded with inflation and equipment was commonly obsolete. These disadvantages served to intensify the loyalty to the institution. The officer corps believed itself above petty politics, although in reality they mired in them. Officers swore to defend the nation, but disdained the people they vowed to protect.

(continued)

(continued)

Many of the officer corps came from small towns in the interior. Others were super-patriotic second-generation Argentines. Many sons of officers followed their fathers into the military. They lived in an insular world with comprised of military friends and family. These officers did not trust civilians. It was the military against the rest of the world. The perceived threat of leftist terrorism in the 1970s struck hard at their psyches, traditions, and beliefs. They saw themselves under siege by international communism.

By 1976, the Argentine armed forces were desperate. They intervened in Argentine politics repeatedly since 1930 to little effect. The nation seemed to regard them with no respect. Peronism was a sore that would not heal and he was by then dead and not a viable option. The international situation was frightening to them, for insurgencies were everywhere: Vietnam, Africa, and elsewhere in Latin America. Fidel Castro sent his comrade Che Guevara to foment (unsuccessfully) revolution in Bolivia. Reflective of their decades of indoctrination and insularity, the officer corps struck hard against its real and imagined enemies. The results scarred Argentina forever.

Slice Of Life

On the Streets of Nuevo Laredo

More than a half of all Latin Americans in 2020 are employed in the informal sector of the economy, which includes petty entrepreneurs selling a broad range of items and providing services, as well as smalltime criminals, prostitutes, and street children. In Peru, almost seventy percent of the working people toil in the informal sector. High unemployment rates, especially among unskilled, inadequately educated people, many of whom are recent migrants from the countryside, left millions of Latin Americans on the economic margins, struggling daily to make a living.

The most well-known petty business folks are the street vendors seen almost everywhere in the large cities, where they fill the public spaces of the underground (subway) and bus stations and the sidewalks of busy neighborhoods. On Sundays in Chapultepec Park in Mexico City, hundreds of vendors line up along the pathways.

Several hundred thousand more people scratch out their subsistence as trash pickers, known as *pepenadores* in Mexico, *cartoneros* in Argentina, *catadores* in Brazil, and *moscas* in Peru. They constitute an extensive recycling enterprise throughout the region, scavenging bottles, cans, and cardboard. On study in 2002 estimated that 150,000 Brazilians earned their living collecting aluminum cans, some nine billion of them a year. In some cases trash picking moved beyond the informal economy. In Mexico City, the pepenadores have their own union, which controls the municipal dumps.

The cardboard pickers, known as cartoneros, of Nuevo Laredo, Mexico, while not entirely typical of the informal economy, nonetheless, provide us with a graphic insight into its operations. Nuevo Laredo is a city of 373,000 people in the State of Tamaulipas, in northeastern Mexico directly across the Río Grande River from its twin city Laredo, Texas. For a century and a half, Mexicans recovered wastes from both cities. According to Martín Medina, who meticulously studies the cartoneros of Nuevo Laredo, Mexican scavengers collected cardboard in Laredo, since before World War II. Medina's informants describe a large number of cartoneros collecting in Laredo and bringing the cardboard across the border during the 1940s. Because U.S. sanitary regulations did not permit them to bring their horses into the United States, the collectors had to use pushcarts.

As the result of the considerable expansion of Laredo as a retail center and the establishment of border manufacturing plants, known as maquiladoras, in northern Mexico, the amount of cardboard boxes grew enormously. During the 1950s, a Catholic priest in Laredo helped to found a cartonero cooperative, the Sociedad Cooperativa de Recuperodores de Materiales de Nuevo Laredo and to negotiate a legal working arrangement with local government in Laredo. The scavengers suffered a setback in the 1960s, when the Mexican government outlawed importation of waste cardboard. The cartoneros innovatively smuggled the material by throwing the cardboard into the river and having accomplices pull it out on the other side. During the 1980s the Mexican government instituted a quota system, requiring an expensive permit to transport cardboard within Mexico. The cartoneros, however, circumvented and outlasted all these impediments.

(continued)

(continued)

Recycling paper products in Mexico is an important business. The paper industry was chronically short of raw materials, as a consequence of the high cost of logging. Only twenty percent of the fiber used in Mexican paper came from wood pulp. Eighty percent is from recycling. What began as informal economy became crucial for the formal economy, the paper industry.

The cartoneros earn more than one might expect. They do not sell directly to the paper industry, but to middlemen, who in turn sell to industry. These types of arrangements rarely are to the advantage of those who do the actual work. But Medina conducted a survey in the mid-1990s that presented a picture of the average cartonero. He is a forty-year-old married male literate in Spanish, with only four years education. Most are male because the usual method of transporting the cardboard is a three-wheel cart, known as a tricicleta, which requires sufficient strength to push eight hundred pounds of cardboard. The cartoneros work 8 or 9 hours, six days a week. Many augment their income by scavenging other recyclable materials. Occasionally they assist smugglers, moving mostly electronics across the border. Three quarters own their own homes. They earn a median income higher than that of a resident of Nuevo Laredo.

The example of the cartoneros illustrates that it is possible to make a living income in the informal economy and that those in this economy at the margins provide useful services to society. They are also yet another case of the resourcefulness of people in poverty.

Nature's Way

Hurricane Mitch, 1998

Hurricane Mitch was the deadliest Atlantic Hurricane since 1780, hitting the Honduran coast on October 28, 1998 with winds at 98 miles an hour and a storm surge of 12 feet. Before it made landfall it swept around the Caribbean for ten days. Eventually, its sustained winds were over 180 miles per hour and gusted up to 200 m.p.h. After it struck the coast, over the next week, it meandered slowly through Honduras, Nicaragua, Guatemala, Belize, and El Salvador. Because it moved so slowly over the mountains, it produced enormous rainfall in Honduras and Nicaragua. One town recorded nearly 40 inches of rain. Some unofficial reports estimated the rainfall as high as 75 inches. The storm hovered over the region for thirteen days, then crossed into Mexico and reconstituted in the Bay of Campeche on November 2. It made landfall again on the northwestern coast of Yucatán on November 4. It went into the Gulf of Mexico and made landfall one last time in Florida. It did not dissolve until November 9 off the northern coast of Great Britain, more than three weeks after it constituted.

Hurricane Mitch killed an estimated 11,000 Hondurans, with another 9191 missing. The accompanying mudslides and floods razed tens of thousands of homes. The hurricane affected an estimated twenty percent of Hondurans, about 1.5 million, with 285,000 homeless. It erased 25 small towns. It also badly damaged the country's transportation infrastructure, perhaps 70 percent of it destroyed. Reportedly, old road maps were no longer usable, because the destruction was so widespread. Honduras endured $US 3.8 billion overall damages. The hurricane wiped out seventy percent of Honduras's crops, with losses of over a billion dollars. Thousands of cattle and other animals died in the deluge. It nearly ruined the shrimp industry, which was a major employer in the southern region of the country. It brought about food and water shortages, dangerous sanitary conditions, and outbreaks of malaria, dengue, cholera, hepatitis, and other afflictions of the respiratory and gastrointestinal systems. Starvation was a real threat for many dependent on agriculture.

The storm ruined the banana crop. Banana plants died when their roots were underwater for more than 48 hours. The flooded land was unfit for replanting for at least a year. The major banana producers, the multinational companies Chiquita and Dole made the situation worse by laying off almost their entire workforce, some 20,000 people. At a time when jobs were virtually non-existent, banana workers faced life and death conditions.

Nicaragua suffered as well with an estimated 800,000 people affected or 19 percent of the population. Mudslides buried several towns near Las Casitas Volcano in the northeastern region. At least 2000 died. Additional losses included more than 20,000 homes, 340 schools with another 500,000 homes damaged. Sanitary conditions were unspeakable. The hurricane inflicted similar damages in Costa Rica.

Experts concluded that the deadly mudslides were the result of the widespread use of slash and burn agriculture in Honduras, which cut down forest lands which normally absorb rainfall. Among the major culprits were the foreign-owned banana plantations.

(continued)

(continued)

The catastrophe spurred the governments of both Honduras and Nicaragua to pass legislation establishing institutions to prepare for future disasters. Honduras created the National Risk Management System and Nicaragua the National System for Prevention, Mitigation, and Attention to Disasters in 2000. It also stimulated community organizing. While some of the new activism continued over time, assisted by the NGOs, critics maintained that region relied too heavily on outside resources. One complained: "Six months after Hurricane Mitch, poor people no longer received provisions and food supplements. Many were hungry and struggling…"

Non-Governmental Organizations (NGOs) and foreign governments pledged a staggering US$ 25 billion in aid, but the process did not go smoothly. The U.S. aid package bogged down in Congressional disputes over budgeting and the European Union had not delivered any of its promised $US 180 million eighteen months after the hurricane. The NGOs bickered with the Nicaraguan government over where the funds targeted.

In Nicaragua, the government left immediate aid almost all to the NGOs. Half of the recipients of food aid, approximately 400,000 people, got it from the United Nations relief agency. Fewer than ten percent of all aid recipients received it from the Nicaraguan government. It was a spectacular failure. In the aftermath of the disaster, those communities that previously were well organized fared the best.

One scholar, Julie Cupples, traced the impact of the hurricane and recovery on women. She found that the recovery undermined "existing gender identities." In one village, the children ate at a dining hall, which perhaps eroded women's identity as mothers. Some of the women resisted. Unemployment caused by the storm, such as in coffee processing plants, undermined their identities as paid workers. On the other hand, women came to the fore organizing reconstruction.

As in the occurrence of other natural disasters, Hurricane Mitch starkly brought forth all of the weaknesses and vulnerabilities of national and local governments. In so many cases, governments fell short in their duties to protect and enhance the lives of their citizens. And, like, in so many other instances, these disasters also featured the capabilities and courage of everyday folks.

9

Globalization and Everyday Life, 1959 to the Present

The dominant aspects of everyday life in Latin America in 2020 were the improving, but still unacceptable levels, of poverty; the stunning inequities in the distribution of wealth; the all too common high instance of violence, both criminal and state-sponsored; the inability of national economies to provide employment; the vast movements of people both from the countryside to the city and transnationally; continuing super-urbanization; and the consistent failure of governments to invest in human capital, such as education and health care.

The half century after 1959 brought stunning change. Extraordinary innovations in communications, technology, transportation, energy, data processing, and more transformed how people lived and worked. Consumerism and popular culture carried first by the mass media and then through the internet from the United States in particular, challenged and altered all aspects of tradition. Latin Americans, as much as people anywhere, experienced these revolutions.

For thirty years between the 1960s and 1990s, millions of Latin Americans in Argentina, Brazil, Chile, and Uruguay lived in fear and uncertainty. In Central America, Colombia, and Peru people struggled in the midst of brutal civil wars. The violence certainly was costly in terms of deaths and displacements and physical and economic damage, but, also, in terms of the kind of post-traumatic stress syndrome it inflicted on whole societies. Few people in Argentina or Guatemala, for example, did not know anyone who "disappeared." Every village in highland Peru in the early 1990s cringed at the possibility of the Shining Path guerrillas entering. To make matters worse, the neo-liberal policies initiated heavy-handedly by rightist regimes were often destructive of local commerce and industry, leaving many jobless. During the years of terror and war, Latin Americans suffered an unprecedented decline in their standard of living, economically and psychologically.

Democratization did not immediately improve Latin American lives, but by the late 1990s and into the new millennium a period of sustained growth and new directed social programs lessened the dire inequities, by decreasing the numbers of desperately poor and narrowing the gap between rich and poor.

Population [birth rates increased then decreased]

At mid twentieth century, Latin America's population exploded, because birth rates increased substantially, while death rates declined rapidly. The annual growth rate for the region reached 2.8 percent during the 1960s. Though these rates slowed considerably after the 1970s, the population tripled between 1950 and 2000. The whole region has a total population of 626,741,000 people in 2020, with Brazil and Mexico together accounting for almost half. Uruguay and Panama are the least populated with around 7.5 million people (Tables 9.1 and 9.2).

Brazil's population more than tripled from 54 million in 1950 to 171 million in 2000. Mexico's population tripled between 1950 and 1990, as did that of Colombia and Venezuela. Cuba and Uruguay at about a fifty percent rise and Uruguay were the only countries that did not at least double their populations.

Demographic trends comprised two distinct stages after 1945. Through the 1960s, fertility rates were high, an average of six children per woman. Improved health care and younger marriage age were likely causes. Starting in the 1970s, the fertility rate fell to around three children per woman. The extent and rate of decline of fertility rates were not the same everywhere. Brazil, Colombia, Mexico, Peru, Costa Rica, Ecuador, Dominican Republic, and Venezuela experienced sharp drops from 6.1 to below 3.0. The decline was slower and less in Bolivia, Haiti, Central America, and Paraguay.

The *Population Bulletin* maintains that Latin America's fertility decline owed to "social and economic changes… primarily by molding values and attitudes toward childbearing." Family planning in the form of contraception played a critical role. In 2002 seventy percent of married women ages 15 to 44 in the region used family planning, well above the percentages in the rest of the world. This was the consequence of considerable efforts on the part of Latin American governments to reduce the birth rate. The Mexican government program to encourage the use of contraceptives resulted in more than a

Table 9.1 Population growth in Latin America, 1950–2000 (Millions)

Country	1950	1960	1970	1980	1990	2000
Argentina	17.2	20.6	24.0	28.1	32.5	37.0
Bolivia	2.7	3.4	4.2	5.4	6.6	8.3
Brazil	54.0	72.8	96.0	121.7	148.0	170.7
Chile	6.1	7.6	9.5	11.1	13.1	15.2
Colombia	12.6	16.9	22.6	28.4	35.0	42.3
Ecuador	3.4	4.4	6.0	8.0	10.3	12.6
Paraguay	1.5	1.8	2.4	3.1	4.2	5.5
Peru	7.6	9.9	13.2	17.3	21.8	25.9
Uruguay	2.2	2.5	2.8	2.9	3.1	3.3
Venezuela	5.1	7.6	10.7	15.1	19.5	24.2
Costa Rica	0.9	1.2	1.7	2.3	3.0	4.0
El Salvador	2.0	2.6	3.6	4.6	5.1	6.3
Guatemala	3.0	4.0	5.2	6.8	8.7	11.4
Honduras	1.4	1.9	2.6	3.6	4.9	6.5
Mexico	27.7	36.9	50.6	67.6	83.2	98.9
Nicaragua	1.1	1.5	2.1	2.9	3.8	5.1
Panama	0.9	1.1	1.5	2.0	2.4	2.9
Cuba	–	5.9	7.0	8.5	9.7	10.6	11.2
Dominican Republic	2.4	3.2	4.4	5.7	7.1	8.4
Haiti	3.3	3.8	4.5	5.5	6.9	8.4
Latin America	167.0	218.3	284.8	361.4	440.7	520.0

Source: Jorge A. Brea, "Population Dynamics in Latin America," *Population Bulletin* 58:1 (March 2003): 1–36. This article provides much of the data for the discussion of population, labor, and migration
*Population statistics are at best estimates, compiled from various sources at a particular time. No two sources provide the same figures

two-fold increase in their use from 1976 to 1995 (30.2 percent in 1976 to 66.5 in 1995). Of course, not everyone was willing. Sylvia Chant provides the example of Melia, a twenty-seven year old woman, who lived in a one-room hut in a barrio in Puerto Vallarta, Mexico, with her husband, a construction worker, and six children ranging from ages 3 to 9. A devout Catholic, Melia did not use contraceptives, nor did she plan to in the future. Her offspring were to her "gifts of god."

The decline in mortality rates contributed much to the growth in population. By the end of the twentieth century, they fell from the low teens in the 1950s to six. Life expectancy showed remarkable gains, going from 52 years in the late 1950s to 71 years in the late 1990s. The highest life expectancy was in Cuba, Chile, and Costa Rica at seventy-five in 2002. The lowest was sixty-five in Bolivia, Guatemala, and Haiti. Latin American nations drastically improved their ability to prevent and treat infectious and parasitic diseases, reducing the number of fatalities from malaria, tuberculosis, pneumonia, influenza, measles, diphtheria, tetanus, and typhoid.

Table 9.2 Population of Latin America, 2020 (In Millions)

Brazil	212.560
Mexico	128.930
Colombia	50.880
Argentina	45.380
Peru	32.970
Venezuela	28.440
Chile	19.120
Ecuador	17.640
Guatemala	16.850
Bolivia	11.670
Haiti	11.400
Cuba	11.330
Dominican Republic	10.850
Honduras	9.900
Paraguay	7.130
Nicaragua	6.620
El Salvador	6.490
Costa Rica	5.090
Panama	4.310
Uruguay	3.470

*Population statistics are at best estimates, compiled from various sources at a particular time. No two sources provide the same figures

Causes of death

Women live longer than men do in Latin America, like in the rest of the world. In Uruguay, they live eight years more. In Bolivia, however, the difference is only three years. It is likely that much of the gap in mortality between men and women lies in the young adult age group, for men that age are most probable to fall victim to violence or accidents. Before the 1940s, the rate of deaths in childbirth among women 15 to 49 was very high in much of the region. However, from 1970 to 1989 the risk of dying in pregnancy decreased by 54 percent.

Perhaps, the crucial component of increased life expectancy is the decline in infant mortality. For Latin America and the Caribbean, it fell from 128 deaths per 1,000 live births in the 1950s to 30 in 2002. The lowest rate was in Cuba at 6 deaths. The highest were Bolivia at 61 and Haiti at 80. This was marked improvement from the mid-1990s, when it was 102 per 1000 births in Bolivia and 138 in Nicaragua.

The statistics tell us that the region entered the new industrial age, because where life expectancy is seventy-five or better, non-communicable diseases (heart disease, cancer) cause two-thirds of the deaths. Poor, less-educated, rural people who reside in less wealthy areas still are subject to communicable diseases. In the dark years of the 1980s, the occurrence of communicable

disease

diseases, such as dengue, rose. Reports of bubonic plague resurged in Peru and yellow fever and malaria in the Amazon.

The distribution of ages within a population is very important to economic development. The critical groups are those under fifteen and those over sixty-five. The larger those groups the greater the burden on the 16 to 64 working population. The improvement of infant mortality expanded the younger cohort, while the extension of life expectancy enlarged the 65 and over cohort. The reduction in fertility during the late 1960s and afterward shrank the percentage of people under 15 from 43 percent in in 1965 to 32 percent in 2000. The proportion of the population over 65 increased. In three countries, Uruguay, Cuba and Argentina, they count for over ten percent. Economists maintain that when countries have a majority of the population in the 16 to 64 range, the working age, this provides an opportunity for dynamic economic growth. For Latin America, they predict this opening will last until 2040.

Poverty

The poor are for the most part children, adolescents, women, indigenous, Afro-descendants, rural dwellers, and unemployed. The poverty levels in the countryside over time were twice those in the cities. Women are more likely to be poor than men. Indigenous poverty was and is an extremely high percent, 72 in Bolivia in 2002, 90 in Mexico, and 65 in Peru.

From 1950 to 1980, per capita income rose by an average of three percent a year. This decreased the percentage of people living in poverty from an estimated 65 percent in 1950 to 25 percent in 1980. However, after 1980 dictatorships and the adoption of free market, neo-liberal economic policies took a heavy toll. From 1982 to 1993, the number of people living in poverty in Latin America increased from 78 million to 150 million. Relatively speaking, the wealthiest nations in the region, Argentina, Uruguay, and Venezuela, experienced the sharpest rise in poverty. Economic stagnation or decline, rampant unemployment, widespread underemployment, and inflation characterized these years of the terror and subsequent incipient re-democratization. During the 1980s, the per capita gross national product fell more than twenty percent in Argentina, Bolivia, Nicaragua, Peru, and Venezuela. The only countries that did not suffer a net decline in gross national income from 1980 to 1992 were Chile, Colombia, and Uruguay. In Latin America in 1990, per capita income was fifteen percent below the 1980 level. As a result, the number of poor rose to 210 million by the mid-1990s. Clearly, the rule of right

Table 9.3 Latin Americans living in poverty and extreme poverty, 1980–2002

Country	Percentage of population in poverty			Percentage of population in extreme poverty		
	1980	2002	2006	1980	2002	2006/2007
Argentina	10.5	45.4 (Urban)		2.8	20.9	
Bolivia		62.4			37.1	31.2
Brazil	45.3	37.5	33.3	22.6	13.2	8.5
Chile	45.1	18.8	13.7	17.4	4.7	
Colombia	42.3	51.1	19.2	17.4	24.6	
Costa Rica	23.6	20.3		6.9	8.2	5.3
Ecuador			43.0			16.0
El Salvador		48.9			22.1	
Guatemala	71.1	60.2	54.8	39.6	30.9	
Honduras		77.3	71.5		54.4	45.6
Mexico	42.5	39.4	31.7	15.4	12.6	8.7
Nicaragua		69.4			42.4	
Panama	41.0		29.9	19.7		12.0
Paraguay		61.0			33.2	31.6
Peru	34.0	54.8	44.5	17.4	24.4	
Republica Dominicana		44.9			20.3	
Uruguay	14.6			4.0		
Venezuela	25.0	48.6	30.2	8.6	22.2	8.5
Latin America	40.5	44.4		18.6	19.4	

Source: Economic Commission for Latin America and the Caribbean (ECLAC), Statistical Yearbook for Latin America and the Caribbean, 2004 (LC/G.2264P/B), Santiago 2005, figure 50.0, pp. 118119. United Nations Publications, Sales N° E/S.05.II.G.1

increased poverty after dictatorship

wing regimes or the presence of prolonged insurgencies correlated closely with the impoverishment of the population. The percentage of people below the poverty line in Chile, for example, went from 17 in 1970, the first year of the government of Salvador Allende, to 45 in 1985, after a dozen years of the Agustín Pinochet dictatorship. Thirty years of war in Guatemala immersed sixty percent of the population of ten million in poverty (Table 9.3).

Democratization improved the lot of the poor. The Pink Tide, with its emphasis on mitigating the harshest aspects of free market capitalism, reallocated funds to those most in need. One of the crucial improvements accompanying the Pink Tide was the easing of inflation. Prior to 1995 double-digit inflation was extremely common. No other phenomenon of the post-1959 era damaged the status and well-being of the lower and middle classes more than inflation. It reached staggering proportions during the 1970s and 1980s. Bolivia's consumer price index, for example, rose an average of 610 percent between 1980 and 1985, with the largest increase in 1985 at over 11,000

inflation

percent. Brazil's inflation topped 1,500 percent in 1989, Nicaragua's 9,700 percent in 1988, and Peru's 3,398 percent in 1989. Only Colombia, Guatemala, Honduras, Panama, and Paraguay escaped rates of inflation of more than 30 percent a year during this era. Inflation badly eroded real wages and purchasing power. No one could live without dire difficulty during these periods of hyperinflation. Since the Pink Tide, only Venezuela endured crippling inflation. Only once, in 2008, the year of worldwide financial crisis, was the region's inflation rate over five percent (Tables 9.4 and 9.5).

In 2019, 191 million Latin Americans lived in poverty, 31.8 percent of the population. Of those, 11.5 percent live in extreme poverty or more than 60 million people. The countries with the lowest rates of poverty in 2019 were Uruguay (2.7 percent) and Chile (10.7). The worsening of conditions in

Table 9.4 Latin American inflation: regional average 1980–2019

Year	Inflation rate %	Year	Inflation rate %	Year	Inflation rate %
2019	2.76	2006	4.27	1993	10.75
2018	2.43	2005	4.69	1992	11.21
2017	2.31	2004	4.32	1991	21.78
2016	1.69	2003	3.81	1990	21.74
2015	1.68	2002	3.75	1989	11.43
2014	3.40	2001	4.36	1988	8.27
2013	2.61	2000	4.69	1987	12.32
2012	3.90	1999	3.47	1986	11.83
2011	5.04	1998	5.19	1985	15.06
2010	3.52	1997	7.05	1984	11.73
2009	2.59	1996	8.57	1983	10.91
2008	8.25	1995	10.66	1982	8.40
2007	4.99	1994	10.59	1981	14.45

Source: Macrotrends, Latin American Inflation Rate 1967–2020. http://www.macrotrends.net/countrie/LCN/latin-america-caribbean-/inflation-rate-cpi

Table 9.5 Inflation (Average annual rate) selected Latin American nations

	1970–1980	1980–1985	1985	1992	1995	2000	2003
Argentina	118.5	322.6	672.2	17.6	1.6	-0.7	13.4
Bolivia	18.8	610.9	11,749.2	10.5	12.6	3.8	3.3
Brazil	34.2	135.1	301.8	1,149.1	22.0	5.5	14.7
Chile	130.2	21.3	30.7	12.7	8.2	4.7	14.7
Colombia		22.3	24.1	25.1	19.5	8.8	7.1
Mexico	16.5	60.7	57.8	11.9	52.1	8.9	4.5
Peru	30.3	102.1	163.4	56.7	10.2	4.0	2.3
Latin America				414.4	25.8	8.7	

Source: *ECLA. Statistical Yearbook for Latin America and the Caribbean, 1990*, pp. 98–99; 2000, p. 751; 2005, 136

Brazil and Venezuela caused the increase of 2.3 percent in poverty in the region between 2014 and 2018. In the rest of the region, poverty lessened, because of government programs and remittances from abroad.

Malnourishment, disease, and high infant mortality are inescapable facts-of-life for the poor. In 1980, more than 50 million people in the region had a daily caloric intake below the standards set by the World Health Organization (WHO). Twenty million were seriously malnourished. In Mexico, the diets of 52 percent of the population did not meet WHO standards. Urbanization and globalization worsened dietary insufficiencies. In 1960, for example, Mexicans ate mostly tortillas, bread, beans, and small quantities of vegetables, eggs, and meat. Two decades later, poor city dwellers consumed more processed food (such as white bread) and soda. Consumption of milk in Mexico fell about ten percent during the 1980s, while consumption of beans dropped even more. Mexicans ate only minimal amounts of eggs, fruits, and vegetables, and 60 percent ate no meat at all, leaving them easy prey for dysentery, malnutrition, and anemia. Their diets consisted of less and less protein and more sugar. The complex combination of corn (tortillas), beans, and chili, which provided their sustenance since the beginning of civilization, gradually gave way to widely advertised Pan Bimbo (the equivalent of Wonder Bread) and Coca-Cola. Maternal malnutrition was the primary cause of high child mortality rates.

Not having enough to eat was only the most urgent circumstance. Lack of health care was equally as important. Routine health services are not available to one third of all Latin Americans. Millions die from preventable causes. Neo-liberal cuts to government expenditures exacerbated these shortcomings. Growing up in the slums without clean drinking water and sanitation facilities leave children susceptible to dengue, cholera, hepatitis, typhoid, tuberculosis, influenza, measles, and respiratory infections. Crowded conditions, living three or more to a bedroom, lead to rapid spread of these diseases. In the early 2000s in Brazil an estimated 200,000 children live on the streets.

Governments have taken measures to alleviate poverty since the 1990s. Between 2011 and 2018, social spending by central governments increased from 10.3 to 11.3 percent of GDP, more than half of all public spending.

Indigenous

Census data in 2010 estimated the number of indigenous at 42 million. One estimate guesses perhaps 500 different ethnic groups. Eighty percent of the indigenous reside in four countries, Mexico, Guatemala, Peru, and Bolivia.

Although they comprise 8 percent of the total population, the indigenous make up 14 percent of those in poverty and 17 percent of those in extreme poverty. Forty-three percent of the indigenous people were poor, approximately twice the proportion of the rest of the people. The rate of extreme poverty was 2.7 times greater. A little less than half live in urban areas. Their access to education and health care were far less than the general population. Employment tended to concentrate in low skilled, highly unstable jobs. Only 20 percent of indigenous Brazilians have access to primary education; 2.1 percent to secondary education; and less than 1 percent to higher education.

Brazil has approximately 900,000 indigenous people in over 300 tribes. The government (supposedly) set aside nearly 13 percent of the nation's land, almost all in the Amazon area, for them. The Guarani, who live in southern Brazil, are the largest group, numbering 51,000. The largest Amazon group is the Tikuna who count 40,000. Extraordinarily, more than 100 "uncontacted peoples" inhabit the Amazon. These peoples are extremely vulnerable to violence from outsiders and disease. Commercialization of agriculture endangers indigenous people in Brazil. Over the past century an average of one tribe a year became extinct. Development surrounding the construction of hydro-electric dams, cattle ranching, soy farming, road building, and mining deprived indigenous of their lands, livelihoods, and often their lives.

Mexico has the largest indigenous population in Latin America, 12.7 million people, 15 percent of the total, who speak 62 languages. Chiapas with 1.1 million has the most of any state. Conditions there are appalling. Half of Chiapas's indigenous earn no income and another 45 percent less than $US5 a day. Seventy percent lived in a high level of malnourishment. Twenty percent are illiterate, 90 percent have no electricity or plumbing. Their healthcare is substandard. Recently, Mexico's indigenous experienced some improvements. The percentage of indigenous covered by health insurance rose from 14 to 62 percent from 2006 to 2012, because of a new program *Seguro Popular*. Infant mortality rates declined as did the incident of child malnutrition. Nonetheless, wide discrepancies between indigenous and non-indigenous continue in healthcare.

Indigenous Mexicans are highly likely to migrate from their homes to elsewhere in Mexico, usually to toil in the fields, often replacing labor that went to the United States to work in agriculture. These are seasonal subsistence jobs. They also migrate to the cities where they work in construction, as domestics, and vendors. Internal migration at times was the first step toward the United States.

Inequities

Latin America has the most inequitable distribution of wealth and income of any region in the globe. This is of particular interest, because experts long maintained that one crucial element for promoting economic development (and attainment of a place among the advanced nations) is fostering the expansion of the middle sectors.

During the difficult times between 1970 and 1982, the share of the income of the wealthiest 20 percent fell, and the share of the poorest rose 10 percent. Income inequality dropped significantly from 2002 to 2014. In 2016, however, it worsened, as economic growth slowed.

Between 2002 and 2017, according to ECLA, the share of the low-income strata as a proportion of the total population fell from 70.9 percent to 55.9 percent. This group includes the people in poverty and extreme poverty and those non-poor lower strata. At the same time, the share of the middle strata (divided into lower middle, intermediate-middle, and upper-middle) grew from 26.9 percent to 41.1 percent. The people in the high-income strata rose from 2.2 to 3.0 percent.

During the first two decades of the twenty first century, the middle class expanded all over Latin America. Unfortunately, the folks who rose in class were in a precarious position at best. More than half of the middle-income sector had not finished their secondary studies. In addition, 36.6 percent of the middle class were in occupations considered to have a high risk of "informality and precariousness," such as non-professional self-employed workers, non-professional salaried workers in microbusinesses, and in service industries. Only half of all economically active people had access to a pension system. The middle strata worker on average earned $664 dollars a month. The low strata earned $256 dollars a month. "A high proportion of the middle-income population experiences significant deficits in terms of social and labor inclusion and a high degree of vulnerability to falling back into poverty due to changes prompted by unemployment, a decline in their income, or other catastrophic events such as grave illness or disaster," according to ECLAC.

The share of the wealthiest people grows inexorably. In Brazil, for instance, the share of the wealthiest 1 percent of the population in the country's overall income rose to 27.5 percent in 2017. In Chile taking both financial and non-financial assets into account the share of the wealthiest 1 percent in the country's net wealth amounts to 26.5 percent. Unlike those countries, the proportion of social wealth controlled by the richest 1 percent only equals 17.5 percent in Uruguay, a country ruled by leftist governments for 15 consecutive years.

Table 9.6 Gini coefficient for Latin America 2018

Country	Gini coefficient
Brazil	53.9
Honduras	52.1
Colombia	50.4
Panama	49.2
Guatemala	48.3
Costa Rica	48.0
Nicaragua	46.2
Paraguay	46.2
Ecuador	45.4
Mexico	45.4
Chile	44.4
Dominican Republic	43.7
Peru	42.8
Bolivia	42.2
Argentina	41.4
Haiti	41.1
El Salvador	39.7
Uruguay	38.6
Venezuela (2017)	46.9

The Gini coefficent depicts a ranking of Latin American countries based on the degree of inequality in wealth distribution. The Gini coefficient measures the deviation of the distribution of income (or consumption) among individuals or households in a given country from a perfectly equal distribution. A value of 0 represents absolute equality, whereas 100 would be the highest possible degree of inequality. As of 2018, Brazil was the most unequal country in Latin America, with a Gini coefficient of 53.9, followed by Honduras with 52.1 (Table 9.6).

Inequality appears to be lessening in 2020. The Gini index went from an average of 0.538 to 0.465. Between 2002 and 2014 the same index fell by 1.0 percent a year and between 2014 and 2018 by 0.6 percent a year.

Violence

Perhaps, the most difficult question in the first two decades of the twenty-first century in Latin America is why at a time when poverty is at its lowest level in more than a generation, the region suffers the world's highest homicide rates. According to most social science theory, the exact opposite should prevail. Five countries rank among the ten with the most homicides, El Salvador,

Venezuela, Honduras, Brazil, and Guatemala. The most dangerous cities in Latin America were San Pedro Sula, Honduras, Ciudad Juárez, Mexico, Ananindeua, Brazil, and Caracas, Venezuela. Few experts agree on the causes of the rising numbers of murders. They posit a number of possibilities: youth unemployment, unemployment (desperation?), weak police and court systems, narcotics commerce, easy access to guns, and the prevalence of machismo (Tables 9.7 and 9.8).

Table 9.7 Homicide rates for Latin America 2020

Country	Homicides per 100,000 people
El Salvador	82.84
Honduras	56.52
Venezuela	56.33
Brazil	29.53
Guatemala	27.26
Colombia	25.50
Mexico	19.26

Source: "Homicide in Latin America and the Caribbean: Statistics and Facts," Research Department, *Statista*, April 23, 2020

Table 9.8 Global peace index

Country	Score	Global rank
Costa Rica	1.691	32
Uruguay	1.704	35
Panama	1.875	56
Argentina	1.978	74
Paraguay	1.991	75
Dominican Republic	1.992	76
Peru	2.066	84
Bolivia	2.074	86
Cuba	2.074	86
Ecuador	2.085	90
Haiti	2.211	111
El Salvador	2.243	113
Guatemala	2.267	115
Honduras	2.288	119
Brazil	2.413	126
Nicaragua	2.553	135
Mexico	2.572	137
Colombia	2.646	140
Venezuela	2.936	149

Source: *2020 Global Peace Index*. The United States. 2.307 #121
The GPI covers 99.7 per cent of the world's population, using 23 qualitative and quantitative indicators from highly respected sources, and measures the state of peace across three domains: the level of Societal Safety and Security; the extent of Ongoing Domestic and International Conflict; and the degree of Militarization

During the height of the Pink Tide, civil unrest was at low levels. As the 2010s progressed, however, it grew, especially in Venezuela, Brazil, and Chile. Demonstrations, protests, and strikes in these three countries made South America the second highest region in the number of such events in the world in 2018. Nicaragua too experienced considerable unrest. In April 2018 government clashes with its political opposition led to 325 deaths and 700 imprisonments.

Doubtlessly the unsatisfactory level of violence eroded the quality of life in the areas affected. It was difficult to conduct business in a climate of lawlessness and accompanying uncertainty. The hundreds of thousands of people who left their homelands because of the violence were a substantial loss.

Employment

As Latin American nations sought to modernize their economies through industrialization, the composition of the workforce changed. The percentage of people who labored in agriculture declined. In 1950, only five countries did not have a majority of the labor force in agriculture, Argentina, Chile, Cuba, Uruguay, and Venezuela. By 2000, only Haiti employed more than half its people in agriculture. By then only five of twenty Latin American nations employed more than a quarter of its workers in agriculture. The most extreme case is Argentina, where one percent toils in agriculture. Industry employed a growing number while ISI predominated. After its abandonment, jobs in manufacturing decreased. With agriculture in sharp decline and manufacturing struggling to hold its own by 2000 the service sector employed a majority of workers in 16 of 20 Latin American nations. The four in which service did not predominate are El Salvador, Haiti, Honduras, and Nicaragua. These are the region's most rural and poorest countries. Even in Honduras the trend is clear. In 1950, agriculture employed 72 percent of its people, while in 2000 this shrank to 35 percent. Service grew from 19 to 43 percent.

Women's participation in the work force rose from 19 percent in 1960 to 28 percent in 2000. This resulted from decrease in agricultural employment and the increase in industrial and service jobs. It also reflected economic hardship. Male unemployment and underemployment meant one source of income was insufficient. Employers pay women less than men earn. One of the sectors with increased demand for cheaper female labor arose in the maquiladoras assembly plants along the U.S. border, where they comprise sixty percent of the workforce. The rise in women's participation in the work force meant gains in independence and changed their role in families

Informal Economy

The informal economy consists of economic activities unregulated by the state, which often compete against other businesses operating legally. Informal enterprises function on the margins; they generally do not generate much income. Street vending is the most visible and well-known category, but other occupations include shoe shining, car washing, small-scale construction, and low technology repairs. The size of the informal sector depended on the condition of the economy. When manufacturing expanded in the 1950s and 1960s and people flooded into the cities the sector expanded, but because other work was relatively plentiful, the percentage of the workers involved did not grow. The downturns of the 1980s and 1990s brought the percentage to thirty percent of total employment.

Neoliberal policies resulted in a substantial increase in the informal sector, because 81 percent of the jobs they created were informal or small enterprises. From 1980 to 1992, in Latin America as a whole employment in small enterprise rose from 15 to 22 percent of the workforce. The informal sector's share went from 19 to 27 percent. With domestic service, these two categories accounted for more than half of the jobs. Employment in large or medium size businesses fell from 44 to 31 percent and public employment from 15.7 to 13.6. The number of street vendors in La Paz, Bolivia doubled from 1967 to 1992. The informal sector accounted for more than 40 percent of the Gross Domestic Product in Bolivia, Colombia, Ecuador, Paraguay and Peru. In Paraguay, the total was nearly 70 percent.

The percentage in informal employment in Latin America and the Caribbean in 2016 was 53.1 percent. Bolivia had the highest share at almost 81 percent. In Ecuador (73.6), Peru (69.5), Paraguay (68.9), El Salvador (68.5), and Colombia (62.1) more than six of every ten workers toiled in the informal sector. Argentina (49.4) had nearly half the workforce. Uruguay had the lowest number with a bit less than a quarter informally employed (Table 9.9).

Petty entrepreneurs fill the streets of Latin American cities, selling items ranging from gum and candy bars to hot food to appliances. The small businesses evolve from a continuum, in which migrants move to the cities, take jobs—if they can find them—as domestics and menial laborers, and, then, when they are more established, start their own enterprises, using skills they learned from parents and other family. They rely first on the unpaid labor of nuclear family and extended networks (much like they did on their plot of land in the countryside). Sometimes they obtain additional labor from the pool of unemployed and underemployed slum dwellers. Some proprietors of

Table 9.9 Informal economy as percentage of total employment in Latin America: Selected Countries 2019

Country	Percentage of total employment
Bolivia	80.7
Ecuador	73.6
Peru	69.5
Paraguay	68.9
El Salvador	68.5
Colombia	62.1
Argentina	49.4

Source: Marina Pasquali, "Latin America and the Caribbean: Informal employment by country, 2019". https://www.statista/statistics/1037216/informal-employment-share-latin-america-caribbean-country

informal sector business rise above poverty. Much of the informal sector, such as the street children, who beg, smalltime criminals, and prostitutes, unfortunately, live lives of struggle and misery.

The informal economy fulfills another crucial function in addition to providing a living for an increasing number of Latin Americans. It supplies the daily needs of much of the population. In the bustling central market of Cuzco, Peru, for example, vendors sell anything a consumer might want, such as watches, hats, medicinal herbs, clothes, and endless quantities of food, some of it prepared and hot. In Lima, the informal sector built most of the public markets and delivers 95 percent of Lima's public transportation. In Bolivia, half the economically active population works in small businesses. In the cities vendors set up anywhere space is available. The sound of bargaining is relentless, as the market women and their customers dicker back and forth over prices. The noisy market, teeming with people and overflowing with the smells of food, is still the very lifeblood of the city.

Women play crucial roles in the informal economy. They run the markets today much as they did before the Europeans arrived five centuries ago. In Cuzco, women operate the stalls, caring for children, gossiping, and helping their neighbors all at the same time. The women commonly start off, when they arrive from the countryside, as domestic servants, then moving on to itinerant peddling, and lastly to the market. The necessary skills, including the ability to haggle relentlessly with customers to obtain the best prices for her merchandise, pass on from mother to daughter or aunt to niece. Work in the market provides women with an income, flexibility for childcare, and autonomy from men. Some work part-time in the market and hold other jobs, as well, others journey from their farms to sell their crops. A few have funds enough to invest in a license for a permanent stall in the market.

Life is not easy for the vendors. Many are single mothers or widows. Competition with other sellers is relentless. The women must be shrewd in their dealings with local authorities. The hours are long. The pressure on them is great. As one market woman put it: "From the time I wake up until I go to bed, it's the preoccupation a mother has to feed her children, to find food for her children, whether we sell or not, because if we do not sell, there's no food to eat."

A few examples illustrate how men and women make the complex adaptations the informal economy requires. Dona Avenina Copana de Garnica is an artisan in La Paz, Bolivia. Although born in the city, she nonetheless speaks Aymara, an indigenous language, as well as Spanish. She, her husband, and six children live in small, rented quarters above their small, artisan workshop in an artisan district of the city. The upstairs has one bedroom with bunk beds. They sleep and work there. The shop has a small stove for soldering and shares space with a cooking area demarcated by a piece of cloth. The Garnica family uses metal, cardboard, and cloth to make numerous items used in rituals and celebrations, including masks, noisemakers, whips, and costumes for miniature figures. Avelina's parents live across the street, and the whole family works in the business. Avelina comes from a family of costume makers, so she learned the trade from relatives. She embroiders the costumes for the miniatures. She also cuts and pastes the decorations for the costumes. Her husband, a tinsmith, makes objects out of sheet metal. He learned his trade from her aunt. The family employs seasonal workers. Avelina also keeps the books and supervises the workers. The latter requires that she often ride buses as much as forty minutes to inspect their work, which is done in their own homes. The Garnicas actively promote their products through sponsorships of local fiestas, selling to tourists in the cities, and even traveling to Peru.

Like Avelina, Sofía Velásquez, who grew up in La Paz, Bolivia, earns her livelihood in the informal economy. She began her working life helping her mother sell candles in the markets and then sold vegetables there on days when there was no school. Later, she sold eggs, beer, onions, mutton, and pork. Separated from her husband, she earned enough to send her one daughter, Rocío, a teenager in the early 1990s, to private school. She continues to buy and sell pork, but she and her daughter supplement their income by working as food vendors. Rocío cooks and Sofía sells the food in front of their home. Sofía plays an active role in the community, heading an organization that controls the local market. This position carries with it the responsibility and considerable expense of sponsoring local fiestas.

One of the major categories within the informal sector is domestic service. In 2020 in Latin America and the Caribbean, between 11 and 18 million people engaged in paid domestic work, of these 93 percent are women. Domestic work accounts for 14 percent of women's employment in the region. Over 77.5% operate in the informal sector, which means that a significant proportion of them work in precarious conditions and without access to social protection. The income of women employed in domestic service is also equal to or less than 50 percent of the average for all employed persons.

The informal sector involves a constant struggle to feed, clothe and shelter. Latin Americans show extraordinary adaptability, resilience, and persistence. Nonetheless, it is a hard life indeed.

Migrations

Since 1950 people have left Latin American nations for other Latin American nations and other regions, some because of revolutions in Cuba and Central America, guerrilla wars in Colombia and Peru, repressive rightist governments in South America, in search of political asylum and peace, and others because they sought better economic opportunities. The largest number, of course, sought refuge in the United States, but a significant group went to Europe, as well.

For many immigrants both the push and pull were strong. They sought to leave their homes, where the jobs were few and those available paid low wages. In some areas like Honduras, half the population lived in poverty. Even if one had employment, violence and corruption constantly threatened.

The compatibility of languages accounts for the preference of emigrants for Spain and Italy. The Dominican Republic, Colombia, and Ecuador sent tens of thousands to Spain because of labor migration agreements. In 2001, more than 200,000 Japanese Latin Americans worked in Japan.

Immigration generally falls into two categories. The first is well educated, constituting a "brain drain." Often this phenomenon was associated with the exiled academics in fields disapproved by rightist regimes. For example, perhaps 15,000 or more Argentine scientists and professionals fled the terror, living abroad during the 1980s. Unskilled labor comprises the biggest group of immigrants. They left their homes for the many reasons discussed earlier.

Migration within Latin America has a varied record, ebbing and flowing dependent on economic conditions. Generally, migrants went from poorer countries to those more prosperous. Southern Cone poor looking for employment went to Buenos Aires, where they were so numerous that eventually in 1994 the Argentine government amnestied over 200,000 illegal immigrants from Bolivia, Peru, and Paraguay. Venezuela was an attraction prior to 2000 for immigrants in the northern tier of South America. The biggest source of migrants was neighboring Colombia, because 1.5 million of its residents fled the violence of the guerrilla war.

Internal displacement emerged in the 2010s as among the most important crises in Latin America. Hundreds of thousands of people fled their homelands annually in the face of unprecedented violence. In Colombia, fifty years of guerrilla war displaced 7.3 million residents. More than 340,000 Colombians were at the same time refugees abroad, mostly in neighboring countries. Few were willing to return, wary of the unsteady peace agreed to in 2016. The situation in Venezuela is, if anything, even worse, as its citizens departed in the millions to escape the collapsed economy. Between 2015 and 2018, three million Venezuelans left their homes. Colombia and Peru between them accepted 1.8 million of these refugees. Ecuador took 250,000. In 2019, approximately one million Venezuelans temporarily settled in towns just on the Colombian side of their border. Brazil, too, experienced internal displacement, with 7.7 million of its people forced out of their homes after 2000 to other parts of the country because of infrastructure projects (dams, highways), violence, and natural disasters. In addition, 52,000 Venezuelans poured into Brazil just since 2017. The Venezuelan migrants met with some hostility in Colombia, although both there and in Peru governments made considerable efforts to arrange temporary legal status for them. Nonetheless, the conditions in the border towns were difficult with shortages in supplies and housing and lack of employment possibilities.

The biggest flow of people originated in Central America the result of the ongoing civil wars and terror campaigns before and after the combatants signed peace accords. If anything, conditions worsened since the peace accords. Before the 1960s, Central Americans moved within the region. More than 350,000 Salvadorans made homes and found work in neighboring Honduras until the mid-1960s, when Honduran authorities deported them. Guatemalan indigenous crossed back and forth across the Mexican border to labor on the plantations in Chiapas. The civil wars, however, changed these patterns, forcing the migrations to the United States and other nations.

The so-called Northern Triangle, El Salvador, Guatemala, and Honduras, sent immigrants north to the United States for fifty years. From 1980 to 2015 the number of migrants from this region residing in the United States increased by an annual average of eight percent. In 2017, their total number was almost three million. During the 2010s, the Northern Triangle's displacement crisis reached troubling levels. Honduras had in 2019 190,000 internally displaced people, or four percent of its population. El Salvador had similar statistics with 71,500 displaced between 2006 and 2016. Many of these people have nowhere to go, because the United States and Mexico tightened their borders and in the case of the United States increased the number of deportations. Mexico, formerly welcoming these migrants, had its own displacement problems caused by rampant violence. In 2017 an estimated 345,000 Mexicans were displaced.

Immigration has advantages and disadvantages. On one hand, it weakens or breaks family and community links and it disrupts support networks in the home countries. It also deprives the originating country of skilled and unskilled labor. On the other hand, immigration can reduce poverty. Remittances transfer needed capital to the homeland. The World Bank reported that in 2014 the poverty rate would have been 12 percent higher in El Salvador without remittances. Evidence indicates that in countries like Guatemala it decreases the likelihood that families would go hungry.

Super-Urbanization

The shift in population from rural areas to the cities after 1950 was remarkable and overwhelming in many aspects. This marks the greatest movement of people, far exceeding that of immigration abroad. Latin America's urban population increased from an estimated 65 million in 1950 to 380 million in 2000, over 75 percent of the region's people. (This is about the same as in the United States.) In several nations, the percentage is even higher. Argentina is almost 90 percent urban, Brazil approximately 80 percent, Chile over 85 percent, Uruguay and Venezuela more than 90 percent. The least urban countries are Haiti, Guatemala, and Honduras where urban dwellers account for fifty percent of the population.

The rural-urban transfer occurred in discernible stages. The first took place between 1950 and 1980, when 27 million Latin Americans, lured by manufacturing jobs created by ISI policies moved to the cities. It was also a time when governments turned away from the countryside focusing attention on the cities. Modern agriculture required fewer workers. The improvement in health care and the accompanying population growth resulted in more people in search of employment. The jobs were in the cities. Government expanded at this time, creating still more opportunities in the cities. Second, migration to the large urban areas slowed during the 1970s and 1980s. The numbers of people who moved during the previous two decades was so high that fewer remained to migrate from the countryside. The changeover from ISI to neo-liberal strategies decreased the work in factories, at that point closing because they could not complete with the flow of cheaper foreign goods. Neo-liberal cutbacks reduced the opportunities for employment in government. Economic downturns added further misery. The city was not as attractive with falling wages and increased unemployment. To make matters worse, urban conditions deteriorated. Pollution, overcrowding, and crime combined to discourage migrants. By the 1980s, the potential migrant could decide between poverty in the countryside or in the cities. By the later 1980s, migrants looked to medium-size cities.

The transformation created giant metropolises. In 1950, only Buenos Aires had more than five million inhabitants. Mexico City was the next largest city with just under three million people. Currently nine Latin American cities have five million or more residents. These nine cities together house more than 100 million people. (These cities are in order of size: Mexico City, Sao Paulo, Buenos Aires, Rio de Janeiro, Lima, Bogotá, Santiago, Belo Horizonte, and Guatemala City.) It is likely that the first four of these metropolitan areas have twenty million inhabitants (Table 9.10).

From the late twentieth century, the growth of medium-size cities outpaced that of the largest and, as a result, the portion of the population in the latter decreased. The number of cities with between 1 million and 5 million residents climbed from 17 in 1975 to 43 in 2000. In 2018, fifty-five Latin American cities had more than one million inhabitants. The population of Mexico City, although it increased, fell as a percentage of the nation's inhabitants from twenty-five percent to approximately sixteen percent. Nonetheless, the mega-cities continue to dominate the economies of their nations.

What is it like to live in the super cities? Latin American cities are bifurcated. One part is for the rich, the other for the poor. Lima, for example, has a modern downtown with skyscrapers lining paved streets. Twenty-five percent (160 million) of Latin America's urban population lives in slums. Lima's *barriadas* or squatter settlements (known as *barrios* or *colonias* elsewhere in Spanish America or *favelas* in Brazil) surround the center. The settlements

Table 9.10 Latin America, largest cities

1	Mexico City	Mexico	22,976,700
2	São Paulo	Brazil	20,847,500
3	Buenos Aires	Argentina	15,481,800
4	Rio de Janeiro	Brazil	12,460,200
5	Lima	Peru	10,674,116
6	Bogotá	Colombia	9,135,800
7	Santiago	Chile	7,164,400
8	Belo Horizonte	Brazil	5,595,800
9	Guadalajara	Mexico	4,687,700
10	Caracas	Venezuela	3,260,200

were rural into the 1940s and 1950s. Gradually, as the population expanded and sought quarters, the cities expanded and what was once farmland disappeared. The residents arrived from the Andean highlands. Dirt roads meander between houses built using scrap lumber, woven mats, and other scavenged materials. The stink from open sewers and the loud noises permeate the air.

Beneath the hustle, bustle, odors, and apparent squalor reside real communities. It is in the barriadas and other such settlements that the twenty-first century version of the struggle for control over everyday life occurs. In the squatter towns people assist each other in much the same way they did when planting and harvesting on collectively owned farms in the Andean highlands or in the villages of Morelos, Mexico. Networks of relatives and friends, usually from their home villages, make these difficult lives more bearable. When Jorge and Celsa settled in Lima's Chalaca barriada, for example, Jorge's sister and brother helped them build a house on the same plot where the sister and her husband lived. An aunt also provided support. Later, Celsa's sister, her husband, and four small children moved in.

Most of the families in the barriadas start with next to nothing. They built their houses painstakingly, board by board. The typical house first had one story built with reed matting or wooden boards. Later residents reconstructed with wood or perhaps brick and cement. Rarely, do the residents have formal titles to the land. In Callao, the port for Lima, dwellers salvaged bricks and wood from the structures destroyed by the earthquake in 1967. Barriada residents cooked their meals over small fires or kerosene stoves. Only a few dwellings had electricity, initially pirated from main lines. Because they had no refrigeration, residents bought their food every day at the market. Not many had enough money to buy more than that, the storage problems notwithstanding. Furnishings varied depending on the economic situation of the inhabitants and were usually few in number and purely functional. A typical home might have a table. Utensils hung from the wall. Sleeping areas consisted of cots or beds with straw mattresses. The residents hung their clothes from poles or lines strung overhead. Boxes or trunks provided storage. People shared the courtyard with goats, sheep, and pigs. In Lima, they raised guinea pigs, a traditional Peruvian delicacy.

The giant metropolis Mexico City grew during the twentieth century from 23 square kilometers to 154,710 square kilometers, most of which poor people occupy. The sprawl annexed all the neighboring towns and villages, stormed up the surrounding hillsides, and swarmed over the dried up lakebeds. In the nineteenth century in the core of the city crowded tenements known as *vecindades* provided housing for the poor. As the city spread, out new neighborhoods arose. According to Priscilla Connelly, five types of slums emerged: colonias populares, vecindades, ciudades perdidas, cuartos de azotes, and deteriorated housing projects. The colonias are by far and away the most important, housing perhaps two-thirds of the capital's people. The colonias are unauthorized developments with uncertain land titles with spotty services, at least initially. The government usually leaves them to their own devices, and after a while some regular infrastructure materializes. These are not shanty-towns. From 2001 a successful Federal District government program provided credits for home improvements. The oldest of the housing for the poor are the vecindades, rental apartments mostly in the central city, comprised of old homes once occupied by the wealthy. They house about one-tenth of the city's people. The ciudades perdidas are small-scale shantytowns put up on undesirable vacant lots. The cuartos are makeshift arrangements on rooftops, sometimes for domestics. The latter two accommodate only less than one percent of the population. Housing projects, which hold fifteen percent of the people, suffer from poor construction, neglect, and overcrowding. Most of the housing for the poor is occupant owned. In general the housing for the poor is precarious in that the threat of flooding, accompanying landslides, is considerable and poor, erratic services, and overcrowding predominate.

In Netzahuacoyotl, an enormous barrio of three million people in Mexico City, I visited the home of a street vendor. It was on a muddy pothole marred street on a hill. The owner had built the house with concrete blocks, purchased one at a time. Many of the blocks were not joined by mortar, because the owner had not saved enough to buy cement. The residence occupied one third of the lot with a concrete block enclosed courtyard making up the rest. It had one room, divided into kitchen, dining and sleeping areas. A table stood in the middle of the room. The vendor's spouse cooked on a stove. She had an oven, but used it for storing pots and pans only. The courtyard sheltered the outhouse, a small garden, a goat, and some chickens. The owner had begun work on a second floor. A water pipe stuck out in the middle of the courtyard.

The story of Percy Hinojosa (related by Jorge Parodi) of Lima, Peru illustrates the plight of hundreds of thousands of Latin Americans who left their homes in the countryside to better their lives in the cities. He migrated at fifteen, because all that his home offered was endless poverty. Like most migrants to Lima, he had barely an elementary education. How then could he find employment? Unfortunately, he lacked relatives or friends in the city who might help him. He toiled for twelve years in one job after another, until he obtained a steady position in a factory. Percy started as a domestic servant, attending school at night. Then he worked successively at a Coca Cola plant, a bakery, in small shops, furniture shops, and carpentry. No job lasted for more than a few months, when the business would let him go. His jobs entailed packing notebooks, counting bottles, and sanding furniture. He earned just enough to get by, but nothing more. He tried his hand at construction, which paid better than other trades, but it also meant that he was out of work for long periods. He apprenticed as an auto mechanic, but quit when he too loudly asked for a raise. Percy returned to the countryside for a year. Eventually, with a contact acquired from his earlier time as a domestic, he secured a factory job. Like so many others in Latin America, Percy did whatever was necessary.

The cities grew too fast. Governments have not provided the necessary services for the new residents. The cities are so big that public transportation is insufficient. Even in Mexico City, where the Metro carries almost four million riders a day, the transportation network is inadequate, because it does not cover vast areas of the Federal District. Electricity is inadequate. So is internet access.

Environment

Latin America confronts the global issues of warming within the context of the need for development. The cost of industrialization and commercialized agriculture is high. Air and water pollution, deterioration of croplands, and the destruction of tropical rainforests areas are among the region's environmental disasters. One estimate is that 200,000 people died between 2017 and 2019 because of pollution.

Mexico is the prime example of environmental degradation. The air is dangerous to breathe. The World Bank estimates that air pollution kills 33,000 Mexicans annually. About two-thirds of these deaths result from outdoor air pollution, but the remainder are the consequence of indoor pollution in rural areas, caused by in home cooking with wood and other solid fuels. In Mexico City, the smog is so thick that residents rarely see the beautiful mountains that surround the city. An estimated five million cars clog the streets of the capital (for the metropolitan area as a whole the number may be closer to ten million), often bringing traffic to a standstill. Their exhausts are the major cause of air pollution, emitting enormous quantities of contaminants. The government tried various strategies to clean up the air, such as prohibiting the individual usage of autos, testing emissions, and cleaner fuels. Some improvements resulted, but some days the government warns people to stay home, because the air quality is too dangerous to breathe. Capitalinos (residents of Mexico City) regularly wear facemasks for protection.

One crucial problem is safe drinking water. According to the United Nations, 36 million people in Latin America live without clean, safe drinking water. This is not a result of lack of water resources. These are bountiful. "It is the poorest of the poor who live without access to drinking water." The poor do not have influence and struggle to apply pressure to politicians to remedy the situation. It is common for the water that is pumped into homes is unsafe, even though statistical data does not count it as so. In Mexico City, for example, in the upper-middle class neighborhood Condesa, homes have running water but" no one drinks the water even the people of the barrios, the slums." (Charles Fishman). In Mexico City, the pipes for drinking water and sewage were laid underground long ago side by side. The pipes corroded and sewage and drinking water intermingle." The water comes out of the treatment plants clean, but it becomes undrinkable. In other places, water is available only a few hours a day. Only 28 percent of Latin America's sewer water is treated. More than 77 percent lack safe sanitation.

Waste disposal is another seemingly unsolvable problem. In Mexico City, thirty percent of solid waste is not collected. People dump it into the streets, rivers, lakes, and open fields. Lake Guadalupe, the closest lake to the Federal District is essentially a huge septic tank. Unspeakable wastes pollute its thirty million cubic meters of residual waters. Consequently, agricultural products produced in the region of the lake are dangerous because harmful microorganisms from the lake water used to irrigate crops infest them.

Human Capital

Latin American nations notoriously underfund investments in human capital, which includes education, health care, and nutrition. This is a result of several factors. First, government revenues are usually insufficient. Second, no tradition of public investment in these areas existed. In the past, governments left schools and hospitals, for example, to the Catholic Church. Third, until the adoption of the ISI model of development, the commodity export strategy did not require an educated workforce. The commodity export model actually diminished production of staple crops crucial to basic nutrition. One exception was in Mexico, where in the 1970s the administration of President José López Portillo built 2,000 rural health clinics and thousands of government stores to supply subsidized basic foods. Two decades later President Carlos Salinas de Gortari established Pronasol, a program that funded 80,000 new classrooms, renovated over a 100,000 schools, awarded scholarships to 1.2 million poor students, and built 300 hospitals, 4,000 health centers, and

1,000 rural health clinics. From the transition to democracy from the late 1980s through the Pink Tide, governments changed course and invested in human capital. The mechanism adopted was the so-called CCTs or conditional cash transfers.

The most well-known and scrutinized CCTs are Mexico's *Prospera* and Brazil's *Bolsa Familia*. Founded in 1997, by President Ernesto Zedillo, as *Progresa*, renamed *Oportunidades* in 2001 and *Prospera* in 2010, it granted cash to mothers in return for their sending their children to school and periodically bringing them to health centers. It covered 300,000 households in 6,344 rural municipalities in 1997 with an expenditure of US$3.62 billion. By 2015, it reached 6.1 million households, effecting 28 million people or about 25 percent of the nation's population. Initially the government payment took place at distribution points in towns in cash. This practice proved inconvenient and risky, because it often required long travel and waiting lines and made recipients vulnerable to robbery. Subsequently, the program adopted electronic transfers. The crucial aspect of the program was the centrality of "co-responsibility." The government provided assistance, but only so long as the family benefitting did their part keeping the children in school and taking them to clinics. The agreement included provisions that all members of the family had to use preventive health services.(These included pre- and post-birth care for mother and child, etc.) Prospera increased the percentages of children in school, lessened the rate of childhood diseases, and lowered the rates of poverty and extreme poverty. It also seemed to escape the corruption common to many Mexican government endeavors.

The Bolsa Familia in Brazil originated in the mid-1990s in Campinas and Brasilia, expanded as the Bolsa Escola in 2001 and finally became the Bolsa Familia in 2003. Currently, it reaches 13 million families and 50 million people. Its conditions for participation are, basically, the same as for Progresa in Mexico. Criticism of the program arise in two areas (which may be applicable to the Mexican case as well, but the evaluation data is more complete for Brazil). First, while the program successfully keeps children in school, the education they receive is of low quality. Second, although more children finish secondary school, the economy is not expanding sufficiently to provide employment for them. Consequently, too few jobs exist for too many graduates, a situation which drives down wages for these jobs.

Particularly in the first decade of the twenty-first century, when the Pink Tide governments benefited from economic growth, they increased funds expended for public education. On average, they spent 3.7 percent of GDP and 14.8 percent of all government expenditures on education during these years. Some Latin American countries expended more than others did: Mexico

23.8 percent of government funds, but Panama and Bolivia only 8 percent. The money went mostly to primary education. This raised the percentage of children who completed primary school from 85 to 92 percent from 2001 to 2013. Wealthier nations, such as Argentina, Brazil, and Uruguay focused more on secondary schools. Brazil expends 25 percent on universities, which have only 2 percent of the pupils. This difference in strategies reflects the dilemma of public education. On one hand, primary education is the foundation upon which the rest builds. If children are not literate they have no hope of better (or any) employment. On the other hand, in the globalized, high technology world economy, the need is for skilled, more educated employees.

The New World of Communications

Latin America entered the mobile phone and internet age in the late 1980s. Given the difficulties in acquiring landlines before then—one might wait years for a telephone in Mexico City—, the availability of mobile phones brought about a revolution in communications. In 2015 Latin Americans spent over $US 100 billion on mobile phones and averaged more than one mobile phone per person. Argentina averaged almost one and a half per person. When we consider that in Argentina only one-third of its people had access to banking services and 22 percent to credit cards, the statistic becomes even more remarkable. The mobile industry created 350,000 jobs. Latin America has not kept the pace in the use of smartphones, however, though rapidly catching up. One difficulty arose in mobile phone use in that competition tended to be restricted. One company in Mexico, Telcel (America Movíl) controls almost 70 percent of the market. In Colombia America Movil controls 60 percent. The business is more competitive elsewhere in the region.

Internet use has exploded as well. Over 150 million Brazilians, 89 million Mexicans, and approximately 200 million other Latin Americans use the internet. In 2015, slightly more than half of all Latin Americans used the internet, up from just over thirty percent in 2010. The percentage of the population that uses the internet grew over ten percent a year from 2000 to 2015. Over forty percent of households connected to the internet in 2015, nearly doubling this number in five years. The development distributed unevenly, however. Of 24 countries (Latin America and the Caribbean) three had internet penetration less than 15 percent and fifteen were between 15 and 45 percent. Only Chile, Costa Rica, and Uruguay reached 60 percent. The vast majority of internet users are under thirty-five years. Internet access in rural areas is also not as extensive as in urban areas. In 2020, Latin America has 62 million subscribers to streaming video services. Netflix was first, joined by Amazon Prime and Apple TV, which arrived successively in 2016 and 2017. Brazil is Netflix's second largest foreign market next to the United Kingdom.

Art

Latin American artists developed innovative style and techniques into the twenty-first century. The stark political art of the 1930s and 1940s gave way temporarily to geometric and abstract art by the 1950s, but neither proved satisfactory to artists concerned with contemporary conditions, In Mexico, led by José Luis Cuevas, who believed the world more complicated than that depicted by Diego Rivera and David Alfaro Siqueiros, artists rebelled against the great muralists. Instead of portraying a world of simple contrasts between heroes and villains, these artists painted humans as victims of greater forces. Perhaps the most famous artists who emerged from this era was Colombian Fernando Botero who also abandoned socialist realism. Botero employed exaggeration and parody to his portrayal of characteristic types in Colombian politics and society.

By the 1960s, Latin American artists again embraced social protest, but they applied this new protest more diversely than that of the earlier generation's socialist realists. According to art historian Jacqueline Barnitz, however, some artists working under brutal regimes of the 1970s through the 1980s, employed a "strategy pf self-censorship" in which "they invented new symbols or invested previously used ones with new meaning." For example, Brazilian Antonio Henrique Amaral painted bananas in the 1970s, as a parody of Brazil as a banana republic, a tinhorn dictatorship that deferred to the United States. Other artists challenged not the political state, but the commercialization of art and official art institutions. This conceptual art provided the means for ideological expression without actually confronting the terrifying regimes in power. Some artists, nevertheless, paid a high price for even veiled protests. After the Chilean coup in 1973, the government arrested, imprisoned, tortured, let go, and then watched closely Guillermo Nunez. After it jailed and tortured him a second time two years later, the regime sent him into exile.

Latin American artists in the late twentieth century struggled and succeeded brilliantly in forging their own art out of the different strains of influence from their home lands and abroad. They fought to make sense out of a world of bitter poverty and profound disappointment. They explored their past and future with the same persistence, courage, and humor displayed by their ancestors for the preceding 600 years.

Sports

Soccer, which came to Latin America with the influx of immigrants from Europe during the late nineteenth century, is by far and away the most popular sport in the region. It became a unifying force, transcending race, class, and culture. Somehow, when on the soccer field or in the spectator stands, people seem to abandon (at least temporarily) their prejudices. Three Latin American nations reached the pinnacle of the sport, winning the World Cup championship: Uruguay in 1930 and 1950; Argentina in 1978 and 1986; and Brazil in 1958, 1962, 1970, 1994, and 2002. Of 21 World Cups, Brazil won the most, almost one quarter of the championships, Latin America's 9 wins were 40 percent of the total. Five Latin American nations hosted the Cup 7 times, one third of the tournaments. Arguably the three greatest soccer players of all time were Latin Americans: Diego Armando Maradona, an Argentine, Pele, a Brazilian, and Lionel Messi, an Argentine. All won World Cups; Pele won three. *Time Magazine* ranked Pele one of the 100 most important persons of the twentieth century. Pele played on the 1970 Brazilian World Cup team that some consider the greatest of all time.

Some regard the goal Maradona scored in the 1986 World Cup against England as the greatest of all time. It was particularly noteworthy because England humiliated Argentina in the Malvinas War only three years before and Argentines still were in recovery from the years of terror. The victory and Maradona's feat undoubtedly assisted the healing process and the transition to democracy. They restored a considerable degree of national pride.

Soccer is big business. The market value of the Brazilian national team in 2020 was almost one billion dollars. The Argentine team was valued at US$656 million.

Baseball is another import, from the United States. It is popular in the Dominican Republic, Venezuela, Cuba, and Mexico. Latin Americans took to the game to such an extent that they comprise 27.4 percent of all major league players, 254 in all. The Dominican Republic supplied 83 major leaguers, approximately ten percent of the total. Several leagues operate in Latin America, such as the Mexican Baseball League with 16 teams, the Mexican Pacific Baseball League with 10 teams, and the Venezuelan Baseball League with 8 teams. Seven leagues compete in the Caribbean World Series.

No better example of the globalization of popular culture exists than baseball. Originally, an American game, it became very popular in the Caribbean region and eventually an important supplier of players for all of professional baseball. Most teams in the big leagues operate bilingually.

Music

Music is another area of intense globalization. Latin American music deeply influenced music (and dance) everywhere. In turn, American popular music profoundly shaped music in Latin America. Latin American music was from the 1500s an amalgamation of traditions from the Americas, Africa, and Europe.

Out of the working class at the turn of the twentieth century in Buenos Aires emerged music and dance that was obscene (for the time) and pessimistic, the tango. It reached its height of popularity in the 1920s and 1930s. It had a revival in the 1980s with the Broadway show *Tango Argentino*, which was a smashing success. Another Broadway show *Forever Tango* played in the 2010s.

Most popular Latin American music during the 1950s and thereafter originated in the Caribbean and Brazil. The "Son" fused the music of Spain and Africa and led to the danzon, then the mambo and the chachacha. The mambo was all the "thing" in the 1950s. (I remember my parents practicing for us in our living room.) Son became salsa in the 1970s. The samba came from Brazil's African enslaved. The upper classes tolerated it (as they had the tango in Argentina) and later adopted it. Samba combined with jazz in the 1950s to create the bossanova. Mexico's contribution is mariachi, which merges indigenous and European folk music.

Conclusion

Most Latin Americans continue to struggle. Although in the first two decades of the twenty-first century their lives improved in statistical terms, at least, the gains achieved were by no means sufficient or permanent. The rise of millions from poverty and extreme poverty was uncertain at best. The majority of employment remains in the informal sector and by their very nature insecure. The majority of the population is at the mercy of erratic commodity prices and unsteady government revenues. Substantial improvements in education and health care are offset by the lack of steady employment. Most Latin Americans live on the edge.

How Historians Understand

From the Countryside to the City

The vast movement of Latin Americans from the countryside to the cities since the 1940s left historians with many questions. Who were/are the migrants? From where did/do they come from? Why did/do they leave rural areas? Three types of analysis arose to explain the phenomenon. The first interprets migration as a "rational" act by people seeking to better their economic situations. The second sees wider forces produced primarily by capitalist markets. The third incorporates both individual motivations and structural causes. The generally accepted is the latter, more pragmatic paradigm. The many case studies undertaken reveal that economic betterment, while crucial to any decision to migrate, was not the only reason.

Migrants are difficult to categorize. At first glance, it appears that young, single males are the likeliest to move from rural villages. Some early observers concluded that these men migrated because they had fewer attachments and the best possibilities for employment. In fact, women comprised the majority of migrants, especially in Mexico, Peru, Honduras, and Costa Rica, despite their lack of education, gender discrimination, and fewer job prospects. No pattern regarding marital status or age emerges. It is not even certain that the poorest migrated. Some analysts maintain that migrants are a select group of the "more dynamic members of the rural population."

Considerable disagreement exists about the geographic origins of migrants. Some investigators found that migrants arrived in the cities directly from the countryside. Others claim a pattern of movement from village to small town, such as a provincial capital, and then to the larger cities. Proponents of the first theory observed that the migrants were unprepared for city life. Proponents of the second theory took the opposite view that the migrants were "pre-urbanized." Small cities were, nonetheless, not the same as large cities, so the posited step-by-step process of acculturation was never easy. Clearly, both observations are likely correct. Migrants came from villages, towns, small cities, and larger cities. Specific conditions affected their plight. What is not so certain is how the circumstances and patterns changed over time.

Leaving one's home, abandoning what one knowns for the unknown was/is an act of enormous courage. Why would someone pull up roots? Was the motivation the "push" of unfavorable situations in their homelands or the "pull" of the promise of better lives elsewhere? We know that demographics were one push factor. Too many people sought to own or work on the land. In many places, the quality of the soils deteriorated. Commercialization and modernization of agriculture lessened the demand for labor in rural areas. The pull factors were evident, as well. Jobs were in the cities. Better education and health care were in the cities. Interestingly, one survey of migrants found that they mentioned economic concerns as the cause for leaving in less than half the responses. Migration had more to do with family, to rejoin a spouse, find a partner, or escape civil war. The same survey discovered that the migrants were unable to delineate clearly their motivations. No one reason seems to explain why a person or family left the countryside for the cities. No one pattern emerges. The migrants themselves do not experience or depict their lives in a linear way. As historians, neither should we.

Latin American Lives

Women Rebels

In the darkest times, women all over Latin America mobilized to combat oppression. They led the resistance to the dictatorships in Argentina, Brazil, and Chile. They joined the revolutions in Central America. Women went to the streets to protest in Bolivia and Mexico. They fought time and time again to protect their families and themselves from economic crisis and political and gender oppression.

Two of these women, Vilma Espín and Doris María Tijerino, are examples of the endurance, sacrifice, and extraordinary courage and leadership women provided to movements for social justice. Vilma Espín Guillois (1930–2007) was a chemical engineer with degrees from the University of Oriente in Cuba and the Massachusetts Institute of Technology, whose father was a high-ranking executive in the Bacardi Rum Company. In 1955, she joined the 26th of July Movement in Cuba, led by Fidel Castro. As a student, she participated in the protests against Batista, wrote and distributed antigovernment pamphlets, and joined the National Revolutionary Movement. She was in Mexico briefly when Castro was in exile there, and when the 26th of July Movement struggled in the Sierra Madre mountains during 1956 and 1957, she was a member of its national directorate, along with two other women, Haydée Santamaría and Celia Sánchez (later Fidel Castro's longtime companion). Working on the cities, she went underground, narrowly escaping arrest in May 1957. Espín coordinated the group's work in Oriente province and took over much of the overall leadership in the area when police killed Frank País, her boss. Espín was one of the leaders of a national strike in April 1958, which failed. She married Fidel Castro's brother Raúl, one of the rebel commanders, after the triumph of the revolution in 1959 (the couple separated in the mid-1980s). In 1960, she became director of the Federation of Cuban Women (FMC), a post she held during the 1990s. The FMC eventually included three million members, 80 percent of Cuban women. She also served as a member of the Central Committee, the Council of State, and the Politburo, the highest leadership group of the Communist Party. Espín spoke out against the sexual double standard and other gender inequities that still prevailed in Cuban society. She was one of only a few women to hold leadership posts in the government and the Communist Party, a clear indication of the at best mixed success of the Revolution in attaining equal rights for women.

Doris María Tijerino Haslam (b.1943) was one of the earliest Sandinistas. Her father worked as an engineer for the Nicaraguan National Guard, which was notorious for its corruption and oppressive tactics. A veteran of the guerrilla insurgency from the late 1960s, Tijerino endured arrest, jail, and torture at the hands of the National Guard. She was in prison until 1974, when the Sandinista raid on a high society Christmas party obtained her release in 1974. The government captured her again in 1978. Another daring raid, which took over the National Palace, secured her release. Tijerino received the rank of full commander in the Sandinista army, the only woman to earn this honor. She paid a terrible price for her achievements however, for the Somoza government murdered her first two husbands. In post-revolutionary Nicaragua she headed the National Women's Association, the national police, and served in the national legislature. She kept her Senate seat even after the Sandinistas defeat in 1989. Tijerino, like Espín, suffered from discrimination by the very revolutionary government she helped place in power and then helped lead, because its men would not allow women to attain the highest ranks of the government, despite their obvious ability to lead and the wrenching sacrifices they made.

Slice of Life

The Barrio/Favela

Super-urbanization, the great migration to the cities and the creation of the great metropolises, was perhaps the most important development of Latin America since the 1940s. Gigantic, unmanageable megacities emerged. Shantytowns, known as barrios in Mexico, barriadas in Peru, and favelas in Brazil, shelter hundreds of thousands, who exchanged the misery of the countryside for the filth and clamor of the slums. Within these seemingly hopeless, crowded neighborhoods unending resourcefulness and resilience merge. Impoverished people survive and sometimes prosper with humor and dignity. One of the great mystery of contemporary times is why they have not erupted into bitterness, resentment, and violence.

The shantytowns popped up in empty spaces owned by absentee landlords or by local governments, appearing overnight as people heard by word of mouth that land was available and assembled to occupy it. New residents constructed their hasty abodes with materials salvaged from others' trash, such as scrap wood, corrugated metal, cement blocks, and sometimes cardboard and cloth. Unrecognized by municipal authorities, the settlements initially lacked water, electricity, or sewers, or schools or medical facilities. If fortunate, inhabitants queued up for hours to fill their cans and bottles with water from a community spigot or a visiting truck. Residents stole their electricity, tapping power lines.

The shantytowns built where no one else would live, on the outskirts, up the steep sides of hills and mountains, in flood zones. The residents made something of nothing. After some time, if the people organized and lobbied successfully, they might gain services, roads, schools, and a mobile market. A few attained status as municipalities. Netzahualcóyotl, or Netza as called by its citizens, a municipality in the northeast corner of Mexico City began as a squatter settlement on the dried-out bed of Lake Texcoco, where winds swirl volcanic soil and flooding is chronic. It has a population of over one million. The government sold the land in the 1920s to developers who never followed through. Later, real estate promoters illegally sold 160,000 plots to low income people. Ciudad Netzacualcóyotl incorporated forty irregular settlements in 1964. In the 1970s, still with no services, the residents protested by withholding mortgage payments. Eventually, the government provided services and granted legal titles. Residents in other cities banded together to protest the lack of basic services and the need for legal titles. Landlords and governments often used violence to silence the protests.

In Rio de Janeiro the seeming chaos hides innovation and resourcefulness. Dwellers employ clever techniques to maximize space. They build their homes brick by brick as they accumulate enough money to acquire more building materials and add to their structures, making them more permanent. The favelas are not obsolete, retrograde remnants of rural culture, but are rather places of transition and persistence.

The shantytowns may very well be twenty-first century versions of rural villages. Just as country folk fought to maintain local autonomy and traditions, the residents of the shantytowns struggle to assert their control over their everyday lives.

Nature's Way

Itaipú, a Modern Wonder

Nowhere do the complexities of reaching a balance between economic development, environment, and humanity come into to view more than in the discussions about the construction and operation of the enormous Itaipú Dam on the Paraná River in Brazil and Paraguay.

Conceived of in the early 1960s, the result of long, difficult negotiations between two nations that fought a brutal war a century before and that bickered over boundaries ever since, the Itaipú Dam took nine years, 40,000 workers, and eighteen billion dollars to build. Engineers regard it as one of the seven modern wonders of the world.

The issues involving the environment and humanity were and are manifold. The construction of the dam and the reservoir behind it required the transformation of a major waterway and ecological system. In and of itself it involved a massive example of Amazon deforestation. The plan called for moving the seventh largest river in the world, the Paraná, forming a reservoir lake of 1,350 square kilometers and 200 meters deep, and in the process destroying the world's largest waterfall, the Guaíra Falls. Not only were the Guaíra Falls one of the most beautiful sites on earth, they provided an important ecological barrier, separating the freshwater species of the upper Paraná from those of the lower Paraná. The dam displaced 129 species of birds, 32 species of mammals, and 9 species of reptiles.

Just as important, the dam relocated no fewer than thirty-eight indigenous communities. Some never received compensation from the government. For others moving was a trauma from which they did not recover. Forty thousand people lost their homes.

Itaipú had many positive aspects. Politically, it represented a path breaking cooperation between two countries long at odds. Its construction, in and of itself was a triumph for two unsavory dictatorships, that of the military in Brazil and that of Alfredo Stroessner (1954–1989) of Paraguay. Neither of these regimes had too many other accomplishments to boast about. Economically, the hydroelectric plant supplies between 20 and thirty percent of Brazil's electricity and over 90 percent of Paraguay's. Paraguay does not produce petroleum, so Itaipú is crucial to its economic development. Brazil is the twelfth largest oil producer (second largest in South America). Seventy percent of its electricity comes from hydroelectric power, a third to forty percent of which Itaipú supplies. Itaipú's production is far more important to Paraguay than Brazil.

Electricity is Paraguay's second leading export, accounting for 23 percent of its total. (Soy is first.) It sells its surplus electricity from Itaipú and the Yacyreta Dam, built in partnership with Argentina, further south on the Paraná. Itaipú generates substantial income to both Paraguay and Brazil. Itaipú Binacional, the company that operates the hydroelectric plant, has a budget of approximately $US 3.2 billion annually, with $US 2 billion earmarked for debt repayment and royalties to each country of $US 320 million. Since the beginning, royalties amounted to $US 5 billion. Paraguay allots half its proceeds to its 17 departments and 250 municipalities, many of which depend heavily on this income. Brazilian municipalities benefit as well.

(continued)

(continued)

Environmentally, the electricity generated saves an estimated 500,000 barrels of oil a day just for Brazil. This is a considerable benefit. The Itaipú Binacional company established a 100,000-hectare preserve. It also planted 44 million trees, a strategy to reduce silt accumulation in the river and reservoir. The company worked with private landowners to mitigate ecological damages. Binacional built a waterway to connect the reservoir to the river that allows migrating fish to reach their spawning grounds. The channel is interspersed with rapids and lagoons, the latter allowing the fish to rest and feed. The rapids became an attraction for adventurous tourists.

Epilogue

What of the Struggle for Control Over Everyday Life?

In a time of rapid globalization, vast movements of people from the country-side to the cities and from one country to another, and increasingly rapid communication, have Latin Americans abandoned their struggle for control over their everyday lives which was central to their political participation for centuries? Has the daily fight for survival overwhelmed their ability or interest to concern themselves about such matters? Latin Americans retain their sense of locality and certainly continue to seek control of their everyday lives. In some cases, local loyalties may have actually helped to save the nation-state from disintegration. The strong sense of local governance and tradition in the Peruvian Highlands, for example, formed the bulwark of opposition to the Shining Path guerrillas during the 1990s. The Shining Path thoroughly alien-ated the countryside by brutally executing village leaders and priests and by intruding on local prerogatives. Peasant village defense organizations were crucial participants in the defeat of the insurgency. The deterioration of the PRI in Mexico owed in great part to its lack of responsiveness to local needs and sensibilities. Governance grew overcentralized in a nation where local tradition was still strong. The opposition PAN to a considerable extent emerged as a regional phenomenon based in the northern states, the residents of which thought themselves badly served by the regime.

M. Wasserman, *Modern Latin America Since 1800*,
https://doi.org/10.1007/978-3-030-96185-5

Unquestionably, contemporary factors altered the unending struggle for the control of everyday life. The vast migration from the countryside to the cities shattered the old ways. Migrants' ties to the villages weakened with each passing generation. Newcomers found it difficult to maintain the traditions of the villages in the face of mass media perpetually advocating consumer culture. Migration brought more people to dwell in the urban barrios than in the villages. Because village identity was not longer central to their lives, the struggle for local (village) autonomy lost its relevance. Instead, city residents of the squatter settlements and more formalized barrios organized to obtain basic services, such as electricity, water, and roads. They replaced the old structures with neighborhood and barrio-wide organizations which continued the struggle.

The struggles to control everyday life both in the countryside and in the cities absorbed heavy blows during the dictatorships of the 1960s and 1970s and the civil wars lasting through the 1990s. In some areas, such as the highlands of Peru, the guerrillas assaulted local autonomy. Right-wing paramilitary hunted down villagers in Guatemala and El Salvador. During Mexico's secret dirty war, the army killed local leaders who did not comply with the PRI. In other regions, such as the remote sections of Colombia, guerrillas seized the governance, pushing out the locals. Barrio leaders often confronted dire threats from both sides of the political spectrum. Bureaucratic authoritarianism left little room for local autonomy. Democratization led to the resuscitation of the struggle for local autonomy and control over everyday life in the emergence of indigenous political movements. In movements like the Zapatistas in Chiapas, Mexico and the Waorani people in Amazonian Ecuador, the concerns were originally local, but widened because of the global implications of their protests, the former its protests against trade agreements and the latter against oil exploration.

Even in socialist Cuba, where the state is highly bureaucratized, local committees are often where governance occurs. Advocacy for local needs is continual.

The apparent end to the Pink Tide by 2020 and resurgence of rightist politics throughout the region (and all over the world) and the simultaneous health and economic crises caused by the Covid19 pandemic cast a pall over prospects for Latin America as it enters the third decade of the twenty-first millennium. The challenge to assert control over their everyday lives will undoubtedly grow more difficult.

Suggested Reading

Arrom, Silvia. The Women of Mexico City. Stanford: Stanford University Press, 1985.

Azuela, Mariano. The Underdogs. Trans. Frederick H. Fornoff. Prospect Heights: Waveland Press, 2002.

Barnitz, Jacqueline. Twentieth Century Art of Latin America. Austin: University of Texas Press, 2001.

Besse, Susan K. Restructuring Patriarchy: The Modernization of Gender Equality in Brazil, 1914–1940. Chapel Hill: University of North Carolina Press, 1996.

Degregori, Carlos Ivan. How Difficult It Is to Be God: Shining Path's Politics of War in Peru, 1990–1999. Madison: University of Wisconsin Press, 2012.

DeJesus, Carlina María. Child of the Dark. NY: Signet, 2003.

Farnsworth-Alvear, Ann. Dulcinea in the Factory: Myths, Morals, Men, and Women in Colombia's Industrial Experiment, 1905–1960. Durham: Duke University Press, 2000.

Fraser, Nicholas and Marysa Navarro. Evita: The Real Life of Eva Perón. NY: W.W. Norton, 1996.

Guardino, Peter. The Dead March: A History of the Mexican-American War. Cambridge: Harvard University Press, 2017.

Gould, Jeffrey and Lauria-Santiago, Aldo. To Rise in Darkness: Revolution, Repression and Memory in El Salvador, 1920–1932. Durham: Duke University Press, 2008.

James, Daniel. DoÑa María's Story. Durham: Duke University Press, 2000.

Klubock, Thomas. Contested Communities: Class, Gender, and Politics in Chile's El Teniente Copper Mine, 1910–1951. Durham: Duke University Press, 1998.

Mallon, Florencia E. Peasant and Nation: The Making of Post-Colonial Mexico and Peru. Berkeley: University of California Press, 1995.

© The Author(s), under exclusive license to Springer Nature Switzerland AG 2022
M. Wasserman, *Modern Latin America Since 1800*,
https://doi.org/10.1007/978-3-030-96185-5

Mattoso, Katia M. de Queirós. To Be a Slave in Brazil, 1550–1888. New Brunswick, NJ: Rutgers University Press, 1986.

Menchú, Rigoberta. I, Rigoberta Menchú: An Indian Woman in Guatemala. Trans. Ann Wright. NY: Verso, 1984.

Moya, José C. Cousins and Strangers: Spanish Immigrants in Buenos Aires, 1850–1930. Berkeley: University of Calif0rnia Press, 1998.

Pérez, Louis A. On Becoming Cuban: Identity, Nationality, and Culture. Chapel Hill: University of North Carolina Press, 2008.

Pérez-Stable, Marifeli. The Cuban Revolution: Origins, Course, Legacy. 3d ed. NY: Oxford University Press, 2011.

Scheper-Hughes, Nancy. Death without Weeping: The Violence of Everyday Life in Brazil. Berkeley: University of California Press, 1992.

Stein, Stanley J. Vassouras: A Brazilian Coffee County, 1850–1900. Princeton: Princeton University Press, 1985.

Timerman, Jacobo. Prisoner without a Name, Cell without a Number. Madison: University of Wisconsin Press, 2002.

Wasserman, Mark. Everyday Life and Politics in Nineteenth Century Mexico: Men, Women, and War. Albuquerque: University of New Mexico Press, 2000.

Womack, John Jr. Zapata and the Mexican Revolution. NY: Vintage, 1968.

Winn, Peter. Weavers of the Revolution: The Yarur Workers and Chile's Road to Socialism. NY: Oxford University Press. Rev. ed. 1989.

Zolov, Eric. Refried Elvis: The Rise of Mexican Counterculture. Berkeley: University of California Press, 1999.

Index

A

Abaitúa Acevedo, Manuel, 172
Abertura (Brazil), 207, 212
Abolition, 104, 124
Agriculture, 4, 7, 9, 26, 47, 67, 68, 73,
    86, 111, 113, 114, 143, 167,
    190, 229, 239, 243, 249,
    253, 260
    See also Haciendas
Aguirre Cerda, Pedro, 152
Agustín Farabundo Martí Front for
    National Liberation (FMLN) El
    Salvador, 201, 202
Agustín I of Mexico, 53, 57
Alamán, Lucas, 105, 187
Alberdi, Juan Bautista, 104
Alessandri, Arturo, 125, 147,
    149, 152
Alessandri, Jorge, 209
Alfonsín, Raúl, 209
Allende, Slavador, 196, 209, 210, 236
Alliance for Progress, 209
American Popular Revolutionary
    Front (APRA), 151, 152, 156,
    157, 203
Anti-Semitism, 161, 162

Argentina, 6, 32, 56–59, 61, 65, 70,
    73, 74, 80, 82, 85, 90, 104, 105,
    107, 114–116, 118–125, 129,
    142, 144, 146–149, 151, 154,
    161, 162, 167, 183, 187,
    205–210, 213, 215–217, 219,
    223, 225–227, 231, 235, 243,
    244, 249, 256, 258, 259,
    261, 263
Aristocratic Republic (Peru), 122,
    125, 148

B

Bachelet, Michelle, 215
Balmaceda, José Manuel, 125
Bananas, 25, 68, 114, 116, 145, 165,
    229, 257
Barrios, 92, 179, 193, 250, 254, 262
Batista, Fulgencio, 153, 155, 197,
    198, 261
Bay of Pigs, 198
Belaúnde Terry, Fernando, 203
Benavides, Oscar, 152
Bolívar, Simón, 32, 34, 35, 39, 40, 43,
    44, 48, 58, 66, 68

© The Author(s), under exclusive license to Springer Nature Switzerland AG 2022
M. Wasserman, *Modern Latin America Since 1800*,
https://doi.org/10.1007/978-3-030-96185-5

Bolivia, 4, 6, 12, 32, 35, 38, 56, 57, 59, 60, 62, 63, 66, 67, 115, 122, 144, 151, 154, 157, 167, 187, 213–215, 217, 218, 226, 232–236, 238, 244–247, 256, 261

Bolsa Familia, 215, 255

Bolsonaro, Jair, 216

Boves, José Tomás, 32

Brazil, 14–16, 18, 22–23, 29, 32, 36–38, 53, 56, 59, 61, 63, 64, 68–70, 73, 74, 79, 80, 82, 86, 89, 114, 115, 118, 119, 121–125, 129, 137, 142, 144–146, 150–152, 155, 165, 167, 171, 181, 182, 184, 186, 187, 195, 196, 205–210, 213–219, 227, 231, 232, 237–242, 248–250, 255–259, 261–264

Buenos Aires, 31–33, 36, 39, 56, 57, 62, 65, 66, 68, 73, 79, 81, 90, 92, 93, 101, 106, 107, 114, 118, 123, 124, 151, 161, 171, 178, 183, 247, 250, 259

Bureaucratic authoritarianism, 206

C

Calderón, Felipe, 212

Calles, Plutarco Elías, 150

Cárdenas, Lázaro, 151–153, 185, 211

Cardoso, Fernando Henrique, 207

Caribbean, 2, 29, 47, 48, 61, 77, 109, 167, 229, 234, 244, 246, 256, 258, 259

Carranza, Venustiano, 130

Carrillo Puerto, Elvia, 163–164, 189

Carrillo Puerto, Felipe, 163–164

Cartoneros, 227, 228

Castello Branco, Humberto de Alcantar, 207

Castillo Armas, Carlos, 202

Castro, Fidel, 155, 197–199, 214, 226, 261

Castro, Raúl, 199, 261

Catholic Church, 11, 35, 42, 45, 50, 80, 109, 129, 196, 254

Chamorro, Pedro Joaquín, 200, 201

Chamorro, Violeta Barrios de, 201

Charles IV of Spain, 30

Chávez, Hugo, 213–217

Chiapas, 5, 211, 239, 248

Chile, 4, 6, 35, 56, 60–63, 66, 68, 77, 105, 115, 122, 125, 137, 142, 144–147, 149, 151, 152, 155, 167, 172–174, 176, 181, 187, 195, 196, 205–210, 213, 215–217, 231, 233, 235–237, 240, 243, 249, 256, 261

Coffee plantations, 86, 173

Cold War, 141, 155, 159, 195

Colombia, 32, 35, 56, 58, 59, 61, 68, 77, 78, 115, 144, 146, 155, 165, 167, 173, 195–205, 212, 217–219, 231, 232, 235, 237, 244, 247, 248

Communism, 145, 151, 155, 159, 195–197, 199, 203, 206, 221, 226

Conservatives, 34, 35, 43, 46, 55, 56, 58, 61, 109, 141, 151, 152, 154, 155, 157, 158, 181, 201, 204, 206, 209, 214, 216

Contras, 200

Copper, 91, 111, 114, 137, 172–174, 176, 177, 210

Correa, Rafael, 213, 215

Costa Rica, 115, 165, 229, 232, 233, 256, 260

Cotton, 3, 5, 68, 99, 111, 121, 135

Creoles, 16, 30–36, 38–40, 43, 45, 66, 120, 184

Cuba, 2, 3, 8, 10, 29, 42, 48, 69, 77, 115, 121, 142, 144, 147, 149, 153, 155, 187, 195, 197–205,

213, 224, 232–235, 243, 247, 258, 261

Culture, 1, 4, 6, 7, 17, 22, 87, 91, 104, 113, 128, 164, 169, 172, 175, 176, 181, 183–186, 189, 223, 224, 231, 258, 262

D

De Collor, Fernando, 207

Debt peonage, 83

Democracy, 50, 61, 62, 72, 122, 123, 129, 141, 143, 146, 147, 151, 155, 196, 198, 205–207, 209, 212, 220, 255, 258

Dependency, 199, 221, 223, 224

Dictatorships, 112, 122, 127, 139, 141, 143, 146, 147, 149, 151, 152, 154, 159, 197, 201, 206, 209, 210, 212, 216, 220, 235, 236, 257, 261, 263

Diffusionists, 223

Disease, 1, 9, 10, 13, 15, 17, 26, 27, 31, 35, 47, 48, 80, 86, 93, 101, 109, 116, 137, 166, 167, 177–180, 233–235, 238, 239, 255

Dominican Republic, 121, 144, 218, 232, 247, 258

Duarte, José Napoleon, 201

E

Economic development, 42, 50, 55, 59–61, 63, 66, 67, 103, 112, 113, 122, 128, 170–171, 196, 207, 211, 213, 216–218, 220, 223–224, 235, 240, 263

Economy, 1, 15, 16, 24, 37, 45, 47, 49, 50, 54, 56, 61, 66, 69, 75, 80, 81, 89, 94, 103, 106, 107, 111–114, 116, 120, 121, 123, 125, 126, 131, 133–135,

141–167, 179, 195–197, 199, 200, 203, 205, 208–210, 212–214, 216–220, 223, 224, 227, 228, 231, 243–248, 250, 255, 256

Ecuador, 6, 35, 36, 43, 44, 58, 61, 77, 78, 115, 118, 167, 213, 215, 219, 232, 244, 247, 248

Education, 36, 119, 122, 150, 153, 170, 179, 181, 185, 186, 197, 204, 212, 213, 219, 220, 228, 231, 239, 252, 254–256, 259, 260

El Salvador, 77, 115, 144, 196, 199–202, 213, 218, 229, 241, 243, 244, 248, 249

El Tenient mine, 138, 172, 174, 177, 178

Everyday life, 6, 55, 63, 79–109, 113, 138, 169, 170, 188, 224, 231–264

Everyday struggles, 55, 113, 138, 169, 170, 251, 262

Export economies, 69, 107, 112, 113, 115, 116, 121, 125, 126, 129, 131, 142, 147, 156, 223

F

Falklands/Malvinas, 208

Families, 6, 7, 10, 11, 13, 16, 21, 26, 31, 38, 43, 62, 65, 70, 75, 78–92, 95, 96, 98–102, 108, 113, 119, 125, 131, 133, 135–137, 152, 159, 165, 166, 170, 172–179, 181, 188–191, 200, 203, 211, 215, 216, 226, 232, 243, 244, 246, 249, 251, 255, 260, 261

Favelas, 250, 262

Federalism, 54, 55, 57, 58, 64

Federal Wars, 58

Feminism, 113, 119, 157, 163, 187

Ferdinand VII of Spain, 2, 11, 30, 34, 37, 40
Fernández de Kirchner, Cristina, 215
Fox, Vicente, 212
Francia, José Gaspar Rodríguez, 73
Frei Ruiz Tagle, Eduardo, 210
Fujimori, Alberto, 204

G

Galtieri, Leopoldo, 208
García, Alan, 204
Goulart, Joao, 206, 207
Gran Colombia, 35, 43, 58
Great Depression, 124, 143, 144, 147, 149, 151, 223
Guatemala, 4, 5, 58, 77, 115, 139, 140, 144, 154, 196, 199, 202, 229, 231, 233, 236–238, 242, 248–250
Guerrero, Vicente, 34, 35, 40, 64, 75
Guzmán, Abimael, 203, 204

H

Haciendas, 18, 21, 24, 25, 27, 33, 43, 63, 65, 67, 82–86, 88–91, 94, 128, 133, 135, 165
Haiti, 29, 38, 47, 48, 115, 116, 232–234, 243, 249
Haitian Revolution, 31, 47, 69
Haya de la Torre, Victor Raúl, 152, 156, 203
Hernández Martínez, Maximiliano, 201
Honduras, 4, 77, 115, 144, 145, 199, 202, 229, 230, 237, 242, 243, 247–249, 260
Housing, 96, 99, 100, 108, 137, 169, 174, 179, 192, 193, 248, 251, 252
Hurricane Mitch, 229–230

I

Ibáñez del Campo, Carlos, 149, 151, 155, 195, 198, 209
Illia, Arturo, 208
Immigration, 85, 104, 112, 120, 121, 199, 247, 249
Import Substitution Industrialization (ISI), 141–167, 196, 216, 220, 223, 224, 243, 249, 254
Income Inequality, 240
Independence, 29, 31–36, 38–40, 42–51, 56–58, 61, 63–68, 70, 72, 73, 75, 76, 79, 80, 94, 96, 103, 104, 106, 107, 112, 118, 120, 121, 125, 138, 141, 159, 171, 176, 197, 198, 243
Indians, 38, 40, 45, 63, 64, 66, 72, 80, 83, 89, 92, 94–96, 99, 102, 104, 105, 125, 127, 128, 152, 156, 157, 171, 184–186, 189, 190
Indigenismo, 128, 184, 185
Industrialization, 68, 113, 114, 116, 118, 124, 141, 143, 145, 146, 157, 158, 169, 183, 186, 221, 243, 253
Informal economy, 220, 227, 228, 244–247
Institutionalized Revolutionary Party (PRI), 192, 193, 210–212

J

Juárez, Benito, 58, 63, 72
Justo, Agustín, 151

K

Kahlo, Frida, 189
Kirchner, Néstor, 215
Kubitschek, Juscelino, 156

L

Labor, 4, 11–15, 18, 22–24, 38, 65, 80, 82, 83, 85, 88, 94, 95, 107, 117, 120, 121, 125, 127, 137, 138, 141, 142, 145, 150, 153, 154, 157, 165, 171, 173–176, 190, 191, 199, 210, 216, 219, 239, 240, 243, 244, 247–249, 260

Labor strikes, 173

Labor unions, 112, 122, 142, 152, 153, 156, 174, 187, 205, 208, 210, 211

Landowners, 13, 21, 25, 32, 51, 54, 56, 57, 65, 67, 68, 80, 82, 87, 90, 94, 112, 113, 115, 117, 120, 123–125, 127, 129, 130, 133, 136, 148, 155, 157, 170, 171, 186, 203, 214, 264

Leguía, Augusto B., 126, 147–149, 152, 154

Liberals, 30, 34, 54–56, 58, 61, 72, 109, 120, 129, 147, 187, 204, 224

Literacy, 119, 157, 170, 195

López Obrador, Manuel, 212

Lower classes, 32, 38, 40, 46, 49, 52–56, 63–66, 70, 75, 76, 103, 104, 106, 107, 112, 123, 124, 130, 138, 141, 142, 146–150, 152–154, 156, 157, 161, 169, 171, 174, 178, 179, 184, 185, 187–188, 224

M

Machado, Gerardo, 147, 149, 153

Macri, Mauricio, 216

Madero, Francisco, 72, 130, 135

Madrid, Miguel de la, 192, 211

Maduro, Nicolás, 214, 215, 217

Maps, 229

Mariátegui, José Carlos, 128, 203

Marriage, 6, 13, 16, 21, 44, 83, 88, 91, 96, 136, 138, 175, 181, 182, 188, 189, 191, 214, 232

Martínez de Perón, María Estela (Isabelita), 208

Medellín, 58, 173, 176

Medici, Emilio Garrastazú, 207

Menem, Carlos, 209

Mexico, 3–5, 12, 27, 34, 35, 39, 40, 45–46, 48, 53, 56–64, 67–70, 72, 73, 76, 80, 82–84, 88, 89, 95, 98, 101–103, 105, 109, 113, 114, 116–118, 120–122, 126–131, 133, 135, 137, 144, 146, 149, 151–153, 163, 167, 171, 172, 181, 185, 187, 189, 192, 193, 198, 202, 210–212, 214, 217, 218, 227–229, 232, 233, 235, 238, 239, 242, 249, 251, 253–262

Mexico City, 3, 5, 12, 21, 24, 33, 36, 39, 45, 46, 48, 61, 63, 64, 75, 77, 79, 81, 92–98, 100, 101, 103, 109, 130, 163, 171, 179, 185, 187, 192–193, 211, 227, 250–254, 256, 262

Middle class, 33, 78, 94, 97, 100, 112, 118, 119, 121–124, 126–128, 130, 133, 142, 147–156, 161, 169, 178–180, 182, 183, 186, 197, 206, 210, 215, 219, 220, 223, 236, 240

Migration, 5, 89, 92–94, 113, 142, 169, 183, 200, 239, 247–249, 260, 262

Military, 2, 4, 5, 7, 8, 10, 12, 32, 36, 37, 44, 45, 47, 51, 57, 59, 61–63, 65, 66, 73, 89, 95, 122–124, 126, 129, 130, 139–142, 147–149, 151–157, 161, 162, 171, 186, 196, 197, 200–212, 215, 216, 225, 226, 263

Military officers, 54, 62, 122, 124, 125, 142, 149, 150, 153, 154, 195, 202, 213, 216, 225–226

Military regimes, 187, 203, 205, 213

Mines, 6, 12–14, 16, 21, 24, 38, 51, 62, 67, 79, 94, 111, 117, 120, 125, 127, 137, 138, 155, 157, 172, 174–177, 181, 190, 219

Morales, Evo, 213–216

Mujica, José, 214

Muralists, 128, 184–186, 189, 257

Murillo, Geraldo, 184

N

Neoliberalism, 204, 216

Neves, Tancredo, 207

Nicaragua, 77, 78, 115, 144, 187, 192, 196, 200, 213, 229, 230, 234, 235, 237, 243, 261

Nitrate mining, 114

North American Free Trade Agreement (NAFTA), 212

O

Obregón, Alvaro, 130, 150, 164, 185

Ortega, Daniel, 200, 201, 216

P

Páez, José Antonio, 58, 70

Panama, 16, 47, 48, 115, 121, 167, 232, 237, 256

Paraguay, 56, 57, 59, 60, 62, 70, 73, 74, 85, 122, 167, 213, 232, 237, 244, 247, 263

Paraguayan War, 59, 63

Parián Riot, 64, 75–76

Parliamentary Republic, 125, 149

Patriarchy, 16, 135, 141, 170–178, 181, 182

Pedro I, 38, 53, 59, 64, 70

Pedro II, 38, 53, 59, 70

Pena Nieto, Enrique, 212

Peons, 63, 82–84, 89, 90, 119

Period, 111

Perón, Eva Duarte de, 154

Perón, Juan Domingo, 154

Peronism, 154, 226

Peru, 3–5, 8, 10–12, 14, 16, 31, 35, 38, 43, 44, 59–64, 68–70, 77, 78, 88, 104, 115, 122, 125, 128, 137, 147, 149, 151, 152, 156, 157, 167, 171, 172, 180, 181, 185, 190–191, 196–205, 217–219, 227, 231, 232, 235, 237, 238, 244–248, 252, 260, 262

Petroleum, 111, 114, 116, 153, 155, 211, 213, 217, 218, 263

Pinera Echenique, Sebastián, 216

Pink Tide, 196, 201, 212–216, 219, 220, 236, 237, 243, 255

Pinochet, Agustín, 236

Plantations, 15, 18, 21–24, 26, 86–89, 108, 114, 121, 165, 173, 229, 248

Political participation, 32, 50, 53, 64, 195

Political stability, 40, 112, 121, 122, 153, 220

Politics, 6, 7, 30, 31, 36, 40, 42, 43, 48–78, 106, 111–167, 169, 189, 195–198, 203, 205, 207, 212, 215, 225, 226, 257

Popular culture, 91, 169, 183, 184, 189, 231, 258

Popular Front (Chile), 142, 152

Population growth, 80, 118, 178, 249

Populism, 142, 147, 149, 152, 156, 159, 185, 187, 205, 220

Poverty, 40, 43, 47, 79, 92, 103, 119, 127, 163, 176, 196, 197, 200, 202, 204, 212–216, 219, 221, 228, 231, 235–241, 245, 247, 249, 250, 252, 255, 257, 259

Q

Quadros, Jánio, 206

R

Race, 1, 19, 32, 40, 102, 118, 258
Radical Party (Unión Cívica Radical),
  123, 147, 148, 156
Railroads, 69, 111–114, 116, 117, 119,
  121, 122, 126, 129, 131, 146,
  154, 163, 186, 211
Ranches, 82, 171
Rebels, 9, 22, 30, 32, 34, 35, 37, 39,
  46, 48, 57, 65, 75, 86, 106, 126,
  129, 133–134, 155, 197, 198,
  200, 202, 210, 261
Revolutionary Armed Forces of
  Colombia (FARC), 205, 219
Río de la Plata, 14, 31, 32, 34, 35, 54,
  56, 57, 61, 62, 67, 68, 70, 73,
  82, 85, 90, 106
Rivera, Diego, 185, 189, 192, 257
Roca, Julio A., 123
Rojas Pinilla, Gustavo, 155
Rosas, Juan Manuel de, 57, 62, 65,
  66, 73, 106
Rousseff, Dilma, 215, 216

S

Sáenz PeÑa Law, 123
Samba, 184, 259
Sánchez Cerro, Luis M., 152
Sandinista National Liberation Front
  (FSLN), 200, 202
Santa Anna, Antonio López de, 57, 58,
  62, 64, 70, 72, 73, 109
Sarmiento, Domingo F., 104, 106, 120
Sarney, José, 207
Scilingo, Adolfo, 225
Semana Trágica (Tragic Week),
  124, 161–162
Sendero Luminoso (Shining Path),
  203, 204

Silva, Luiz Inacío "Lula" da, 215
Slavery, 18, 19, 31, 37, 39, 42, 63, 83,
  86, 104, 124
Slave trade, 18, 66
Social Question, 112, 122, 124,
  146–148, 159, 169, 185, 186
Social structure, 93
Somoza Debayle, Anastasio, 200,
  201, 261
Spain, 2, 11, 12, 14, 16, 17, 29, 30,
  32–34, 36, 40, 42, 46, 48, 57,
  61, 92, 115, 121, 187, 208, 218,
  247, 259
Street vendors, 95, 101, 227, 244, 252
Structuralists, 223
Sucre, Antonio José, 35, 66
Sugar, 15, 18, 21, 22, 24, 26, 47, 68,
  69, 84, 87, 97, 108, 114, 116,
  121, 143, 144, 149, 155, 166,
  197, 199, 238
Sugar plantations, 22, 23, 86

T

Terror, 9, 196, 199, 202, 205–207,
  209, 210, 212, 232, 235, 247,
  248, 258
Texas War, 62
Textile industry, 75, 174
Tijerino, Doris María, 261
Timerman, Jacobo, 162
Toledo, Alejandro, 204
Toussaint L'Ouverture, Francois, 48
Trade, 14, 16–18, 32, 33, 37, 54–56,
  66–68, 79, 94, 115, 116, 126,
  135, 143–146, 151, 199, 212,
  218, 219, 223, 246, 253
26th of July Movement, 195, 198, 261

U

Ubico, Jorge, 139, 154, 202
United Nations Economic Commission
  for Latin America (CEPAL), 223

Upper class, 30, 31, 33–35, 40, 46, 49, 51–53, 56, 57, 63–66, 75, 76, 85, 94, 104–106, 112, 113, 120, 122–131, 133, 138, 141–143, 147–151, 153–159, 161, 169–171, 178, 179, 181–187, 200, 206, 208, 210, 259
Urban areas, 92, 94, 118, 129, 239, 249, 256
Urbanization, 113, 141, 144, 157, 178–184, 186, 238, 249–253
Uribe, Alvaro, 205
Uruguay, 56, 57, 59, 73, 121, 146,. 167, 206, 213–215, 231, 232, 234, 235, 237, 240, 243, 244, 249, 256, 258

V

Vargas, Getulio, 142, 151, 152, 155, 182, 195, 197, 206
Vázquez, Tabares, 214
Venezuela, 16, 32, 35, 40, 58, 68, 70, 77, 106, 115, 116, 122, 144, 155, 167, 195, 205, 213, 214, 217, 219, 232, 235, 237, 238, 242, 243, 247–249, 258
Videla, Jorge, 208
Villaroel, Guaberto, 157

W

War on drugs, 212
Women, 7, 16, 22, 23, 39, 43, 44, 65, 85, 87, 88, 91, 92, 94–100, 108, 113, 118–120, 124, 131, 133, 138, 141, 147–149, 151–153, 157, 158, 163, 164, 166, 170–173, 175, 176, 178, 180–184, 187, 189, 195, 200, 201, 204–206, 208, 210, 215, 225, 230, 232, 234, 235, 243, 245–247, 260, 261
Working class, 68, 75, 106, 112, 117–123, 125–127, 130, 141, 142, 149, 153–156, 158, 169, 179, 180, 182, 186, 196, 210, 259

Y

Yrigoyen, Hipólito, 123, 124, 147–149, 154, 156, 159, 161

Z

Zapata, Emiliano, 130, 131, 153, 163

CPSIA information can be obtained
at www.ICGtesting.com
Printed in the USA
LVHW080107080123
736696LV00004B/63